.STO
ct

National Parks Trade Journal

TAVERLY
CHURCHILL
PUBLISHING

V

NATIONAL PARKS TRADE JOURNAL
SECOND EDITION REVIEWS:

"An invaluable resource to people interested in pursuing careers in the national parks; it is clear cut, well done and has nice profiles on the various parks..."

. . . . . .*National Geographic Society*

"NPTJ gives pertinent information on employee living and working conditions, goes beyond facts and figures with dozens of stories and articles written by park employees..."

. . . . . .*Wilderness Press*

"If you'd like to work in the wilderness but need an income, the National Parks Trade Journal will provide inspiration..."

. . . . . .*Sierra Magazine*

"The Journal gives the reader an intimate look at some of the fascinating and unusual lifestyles available in hundreds of beautiful natural settings..."

. . . . . .*Knapsack Magazine*

"The National Parks Trade Journal will make finding that dream job easier-- not just for the summer, but at any time of year..."

. . . . . .*National Parks Magazine*

Photo by Craig Trachtenberg

Going for it!

I

"National Parks Trade Journal"

1st Edition	© 1984	Taverly-Churchill
2nd Edition	© 1986	Taverly-Churchill
3rd Edition	© 1989	Taverly-Churchill
Revised	© 1990	Taverly-Churchill
Revised	© 1991	Taverly-Churchill

ISBN 0-9616595-0-5

Taverly-Churchill Publishing, Inc.
32282 Big Sandy Drive
Coarsegold, CA 93614
(209) 658-7676

Dedicated to Marie Escola

Paul DeSantis and Bob Snowden

ACKNOWLEDGEMENT

"Our many thanks to the following individuals and organizations
that have made this publication possible"

Lynn Alexander
American Youth Hostels
American Rivers
Allison Ivy Anzalone
Timothy Arnst
Dave Bouchard
California Department of
  Parks and Recreation
Calif. Conservation Corps
Twilly Cannon
Earthwatch
Helen Bruce Frankel
Jack Frankel
Greenpeace
International Red Cross
Alonzo "Johnny" Johnson
Cathy Larson
Phil Lord
Faye Martin
William Penn Mott

Rod Nash
National Geographic Society
National Parks and
  Conservation Association
National Park Service
Nature Conservancy
Bob and Jane Nester
Lillian Nester
Gayle Norton
John Palmer
Peace Corps
Ponderosa Printing
Bertha Quick
Rainforest Action Network
Royal Robbins
Michael Roth
William Shatner
Sierra Club
Bob Weir
Worldwatch Institute

Working Assets Tools for Practical Idealists
...and the crew of the Wawona Store

Special thanks to our own volunteer staff located throughout
national parks and scenic areas around the globe!

"Fantasia" by Royal Robbins appears courtesy of
La Siesta Press: Glendale, California.
Thanks to Royal and Bud Wheelock for permission to use this story.

Cover Illustration by Brian K. Webb

THIRD EDITION STAFF

SENIOR EDITOR

Dave Anzalone

EDITOR

Robert Frankel

ART DIRECTOR

Brian K. Webb

TECHNICAL CONSULTANT

Michael Jones

CONTRIBUTORS

WRITERS

Terry Birch
P. Carol Broadwell
James Cassell
James P. Delgado
Lewis Goldman
Jeff Grandy
Randy Hayes
J.J. Hill
Dick Kemp
Deb Johnson
Tim Messick
Doyle Nelson
J. Emilio Reynoso
Royal Robbins
Kim Saunders
Tina Sonnier
Pam Sweetser
Edgar Wayburn, M.D.
Harvy White
Todd Wilkinson
Rob Frankel

PHOTOGRAPHY

David Ashcraft
Karl Bralich
Alan Busby
Andrew Dixon
Chris Falkenstien
Jeff Grandy
Brian Grogan
Bobby Hicks (ZJIL)
Alan Janzen
Raymond Mauck
Chris Mitchell
National Park Service
Jeff Nixon
J. Emilio Reynoso
Craig Trachenburg
Harvy White
Chris Nishimura - cartoons
Keith Walklet - cartoons

Film Processing by Imperial Color, Kodalux, Mystic Color, Yosemite Photo Express, and Ponderosa Printing.

Typography, Phototypesetting, and Graphics Layout & Pasteup by Ponderosa Printing. Additional Typesetting by Holly A. Brown, Canoga Composition.

All contributions of stories, articles, photos, drawings and cartoons are welcomed. Send yours to the National Parks Trade Journal, P.O. Box 2221, Wawona Station, Yosemite National Park, CA 95389. Sorry, we cannot guarantee return of unsolicited material without a self-addressed stamped envelope included with your submission, 5 x 7 black and white photos are preferred, as is double spaced, typed text.

Contents:

NATIONAL

PARKS

TRADE

JOURNAL

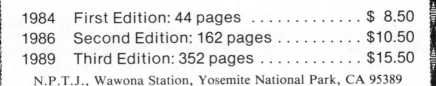

1984   First Edition: 44 pages . . . . $ 8.50
1986   Second Edition: 162 pages $10.50
1989   Third Edition: 352 pages $15.50

N.P.T.J., Wawona Station, Yosemite National Park, CA 95389

INTRODUCTION

The National Parks Trade Journal began in 1981 when a few Yosemite employees felt the need for some kind of employment guide to America's national parks. Questionnaires were formulated and mailed to various private companies (concessionaires) operating within the parks as well as the National Park Service. Research continued for several years, during which time the groundwork was laid for forming a company (Taverly-Churchill Publishing) to handle the printing, advertising and marketing. Early in 1984 Taverly-Churchill published a Spring Guide containing fourty-four pages of information on jobs, meal programs and housing opportunities in various parks.

After a limited printing of 500 copies, one small ad was purchased and displayed in the April issue of Outside Magazine. The results were phenomenal. The N.P.T.J. sold out its first printing with orders from virtually every state and province in North America.

Our Second Edition

Due to the success of the Spring Guide, the N.P.T.J. staff decided to produce a new guide with expanded job listings and to include stories, articles, photos and cartoons from fellow employees. Consequently, the staff grew tenfold, and job listings increased to over 30,000. The staff was delighted to find that national parks offer an unlimited source of fabulous material for the talented writers, artists and photographers working their way through each year.

Thanks to their contributions, the second edition of the N.P.T.J. became the "Number 1 guide to living and working in the national parks" and "one of the most widely read publications by park employees", inspiring twenty-one major national book reviews in newspapers and magazines. Five thousand copies were sold to libraries, bookstores and universities across the country. Thousands of more requests from individuals for single copies reached us as well, plus hundreds of books were donated to public service employment groups.

In that last issue we predicted that we would add "more and more exciting job opportunities from America and around the world."

Our Third Edition

This issue you have in your hands represents the beginning of our effort to reach out. Offering listings for scenic and ski resorts only seems natural, as their seasonal needs for qualified and enthusiastic personnel complement those of the Park Service and its concessionaires.

Preserving and enhancing our park environment has become part of a larger, global challenge, which worldwide volunteer and environmental groups and educational institutions are rising to meet. In this edition you'll find out more about these organizations and how to get involved.Stories, articles and photographs bring to you a taste of their exciting and often exotic work, all in the spirit of making the world a better place to live.

Because they are the finest natural environments on earth, the national parks have been set aside and protected for us all.

On behalf of the N.P.T.J., we wish you a warm and hearty welcome.

Dave Anzalone
Publisher

Rob Frankel
Editor

Inside Trade Journal Headquarters, it's business as usual.

"A book is a handy item to keep with you,
especially one that fits in your backpack."

...a traveling reader

EDITOR'S NOTE

by Rob Frankel

This publication is for, by, and about people interested in living and working in the great outdoors. It has been our goal to put outdoor-related groups, organizations, and companies together with qualified, enthusiastic, and oftentimes experienced applicants, the core of our original readership.

Now, as our readership grows, the National Parks Trade Journal has grown too. Slowly, to be sure, but significantly. We want to appeal to more people, not to just those of us who have the privilege of waking up and finding ourselves ALREADY living in a National Park. Young, old and in between, good employees from our world's cities dream about work and play in exotic locales -- the Journal is meant to bring home that flavor to them, as well.

In these pages you'll find information about the National Park Service, concessionaires, resort operators and both national and worldwide volunteer organizations, all of whom want and need these enthusiastic people to apply for their work opportunities. Interspersed throughout our pages of listings are the contributions of people who live or have lived in beautiful, natural settings around the world.

For an example of how one person decided that the outdoors lifestyle was for him, you can turn to "Shifting Gears in the Great Outdoors." Also displayed are accounts of some of the various outdoor talents of our contributors, whether it be patrolling a frozen lake in Wyoming, skiing an "unskiable" rim-to-floor trail at Yosemite, composing and performing music, or directing a major motion picture.

Working and living in outdoor situations has, for some, opened up a variety of career vistas. Royal Robbins, for example, was at one time a ski lift operator. He continued with his adventures, writing books about rock climbing, opening up a school, two outdoor products/outfitting outlets, and currently manufactures and markets stylish yet comfortable, I hear, clothing. He continues to write fiction, and one of his earlier stories appears in this edition. The San Joaquin Gorge, a more recent story, appears in a recent Royal Robbins catalogue.

Our contributors and volunteers have all been a great inspiration to us at the Journal, and we want to share them with you. Energy, enthusiasm and creativity, coupled with common sense logic and a sense of responsibility, must be encouraged. As for developing interpersonal relationship skills, there is no better substitute for a job in the hospitality, service or public relations fields.

For our younger readers, we hope the Journal opens up new vistas of opportunity for you. For our ever-growing pool of readers already employed or living in the great outdoors, we salute you, and want to hear more from you. For those of you with children or younger relatives who might benefit from work and/or volunteer service experience in our great outdoors, please let them know about us. If you or your company markets a product or service that benefits our readers, we'ld like to know more about it; after all, some of us spend months at a time between visits to a shopping mall. Mail order products and services are desperately needed by our thousands of readers who live far "out of town".

Working together towards a greater outdoors lifestyle, can make a better world, as today we work on making quality tomorrows. Swim in a river. Take a walk in the woods. Climb a mountain or ski down it, while hollering the whole distance. Relax. Write us a letter.

The editor off belay on Wawona Dome

5

William Penn Mott
12th Director of the National Park Service

WILLIAM PENN MOTT, JR.
NATIONAL PARK SERVICE DIRECTOR

William Penn Mott, Jr., was selected in May 1985 to become the 12th director of the National Park Service since its creation in 1916. Mott was appointed by Secretary of the Interior Don Hodel.

In making the appointment, Hodel said "William Penn Mott is one of the most widely respected conservationists in America today with an unparalled record of achievement. America has the finest park system in the world, but Mott's dynamic, experienced leadership can improve even that impressive record."

A career parks professional, Mott joined the National Park Service in 1933 as a landscape architect working out of the San Francisco office. He remained with the Service for seven years.

Mott served eight years as director of the California Department of Parks and Recreation (1967-75), six years as general manager, East Bay Regional Park District (1962-1967), and 17 years as superintendent of parks for Oakland.

He returned to the Park Service as director following service as the President and Executive Officer of the California State Park Foundation, which he founded in 1975. He served as general manager of the East Bay Zoological Society, Oakland, Calif., to show that a nonprofit organization could run a zoo without benefit of government funding. He was appointed to his current position as Director while serving as general manager.

While directing the state park system, Mott was responsible for many innovative changes including opening the park ranger ranks to women and to those whose academic backgrounds were outside of the traditional fields of wildlife management, including archeology, sociology, and dramatic arts. He set up the first ticket reservation system for public campground use and doubled the acreage of the State Park System.

A registered landscape architect, Mott was in private practice, specializing in park and recreation planning and design, in the 1940's. In October 1985, he received the prestigious Alfred B. LaGasse medal of the American Society of Landscape Architects.

In addition to his career assignments, Mott has also been active with a wide range of civic, professional, and conservation organizations. He has been a member of the board of trustees of both the National Parks and Conservation Association and the National Recreation and Parks Association and a director of the Save the Redwoods League.

Among his many honors and awards, Mott received the Department of the Interior's Public Service Award in 1981, the highest honor given to private citizens. He has also received the Cornelius Amory Pugsley Award of the American Scenic and Historic Preservation Society, one of the foremost private park and conservation honors, in 1973.

Born in New York City, Mott holds two degrees in landscape architecture, a B.S. from Michigan State University and a M.S. from the University of California at Berkeley. He has been a resident of Orinda, California, for more than 50 years.

He and his wife, Ruth, have two sons.

8

Government Jobs With The National Park Service

The number one employer within the National Park system is, quite predictably, the National Park Service. Currently, personnel are employed in over 330 National Parks, Monuments, and Recreation Areas, all under the jurisdiction of the Park Service. Year-around, about 9000 full time positions are filled throughout the system. Seasonal and summer openings total close to 11,000 positions. Jobs are as many as they are varied, and include maintenance of roads, trails, and visitor areas, sanitation and water treatment, hazardous tree removal, general administration, visitor programs, law enforcement, rescue operations, and more.

In order to be considered for a National Park Service position, one must first contact and meet the requirements of the Office of Personnel Management (OPM), also known as the Civil Service Commission. Competition for positions is fierce, and there are usually more applicants than jobs available. One should seriously consider his/her qualifications before aspiring for NPS employment. For those (U.S. citizens only) desiring consideration for a career position with the Park Service, acquiring eligibility on the OPM's register, often by means of a specific written test, is necessary.

Listed below are positions available with the National Park Service:

Park Ranger is a highly sought-after position. Consideration, for the most part, is based upon applications from employees already within the Park Service.

Park Aid and Technician. Eligibility exams are given according to need. Contact NPS regional offices (see below) for location and time.

Park Police positions are available in some large and urban areas. Written exams must be passed under intense competition.

Managerial and Administrative positions are available in parks, regional and service offices, and Washington D.C. Written exams determine eligibility.

Maintenance, Trade, and *Craft* positions include laborers, general maintenance, janitors, motor vehicle operators, engineering equipment operators, carpenters, gardeners, painters, electricians, and plumbers, and involve maintenance of trails, roads, buildings, grounds, and equipment. No written exam is given for these positions. Consideration is based on the the type and level of skill possessed.

9

In addition, those seeking jobs as *student assistants* in engineering, architecture, or the sciences, *seasonal* architects, landscape architects, environmental scientists, engineers, surveying technicians, engineering draftsmen, and engineering technicians, may apply to the: Rocky Mtn. Regional Office, NPS, P.O. Box 25287, Denver, CO 80225. Those seeking positions as *seasonal* laborers, trade and craft workers, or lifeguards, should contact the office serving their area of interest for application forms. Apply between September 1 and January 15 for all summer seasonal jobs. For summer clerical positions (mainly in D.C.), contact the Civil Service Commission for exam/application instructions by mid-November.

To receive more information on what Park Service positions are available, application/exam deadlines, necessary forms, and proper procedures, contact either the National Headquarters Office, the Regional Office serving your area of interest, or the NPS Personnel Offices in the parks themselves. Request brochures covering career and seasonal employment. Questions concerning living conditions and related matters can best be answered through the park or office where you desire employment. Generally, however, the Park Service does provide their employees with double occupancy tents, cabins, or dorms with kitchen facilities. One final note, grooming guidelines throughout the Park Service are more leniant then among concessionaires.

Following are the regional and national headquarters Park Service office addresses:

NORTH ATLANTIC REGION
15 State Street
Boston, MA 02109

Serving Maine, New Hampshire, Vermont Massachusetts, Rhode Island, Connecticut, New York, and New Jersey

MID-ATLANTIC REGION
143 South Third Street
Philadelphia, PA 19106

Serving Pennsylvania, Maryland, Virginia, West Virginia, and Delaware

NATIONAL CAPITAL REGION
1100 Ohio Drive S.W.
Washington, D.C. 20242

Serving the District of Columbia and nearby Maryland, Virginia, and West Virginia

SOUTHEAST REGION
75 Spring Street S.W.
Altanta, GA 30303

Serving Alabama, Florida, Georgia, Kentucky, Mississippi, North Carolina, South Carolina, Tennessee, Puerto Rico, and the Virgin Islands

MIDWEST REGION
1709 Jackson Street
Omaha, NE 68102

Serving Ohio, Indiana, Michigan, Wisconsin, Illinois, Minnesota, Iowa, Missouri, Nebraska, and Kansas

ROCKY MOUNTAIN REGION
P.O. Box 25287
Denver, CO 80225

Serving Montana, North Dakota, South Dakota, Wyoming, Utah, Colorado, and Arizona

SOUTHWEST REGION
P.O. Box 728
Santa Fe, NM 87501

Serving Arkansas, Louisiana, New Mexico, Oklahoma, Texas, and Arizona

WESTERN REGION
450 Golden Gate Avenue
Box 36063
San Francisco, CA 94102

Serving Arizona, California, Nevada, and Hawaii

PACIFIC NORTHWEST REGION
601 Fourth and Pike Building
Seattle, WA 98101

Serving Alaska, Idaho, Oregon, Washington, and California

WASHINGTON (NATIONAL) OFFICE
National Park Service
Interior Building, Room 2328
18th and C Streets N.W.
Washington, D.C. 20240

Photo by Robert Frankel

APPLYING FOR A JOB

By Lewis Goldman

Most often, the only opportunity you'll have to "sell" yourself to a prospective employer is through a written application. It may be only one of dozens of applications submitted for a particular job. To be competitive you must submit an application that will set your's apart from the others. This article contains general comments which will be useful for most any written application and also specific comments intended for the National Park Service seasonal application (which may be of use in other applications as well).

First off, read the instructions carefully. No one is going to hire you if you can't follow simple directions. Even a "dumb" error can be fatal. I know of an applicant who was not considered for a position because he mistakenly entered the current year where he should have written his year of birth. The clerk (clerks will not think for you) entered this information into the computer which determined that the applicant was underage and rejected him on the spot. Now, how is your printing? Would you want to read fifty hand printed applications, or fifty typed ones? Unless your printing is impeccable, I strongly advise you to type. Fill in all the blanks (use "N/A" for not applicable). Spell correctly. Use good grammar. When finished, let someone else proofread it. Lastly, identical applications can be submitted to more than one park. It's acceptable to xerox your application. Just make sure your signature on each copy is original.

National Park Service seasonal applications are submitted on form 10-139. The application packet is available from any National Park personnel office or write to this address:

U.S. Department of the Interior
National Park Service
Seasonal Employment Unit
P.O. Box 37127
Washington, D.C. 20013-7127

To obtain applications from other government agencies, I recommend contacting the nearest unit's personnel office. The addresses of private employers are found in this guide.

Here are some tips for completing the 10-139. The comments are listed in the same order that they appear in the application. I've ignored areas that are self-explanatory:

Park Sanitation Specialist Wyly Wood . . . at the helm.

13

Telephone. Make it easy for someone to hire you. Leave a number where you can be reached, if only for a message.

Type of Position. One, two, or three. One referes to interpreters, the rangers who give programs, lead nature walks, etc. Two represents commissioned rangers (an option only if you have law enforcement training). Three is for general positions. This is a catchall. Visitor center staff, lifeguards, resource technicians, fee collectors, etc. are all represented here. You may apply to two of the three position types. Those lacking law enforcement training should put down both one and three. If you are offered a job you don't want, just turn it down.

Lowest Grade Level. Seasonal government jobs are almost all at the GS-3, -4, or -5 level. The pay levels are pre-determined. No one can hire you at a lower level just because you are willing to work at it. This question merely asks "Will you work at a job that pays X per hour?". (For example, GS-3 pays about $5.30/hour, with successive raises of about one dollar per hour for each of the next two grades.)

Availability Dates. If you would be willing to start the "right" job on June 10, consider putting June 1 on the application. If the job begins on June 6, wouldn't you want to be considered? The same goes for less than full time employment. You will only be considered for work at reduced levels if you check the appropriate boxes. Again, you can always say "no" to an offer.

Special Qualifications and Skills. Here is your chance to shine. They are asking you "Why are you so special?" List your hobbies, machine skills, publication and speaking experience, awards, certifications, etc. I recommend that you use a separate sheet of paper (follow the instructions), and list your qualifications like this:

1. Familiar with word processors; type 40 word/min.
2. Associate editor of high school newspaper during senior year. Member of the debate team during junior and senior years.
3. Have been SCUBA diving for eight years and have PADI certification.
4. Enjoy photography and develop own black and white photos. Have recorded travels through Europe (3 mos.) and Africa (2 mos.) and interpret these trips as slide shows for local travel club.
5. Current CPR and Advanced Red Cross cards.
6. Enjoy playing the guitar. Taken lessons for nine years.

I'm sure you get the idea. Notice that I dropped "I have" and "I did". These words are understood.

Skill Levels. Sixty specific skills are identified. Only some, based on

Sign language interpreter Jennifer Jacobs (left) and Naturalist Fermin Salas (right).

weighting factors, affect your score. You get to rate yourself but boldly printed warnings now admonish you to tell the truth or else. Well, I urge you to tell the truth as well but this is no place for modesty. The skill

15

levels range from one (no experience) to five (certified instructor). If you find your skill level somewhere "in between" two levels, give yourself the benefit of the doubt and choose the higher rating.

Work Experience (including volunteer). If you are young then you may feel that your work experience will seem rather weak. Learn to make the most of it. In the work experience block you are asked for a description of your "duties, responsibilities, and accomplishments" and your current position has you working at Harry's Hamburger Stand. You could write "I serve junk food at a greasy spoon" or you could be creative. How's this: "I work part-time as a food server at a local restaurant. I am required to be well-groomed and am responsible for the care and maintenance of a uniform which is worn while on duty. During each shift I contact about two hundred customers, taking orders, serving food, and processing the funds on a model 27 Sweda Electronic cash register. The register contains a bank of $200.00 in bills and coins; I am charged with safeguarding these funds. Each day I take in over $2,000.00 resulting from food sales which are remitted by me at the close of each shift."

Notice that the application has only five lines? It would be difficult to get all of the above in. This is where "cutting and pasting" comes in. Cut out the upper part of the job block and paste it on the top of a blank sheet of typing paper. Under this type in the duties, responsibilities, and accomplishments as we discussed above. Now, xerox this and out comes a custom tailored page. If it's possible to put two or three jobs on one sheet that's fine. Don't elaborate on every job you've had but do emphasize those that will be most useful.

References. Professional references are best, followed by professors and other teachers. Ministers, your doctor, etc., are not very helpful. Friends, relatives, and peers are relatively worthless.

Make sure that the application goes in the mail on time. Park Service summer seasonal applications must be postmarked by January 15; winter seasonal applications by July 15. I recommend sending them by certified mail, return receipt. These things get misplaced so cover yourself. The applications are scored by the individual parks and your name and score are placed on a register. Supervisors begin hiring about three months after the deadline date. The personnel office at the park can usually give you the names of the supervisors. I suggest you follow up by contacting these folks on the telephone. "Hi, my name is Joe/Jane Smith and I'm very much interested in working as an interpreter in Jellystone National Park." It may not seem like much but most supervisors appreciate your enthusiasm and will take extra time to look at your application. Who knows, maybe Zion this summer and Denali the next. Good luck!

NATIONAL PARKS UNDERWATER

By James P. Delgado
Martime Historian, WASO

The units of the National Park System contain more than 2,250,000 acres of submerged land, an area equal to the size of Yellowstone National Park. Yet we know more about the most remote parts of Yellowstone than we do about these underwater areas. There are 80 parks which lie on or near large bodies of water, including well-known parks like Channel Islands, Isle Royale, Virgin Islands, Cape Hatteras, Biscayne or Fort Jefferson. There are lesser known areas, too, including parks on rivers or smaller lakes.

The most famous underwater resources are shipwrecks. The sunken remains of ships, be they Spanish pataches, fregatas, or galleons lost in the 16th or 17th centuries; the battered iron hulls of squareriggers wrecked in the 1880's; or the torn and twisted remains of a World War II warship intrigue and fascinate people. Combined with the thrill of diving, shipwrecks are sunken ghost towns compelling exploration. Sport diving is increasing in the United States; more than three million people are registered divers, and each year thousands more learn. With new diving technology and increased public interest, the undersea world is opening up.

The National Park Service's parks are and will continue to be actively dived. In 1988, 42 parks reported sport-diving activity. In order to properly protect, preserve, and interpret the submerged resources of the National Park System, the Service is working beneath the water. For the past ten years the National Park Service has aggressively pursued an understanding of the submerged parts of the parks, establishing regional and park dive teams and conducting surveys of submerged natural and cultural resources. The National Park Service also has the federal government's only field team of underwater archeologists--the Submerged Cultural Resource Unit--which works around the country and abroad on shipwrecks in and outside of the parks.

Established in 1974 as the National Reservoir Inundated Study at the Southwest Regional Office of the NPS at Santa Fe, New Mexico, the team first worked on prehistoric sites inundated by reservoir construction. Six years later, with that task largely completed and a three-volume study marking their effort, the team was transformed into a servicewide underwater archeological unit, headquartered in Santa Fe. The team is now, as it was then, headed by Daniel J. Lenihan, a New York City-born archeologist and cave diver. Larry Murphy, a Florida native who once worked as a state agent monitoring the destructive activities of treasure hunters in the Caribbean, is one of two other full-time archeologists in the unit. Toni Carrell, a prehistoric

archeologist now working on historic shipwrecks, is the third member of the team. Mike Eng, a former NOAA research diver and park ranger and now the unit's research diving technician, is the fouth full-time member of the unit. Secretary Fran Day runs the office.

Other NPS employees are occasional members of the team. They include archeologist Larry Nordby, Chief of the Branch of Cultural Research at the Southwest Cultural Resources Center, archeologist Jim Bradford, scientific illustrator Jerry Livingston, both at the Southwest Cultural Resources Center, Jim Koza, the park dive officer at Lake Mead NRA, and the author, the service's maritime historian. The Submerged Cultural Resource Unit's ranks swell with many projects, as rangers maintenance staff, and volunteers work in the water and on the boat with the team. Annual dive workshops sponsored by the Service are occasionally taught by unit personnel in the various regions, allowing park staff the opportunity to learn "hands-on" underwater archeological survey and mapping.

In another arrangement, U.S. Navy active and reserve divers work with the Submerged Cultural Resource Unit on archeological projects as part of their regular training. The Navy gets challenging, at times difficult, but always interesting tasks while the Service benefits from their assistance in documenting shipwrecks. Known as "Project Seamark," the Navy-NPS partnership's best-known result was the mapping of the battle-damaged hulk of USS Arizona at Pearl Harbor. Other projects have included work in the Republic of Palau, surveys of shipwrecks at Cape Cod, Golden Gate, Fort Jefferson, and Fire Island, and patching and preparations to raise the sunken

Photo courtesy National Park Service

19

Point Reyes U.S. — U.S. Department of the Interior, National Park Serivce.

historic ferry Ellis Island at Statue of Liberty NM.

The Submerged Cultural Resource Unit, in the past nine years, has worked in more than 25 parks and in the former Trust territories. Major projects have included a five-year survey of ten historic shipwrecks at Isle Royale

21

National Park in Lake Superior. The cold, fresh waters of the lake have remarkably preserved wooden hulls--even human bodies--from wrecks dating from the 1870's, and steel freighters of the 1920's. Other shipwreck surveys have included work at Point Reyes National Seashore and Channel Islands National Park, in California, and documentation of wooden shipwreck remains on the beach at Golden Gate National Recreation Area and Cape Hatteras National Seashore. Individual shipwrecks have been intensively studied, including the near-intact hulk of Frances, a British-built bark wrecked in 1875 that lies in the surf at Cape Cod, and Charles H. Spencer, a sternwheel steamer built, disassembled, and rebuilt in the Arizona desert, only to be abandoned within a few months, whose remains lie at Lees Ferry at Glen Canyon National Recreation Area.

After identifying shipwrecks in the parks, the next priority of work is surveying wrecks in the former Trust Territories and studying wrecks being considered as National Historic Landmarks. A small wooden brig at the mouth of the Columbia River in Oregon, at the request of the Columbia River Maritime Museum was studied by the team in 1987. Identified as the 1830 wreck of the Hudson's Bay Co. supply ship Isabella, the wreck is now pending a decision on National Historic Landmark designation. Work on the two remaining victims of the Japanese attack at Pearl Harbor, USS Arizona and USS Utah, both sunk on December 7, 1941, resulted in these important vessels and national shrines being designated NHLs in early 1989.

While emphasizing report writing and publications in 1989 to more broadly interpret the results of years of National Park Service leadership in American underwater archeology, the unit plans some exciting field projects. A detailed survey at Fort Jefferson National Monument's shipwrecks, similar to that done earlier for Isle Royale National Park, will begin this summer. At the request of the Department of Energy and the Marshall Islands, four members of the team will journey to Bikini Atoll in August to survey and assess some of the 12 major warships sunk by the United States during the epic "Operation Crossroads" atomic bomb tests of 1946.

Wherever they go, and whatever they do, the Submerged Cultural Resources Unit is a highly productive, highly visible program. The ultimate goal is a complete survey of the 2,250,000 submerged acres in the National Park System and the evaluation of the hundreds of shipwrecks thought to be in the parks. The success of the unit, however, relies heavily on cooperation, largely through the involvement of dedicated park rangers and maintenance workers who work side by side with the team and then take the skills they have learned into the field for the day to day challenge of protecting, managing, and interpreting the bold new frontier of national parks underwater.

PRESERVING OUR SUBMERGED HERITAGE
Submerged Cultural Resources Unit
National Park Service

It is probable that a greater number of monuments of the skill and industry of man will, in the course of the ages, be collected together in the bed of the ocean than will exist at any other time on the surface of the continents.

Charles Lyell
1872

For more than half its history, America was explored and settled and its commerce conducted almost solely by ships. By bark and shallop, by galleon and sloop and brigantine the New World was made known, and the peoples of the Old World engaged in the greatest movement of humanity ever made.

Inevitably, there was loss of ships to storms and coastlines, to war and accident. Each wreck became a time capsule, and each added itself and sometimes its contents to the accumulating history of mankind burried by sand and water. These features lay largely unattended and forgotten, until new technologies permitted access to them and brought renewed awareness of what existed beneath the waves. The new accessibility also brought the curious and the treasure seekers, and, inevitably, loss of knowledge about America's past.

Hundreds of these sites lie within areas managed by the National Park Service. In all, 59 parks have identified submerged cultural resources within their boundaries - an underwater realm the size of Yellowstone National Park. Far more sites lie outside Federal jurisdiction. Among the Federal sites are:

• **Cape Hatteras National Seashore**

More than 500 shipwrecks lie along the Outer Banks of Virginia and North Carolina. The earliest is the British *Tiger*, sunk in 1585.

• **Point Reyes National Seashore**

Of more than a dozen shipwrecks here, most significant is the Spanish galleon *San Agustin,* wrecked in 1595 while making a survey of the California coast. It is the oldest shipwreck on the Pacific Coast.

• **Isle Royale National Park**

Ten major vessels lie in the offshore waters of this park, including the side wheel steamship *Cumberland*, sunk in 1877 and the package freighter *Kamloops*, lost in 1927 with no survivors.

- **Cape Cod National Seashore**

The seashore coastline and associated shoals carry the remains of more than 500 vessels, including the *Sparrowhawk* of 1623 and the 64 gun *HMS Somerset*, wrecked in 1778 during the Revolutionary War.

- **Biscayne National Park**

The 18th Century British warship *HMS Fowey* is only one of more than two dozen shipwrecks within park waters.

- **Golden Gate National Recreation Area**

More than one hundred barks, schooners, steamers, and ships lie in offshore waters, including the medium clipper ship *King Philip*, sunk in 1856.

- **Fort Jefferson National Monument**

The story of New World exploration is contained within the park's waters, in vessels dating to the Spanish galleon *Nuestra Senora Del Rosario*, sunk in 1622.

We Americans are the best informed people on earth as to the events of the last 24 hours; we are not the best informed as to the events of the last 60 centuries.

Will Durant

THE SUBMERGED CULTURAL RESOURCES UNIT

With increasing awareness of America's underwater cultural resources, employees of the National Park Service began in the 1960s to investigate shipwrecks with SCUBA equipment and document their locations and condition. This activity accelerated in the 1970s as park managers became increasingly aware of the richness of these submerged resources. In 1980 this effort was formalized within a Submerged Cultural Resources Unit, staffed by underwater archeologists, to provide the expertise needed by the Federal parks.

Its major roles now include:

- inventorying, mapping, and assessing underwater cultural resources in the national park system, with emphasis on historic shipwrecks in marine and Great Lakes parks.

- developing plans for management, preservation, and recreational use of submerged cultural resources.

- coordinating with other agencies on submerged resources.

- working with professional and sport diving organizations regarding submerged cultural resources in Federal park areas.

- cooperating internationally with other countries on similar resource problems.

Attaching baseline to stern of wrecked bork King Phillip (1856-1878) Golden Gate National Recreation Area, San Francisco.

Research vessels approach site of historical shipwreck.

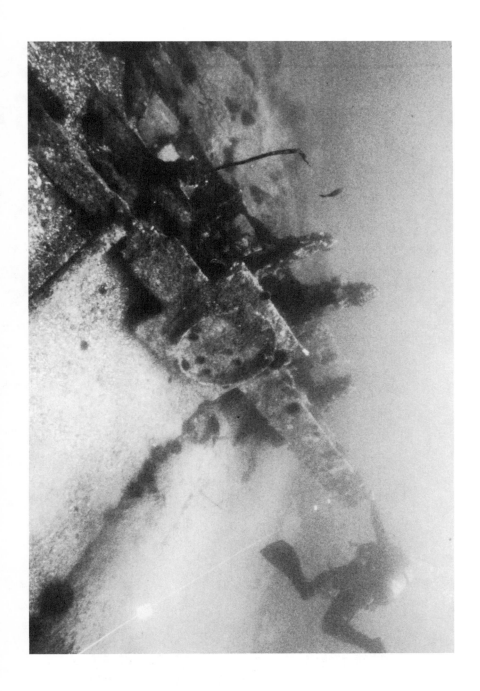

To expand its capability, the Submerged Cultural Resources Unit works extensively with other institutions. In collaboration with the Institute of Nautical Archeology at Texas A & M University, the unit is researching early ships of New World exploration and Columbus landing sites. In collaboration with the U.S. Navy, the unit has begun to locate and map ships and planes at War in the Pacific National Historical Park in Guam and in the Republic of Palau. The National Geographic Society has provided robot equipment for deep, unmanned dives off Isle Royale National Park in Lake Superior, and the U.S. Coast Guard provides invaluable logistical and staff support both in the Great Lakes and along coastlines.

The only way to find the right answers about much of our maritime past is to ask the right questions of the wood and iron time capsules that lay on the bottom of the sea.

Daniel Lenihan

THE FUTURE

The accumulation of submerged cultural resources since Portuguese and British fishermen first plied New World waters is truly staggering. Shipwrecks and their associated artifacts tell of technology and ways of living; they tell of commerce and the relationship among men. Ignored, these windows to the past will inevitably disappear. Attended to, they will bring understanding of how people of the past coped with their lives, and in doing so help us to cope with ours. The increased knowledge these resources represent also holds the promise of a shift in ethics toward their preservation. With the acquisition and dissemination of information about their character there may come a new found respect that will lift resources above exploitation and destruction, and a new found husbandry for the heritage they represent.

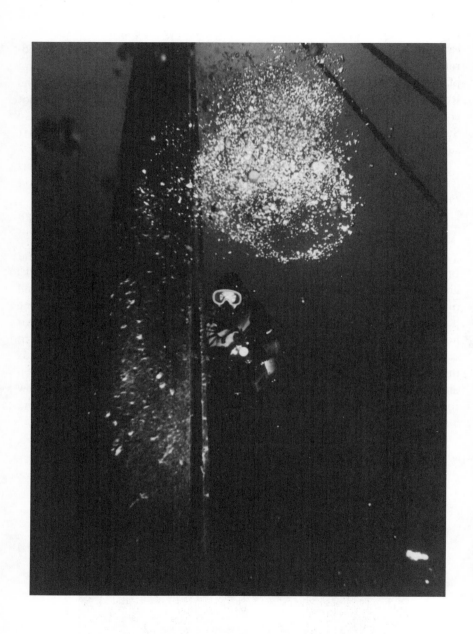

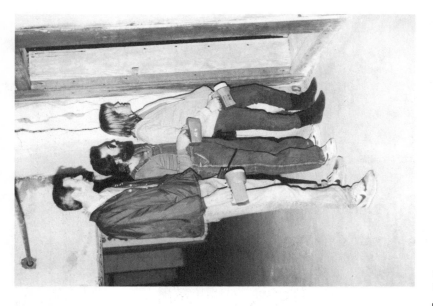

UNDERGROUND ALCATRAZ Collected By *Alan Janzen*

32

"MOTHER CURRY"

Jennie Foster Curry was the heart of Camp Curry where, she said, "I did a little of everything one time or another. I made salads and put up the tents, I was baker and head waitress, postmistress and pantry woman...and it didn't hurt my pride, any of it."

Applicants who are strong and willing and accustomed to work are always welcome . . . The work is hard and calls for people who are rugged . . . If you cannot carry a tray, do not apply for a dining room job. If you cannot make a bed, sweep a room and care for a bathroom exquisitely, do not apply as a maid. If you are not willing to keep the grounds clean, empty the slop-jars, and "rustle" the baggage, do not apply as a porter . . . A desire to spend a summer in Yosemite is not sufficient qualification for a position with us . . . On the other hand . . . many employees return year after year . . . The atmosphere, both climatic and social, the association with interesting people, life in the open where Nature is at her best, all these give a zest to life that offsets the fatigue of labor.

**EMPLOYMENT APPLICATION
YOSEMITE NATIONAL PARK
CIRCA 1920**

Jobs in the Private Sector with Park Concessionaires

Only a small percentage of America's National Parks offer tourist concessions such as lodging facilities, cafeterias and restaurants, showers, stores, service stations, riding stables, and gift shops. When present in a park, these services are run by private (non-government) companies known as concessionaires. These companies perform their own hiring, and, in most cases, provide lodging and meal plans for their employees. Compensation for work is generally minimum wage, with exceptions for skilled positions.

Below is a general explanation of the fact pages on park concessionaires that follow this introduction:

Best Time to Apply will vary from park to park. However, with attrition, summer turnover, and early back to school schedules, an application for employment may be successful at any time.

Seasonal Employment. Because some parks operate in summer, some in winter, and some all year around, the opportunity exists to work in more than one park, or even a year-around position.

General Employment describes the most common types of employment offered, although a few of the larger parks such as Yosemite, Yellowstone, and Grand Canyon offer a wider spectrum of positions.

Employer Provided Lodging. Double occupancy tents, cabins, or dorms are the standard. Bedding and towels are usually provided along with utilities. Lodging rates, as a rule, are very reasonable, rarely exceeding $20.00 per week.

Lodging Restrictions. Since the Park Service requires leashing of pets at all times and forbids them from most hiking trails, and since pets are seldom accepted in concessionaire lodging anyway, it is a good idea to leave all pets behind. Overnight guest policy varies from park to park, but generally a guest registration card and approval from one's roomate is all that is necessary.

Nearby Private Housing. In some cases, Naional Park Boundaries are close enough to private homes and communities where it is possible to arrange an outside-the-park rental agreement. This may involve higher rent, possible security deposits, and, of course, the added cost of commuting.

Employee Meal Programs are provided by most concessionaires. Twenty-one meals a week can be had for approximately $30.00. Cooking quality will vary from park to park, but usually a genuine attempt is made to put forth a well-balanced and nutritious meal.

Employee Cooking Facilities when provided, are usually in the form of a community kitchen, with employees sharing a refrigerator, stove, storage, and a common eating area.

Grooming Restrictions. With a few exceptions, concessionaires, adhere to a more conservative grooming policy than the Park Service. Beards and long hair do not score points with concessionaires, while a groomed moustache is acceptable.

Nearby Religious Services are available in many National Parks, mostly held in small chapels with a multi-denominational congregation.

Courtesy of N.P.S.

So You Want To Work In A National Park
What Concessioners Look For
And What They Provide
By J.J. Hill

Each year hundreds of applications are received by National Parks and "how can I get a job" is a commonly asked question. Obviously the answer varies with different occupations, but there is some common ground that all employers are looking for. This article gives suggestions to help you succeed in obtaining a job with a park concessioner.

Every company, no matter how large or small, is looking for applicants that are conscientious, trustworthy and loyal. How you portray these qualities depends largely on your personality. It is up to you through resume, cover letter and interview to express the "true you". Although an application is merely a tool to review the most basic information, you should give the application your full attention when filling it out. Pay attention to detail. LEAVE NO QUESTIONS UNANSWERED! Type or neatly print your answers. There is nothing more frustrating than trying to decipher the handwriting of a would-be employee. Remember, this may by your only contact with the potential employer.

Should you be granted an interview, there are a few basics to follow:

APPEARANCE: You can never look too good for an interview in the areas of grooming and attire.

PUNCTUALITY: Plan on being five minutes early; five minutes late will leave a poor first impression.

PERSONALITY: Be yourself! An employer is hiring you, not a one time imposter. Be polite, but let the real you shine through. Be pre-

Photo by Chris Mitchell

37

pared to answer questions about your career goals and how to attain them.

Applicants that are enthusiastic about work duties, and have an outgoing personality will succeed in any job.

Concessioners will look at the dates the applicant is available. Applicants are usually expected to be available for a minimum work period of 90 days. Those willing to work the entire season will be considered most satisfactory.

Let's next review the position you are applying for. If you are willing to accept an entry level position, such as roomskeeper, kitchen helper, laundry attendant, etc., you will have the best chance for employment.

Job experience is our final area of concern. Does the applicant have experience working with the public? Can the applicant provide character references? When giving job references, be sure to include correct phone numbers and addresses.

If these requirements are met, you stand a good chance of being hired.

Because of heavy operating requirements during specific seasonal periods, such as Labor Day, employees are expected to work through their commitment dates. Employees who do not fulfill their "commitment dates" are usually not rehired.

Guest Service is the business of park concessioners. Therefore grooming standards are very important. These can vary depending on the park you work at, however, there are usually basics to follow. Men should wear their hair above the collar line. Neatly trimmed moustaches may be allowed. Women are expected to wear their hair in a neat style. Both men and women should maintain a conservative grooming appearance, i.e., no punk hair styles.

Employee housing is often provided. These accomodations are usually dorm buildings, but may also include tents or cabins, depending on the park. Housing is usually shared, so expect a roommate. Blankets, sheets, pillows, pillow cases, towels and a lock may be provided, but again this depends on the concessioner. A list of items provided is usually issued the employee before his/her check-in date.

A minimal rent (approx. $20.00 a week) is usually charged the employee for housing. If there is a meal program, the cost is often deducted from an employees pay check. Housing rent is also handled in this manner. The expense of living in a park is very reasonable. Remember, facilities provided in parks vary.

Housing areas are maintained and supervised by a housing supervisor. Your supervisor will ensure that you are made welcome and comfortable upon checking in. He or she will help you with any problems you might encounter in your housing situation, such as help with locating a compatible roommate, moving to a different housing area, etc. The housing supervisor is also there to enforce the housing guidelines. These guidelines may include no pets, no cooking in rooms, quiet hours, and overnight visitors.

It is wise to bring a minimum amount of belongings. Stereos for example, are not considered essential. It is advisable to leave your valuables at home. A list of things to bring should include the following: windup alarm clock (electricity can go out), flashlight, sturdy but lightweight boots, backpack and accessories, camera and a minimum of electrical

Photo by Chris Mitchell

items. Please leave your pets, firearms, stereos and televisions at home. Plan on enjoying your chosen park for what it has to offer: a great outdoor experience.

Final keys to remember for the first-time employee are:

Be prepared to meet company grooming standards.

Most first-time employees go into entry level positions.

Housing is usually a double occupancy dormitory room. Some parks may house employees in tents or cabins. Rent and meals, if provided, will often be deducted from your paycheck. These charges are very minimal.

Concessioners are in the guest service business and expect employees to remember this and act accordingly at all times. ☐

41

NOW DISAPPEARING AT A LOCATION NEAR YOU.

©Art Wolfe

These sea otters were once on the brink of extinction. They are doing better now, but hundreds of other species are in trouble.

Since 1951, The Nature Conservancy has protected millions of acres of habitat for threatened species in all 50 states. And in a novel way—we've bought it.

A good job . . . but not good enough. Time is running out. Whole species are vanishing every day.

So join us. Write The Nature Conservancy, Box CD0021, 1815 N. Lynn Street, Arlington, VA 22209. Or call 1-800-628-6860.

Conservation Through Private Action

Original concept courtesy of Lewis & Partners, San Francisco

DENALI
NATIONAL PARK
(Alaska)

MAILING ADDRESS:

ARA Outdoor World
P.O. Box 87
Denali Nat'l Park, AK 99755

May-Sept

SEASONAL EMPLOYMENT

0	560	0	0
SPRING	**SUMMER**	**FALL**	**WINTER**

BEST TIME TO APPLY: Year-round

GENERAL EMPLOYMENT:

■ Indicates services and facilities with employment opportunities.

■ Management	□ Administration	■ Housekeeping
■ Gift Shops	■ Front Desk	■ Tour Guides
□ Stables	■ Maintenance	■ Grocery/Supplies
■ Food Service	■ Security	■ Garage/Gas Station
□ Janitorial	□ Gardening	■ Transportation
□ Rental Shops	□ x-c Skiing	□ Alpine Skiing
□ Climbing (Ice/Rock)	□ Camping	□ Boating (rafting, canoeing etc.)

ADDITIONAL INFORMATION:

EMPLOYER PROVIDED LODGING:

■ Dorms   □ Tents   □ Cabins
□ Other:

LODGING RESTRICTIONS:

■ Pets   □ Guests
□ Other:

EMPLOYEE MEAL PROGRAMS:

■ Yes   □ No

EMPLOYEE COOKING FACILITIES:

□ Yes   ■ No

NEARBY RELIGIOUS SERVICES:

■ Yes   □ No

NEARBY PRIVATE HOUSING:

□ Yes   ■ No

GROOMING RESTRICTIONS:

□ Hair   □ Moustache   □ Beard
■ Other: Well groomed

OFF SEASON ADDRESS:

ARA Outdoor World
307 South B St.
San Mateo, CA 94401

Oct. - Apr.

GLACIER BAY
NATIONAL PARK AND RESERVE
(Alaska)

MAILING ADDRESS:

Glacier Bay Lodge Inc.
1600 Metropoliton PK. Bldg.
Seattle, WA 98101

SEASONAL EMPLOYMENT

80	80	80	0
SPRING	**SUMMER**	**FALL**	**WINTER**

BEST TIME TO APPLY: January and February

GENERAL EMPLOYMENT:

■ Indicates services and facilities with employment opportunities.

■ Management	■ Administration	■ Housekeeping
☐ Gift Shops	■ Front Desk	☐ Tour Guides
☐ Stables	■ Maintenance	☐ Grocery/Supplies
■ Food Service	☐ Security	■ Garage/Gas Station
☐ Janitorial	☐ Gardening	■ Transportation
☐ Rental Shops	☐ x-c Skiing	☐ Alpine Skiing
☐ Climbing (Ice/Rock)	☐ Camping	☐ Boating (rafting, canoeing etc.)

ADDITIONAL INFORMATION: 100 ton skippers

EMPLOYER PROVIDED LODGING:

■ Dorms   ☐ Tents   ☐ Cabins
☐ Other:

LODGING RESTRICTIONS:

■ Pets   ■ Guests
■ Other:

EMPLOYEE MEAL PROGRAMS:

■ Yes   ☐ No

EMPLOYEE COOKING FACILITIES:

☐ Yes   ■ No

NEARBY RELIGIOUS SERVICES:

■ Yes   ☐ No

NEARBY PRIVATE HOUSING:

☐ Yes   ■ No

GROOMING RESTRICTIONS:

■ Hair   ☐ Moustache   ■ Beard
■ Other: Neatly Trimmed
Beards allowed in some
departments

OFF SEASON ADDRESS:

Same as above

KATMAI
NATIONAL MONUMENT
(Alaska)

MAILING ADDRESS:

Alaskan Outdoor Services
Box 6927
Anchorage, AK 99502

SEASONAL EMPLOYMENT

0	40	40	0
SPRING	**SUMMER**	**FALL**	**WINTER**

BEST TIME TO APPLY: February

GENERAL EMPLOYMENT:

■ Indicates services and facilities with employment opportunities.

- ■ Management
- ■ Gift Shops
- ☐ Stables
- ■ Food Service
- ■ Janitorial
- ■ Rental Shops
- ■ Climbing (Ice/Rock)

- ■ Administration
- ☐ Front Desk
- ■ Maintenance
- ☐ Security
- ☐ Gardening
- ☐ x-c Skiing
- ■ Camping

- ■ Housekeeping
- ■ Tour Guides
- ☐ Grocery/Supplies
- ☐ Garage/Gas Station
- ☐ Transportation
- ☐ Alpine Skiing
- ■ Boating (rafting, canoeing etc.)

ADDITIONAL INFORMATION:

EMPLOYER PROVIDED LODGING:

☐ Dorms   ■ Tents   ■ Cabins
☐ Other:

LODGING RESTRICTIONS:

■ Pets   ■ Guests
☐ Other:

EMPLOYEE MEAL PROGRAMS:

■ Yes   ☐ No

EMPLOYEE COOKING FACILITIES:

☐ Yes   ■ No

NEARBY RELIGIOUS SERVICES:

☐ Yes   ■ No

NEARBY PRIVATE HOUSING:

☐ Yes   ■ No

GROOMING RESTRICTIONS:

■ Hair   ☐ Moustache   ☐ Beard
■ Other: Neat Appearance

OFF SEASON ADDRESS:

Same as above

Glen Canyon
National Recreation Area
(Arizona)

MAILING ADDRESS:

Wilderness River Adventures
P.O. Box 717
Page, AZ 86040

SEASONAL EMPLOYMENT

25	50	25	0
SPRING	**SUMMER**	**FALL**	**WINTER**

BEST TIME TO APPLY: February thru May

GENERAL EMPLOYMENT:

■ Indicates services and facilities with employment opportunities.

☐ Management ☐ Administration ☐ Housekeeping
☐ Gift Shops ☐ Front Desk ☐ Tour Guides
☐ Stables ☐ Maintenance ☐ Grocery/Supplies
☐ Food Service ☐ Security ☐ Garage/Gas Station
☐ Janitorial ☐ Gardening ☐ Transportation
☐ Rental Shops ☐ x-c Skiing ☐ Alpine Skiing
☐ Climbing (Ice/Rock) ☐ Camping ■ Boating (rafting, canoeing etc.)

ADDITIONAL INFORMATION:

EMPLOYER PROVIDED LODGING:
☐ Dorms ☐ Tents ☐ Cabins
■ Other: N/A

LODGING RESTRICTIONS:
☐ Pets ☐ Guests
■ Other: N/A

EMPLOYEE MEAL PROGRAMS:
☐ Yes ■ No

EMPLOYEE COOKING FACILITIES:
☐ Yes ■ No

NEARBY RELIGIOUS SERVICES:
■ Yes ☐ No

NEARBY PRIVATE HOUSING:
■ Yes ☐ No

GROOMING RESTRICTIONS:
☐ Hair ☐ Moustache ☐ Beard
■ Other: Neatly groomed

OFF SEASON ADDRESS:

Same as above

Glen Canyon
National Recreational Area
(Arizona)

MAILING ADDRESS:

Wahweap Lodge & Marina
P.O. Box 1597
Page, AZ 86040

SEASONAL EMPLOYMENT

200	300	200	0
SPRING	**SUMMER**	**FALL**	**WINTER**

BEST TIME TO APPLY: February thru June

GENERAL EMPLOYMENT:

■ Indicates services and facilities with employment opportunities.

■ Management	■ Administration	■ Housekeeping
■ Gift Shops	■ Front Desk	■ Tour Guides
☐ Stables	■ Maintenance	■ Grocery/Supplies
■ Food Service	■ Security	■ Garage/Gas Station
■ Janitorial	■ Gardening	■ Transportation
■ Rental Shops	☐ x-c Skiing	☐ Alpine Skiing
☐ Climbing (Ice/Rock)	☐ Camping	■ Boating (rafting, canoeing etc.)

ADDITIONAL INFORMATION:

EMPLOYER PROVIDED LODGING:

■ Dorms ☐ Tents ☐ Cabins
☐ Other:

LODGING RESTRICTIONS:

■ Pets ☐ Guests
☐ Other:

EMPLOYEE MEAL PROGRAMS:

■ Yes ☐ No

EMPLOYEE COOKING FACILITIES:

☐ Yes ■ No

NEARBY RELIGIOUS SERVICES:

■ Yes ☐ No

NEARBY PRIVATE HOUSING:

■ Yes ☐ No

GROOMING RESTRICTIONS:

☐ Hair ☐ Moustache ☐ Beard
■ Other: Neatly groomed

OFF SEASON ADDRESS:

Same as above

GRAND CANYON
NATIONAL PARK
(Arizona)

MAILING ADDRESS:

Grand Canyon Nat'l Park Lodges
Personnel Department
P.O. Box 699
Grand Canyon, AZ 86023

SEASONAL EMPLOYMENT

800	1,100	800	600
SPRING	**SUMMER**	**FALL**	**WINTER**

BEST TIME TO APPLY:

GENERAL EMPLOYMENT:

■ Indicates services and facilities with employment opportunities.

■ Management   ■ Administration   ■ Housekeeping
■ Gift Shops   ■ Front Desk   ■ Tour Guides
■ Stables   ■ Maintenance   ■ Grocery/Supplies
■ Food Service   ■ Security   ■ Garage/Gas Station
■ Janitorial   ■ Gardening   ■ Transportation
■ Rental Shops   □ x-c Skiing   □ Alpine Skiing
□ Climbing (Ice/Rock) ■ Camping   □ Boating (rafting, canoeing etc.)

ADDITIONAL INFORMATION:

EMPLOYER PROVIDED LODGING:

■ Dorms   □ Tents   ■ Cabins
□ Other:

LODGING RESTRICTIONS:

■ Pets   □ Guests
□ Other:

EMPLOYEE MEAL PROGRAMS:

■ Yes   □ No

EMPLOYEE COOKING FACILITIES:

□ Yes   ■ No

NEARBY RELIGIOUS SERVICES:

■ Yes   □ No

NEARBY PRIVATE HOUSING:

□ Yes   ■ No

GROOMING RESTRICTIONS:

□ Hair   □ Moustache   ■ Beard
■ Other: Neatly groomed

OFF SEASON ADDRESS:

Same as above

48

GRAND CANYON
NATIONAL PARK
(Arizona)

MAILING ADDRESS:

TW Services, Inc.
451 N. Main
P.O. Box 400
Cedar City, UT 84720

SEASONAL EMPLOYMENT

0	200	200	0
SPRING	**SUMMER**	**FALL**	**WINTER**

BEST TIME TO APPLY: January thru April

GENERAL EMPLOYMENT:

■ Indicates services and facilities with employment opportunities.

■ Management	■ Administration	■ Housekeeping
■ Gift Shops	■ Front Desk	■ Tour Guides
■ Stables	■ Maintenance	■ Grocery/Supplies
■ Food Service	■ Security	■ Garage/Gas Station
■ Janitorial	■ Gardening	■ Transportation
☐ Rental Shops	☐ x-c Skiing	☐ Alpine Skiing
☐ Climbing (Ice/Rock)	☐ Camping	☐ Boating (rafting, canoeing etc.)

ADDITIONAL INFORMATION:

EMPLOYER PROVIDED LODGING:
■ Dorms   ☐ Tents   ■ Cabins
☐ Other:

LODGING RESTRICTIONS:
■ Pets   ☐ Guests
☐ Other:

EMPLOYEE MEAL PROGRAMS:
■ Yes   ☐ No

EMPLOYEE COOKING FACILITIES:
☐ Yes   ■ No

NEARBY RELIGIOUS SERVICES:
☐ Yes   ☐ No

NEARBY PRIVATE HOUSING:
☐ Yes   ■ No

GROOMING RESTRICTIONS:
☐ Hair   ☐ Moustache   ■ Beard
■ Other: Well groomed

OFF SEASON ADDRESS:

Same as above

PETRIFIED FOREST
NATIONAL PARK
(Arizona)

MAILING ADDRESS:

Fred Harvey, Inc.
Box 247
Petrified Forest Nat'l Pk.
AZ 86028

SEASONAL EMPLOYMENT

15	15	15	15
SPRING	**SUMMER**	**FALL**	**WINTER**

BEST TIME TO APPLY: Year-round

GENERAL EMPLOYMENT:

■ Indicates services and facilities with employment opportunities.

☐ Management   ☐ Administration   ☐ Housekeeping
■ Gift Shops   ☐ Front Desk   ☐ Tour Guides
☐ Stables   ☐ Maintenance   ☐ Grocery/Supplies
■ Food Service   ☐ Security   ■ Garage/Gas Station
■ Janitorial   ☐ Gardening   ☐ Transportation
☐ Rental Shops   ☐ x-c Skiing   ☐ Alpine Skiing
☐ Climbing (Ice/Rock) ☐ Camping   ☐ Boating (rafting, canoeing etc.)

ADDITIONAL INFORMATION:

EMPLOYER PROVIDED LODGING:

☐ Dorms   ☐ Tents   ■ Cabins
☐ Other:

LODGING RESTRICTIONS:

■ Pets   ☐ Guests
☐ Other:

EMPLOYEE MEAL PROGRAMS:

■ Yes   ☐ No

EMPLOYEE COOKING FACILITIES:

☐ Yes   ■ No

NEARBY RELIGIOUS SERVICES:

■ Yes   ☐ No

NEARBY PRIVATE HOUSING:

■ Yes   ☐ No

GROOMING RESTRICTIONS:

☐ Hair   ☐ Moustache   ■ Beard
■ Other: Neatly groomed

OFF SEASON ADDRESS:

Same as above

UTAH/ARIZONA'S LAKE POWELL...
As Popular With Seasonal Employees
As With Over 3 Million Annual Visitors

IT isn't a national park but is administered by the National Park Service. Its annual attendance now exceeds such standards as Yellowstone, Rocky Mountain and Grand Teton.

IT is the massive Glen Canyon National Recreation Area, better known as Lake Powell, and it has been discovered by seasonal employees as well as more than three million people a year.

"We average more than four applicants for each of our 500-plus seasonal openings," points out Dave Wood, director of personnel for Wahweap, Bullfrog, Hall's Crossing, Hite and Dangling Rope marinas.

Last spring Wahweap held its first job fair, and about 750 people attended to learn more about 44 job categories at the lake's resorts and marinas. Openings are filled by April.

"The best thing that's ever happened for seasonal employees is the private housing we now have at our three largest marinas," says Wood. "All three offer private rooms with toilet and shower. Two of the three have dining rooms and rec halls, with such outdoor 'fun' things as basketball, volleyball and horseshoe courts."

Wood points out that not only will more qualified employees be attracted to Lake Powell, but as happier employees they will better serve the public.

Also delighted is the National Park Service, which has been underfunded and understaffed at Glen Canyon National Recreation Area since the government predicted (in the mid 1950's) that Lake Powell would draw an estimated 500,000 visitors a year by the year 2000.

Lake Powell, which twists 186 miles from Northern Arizona into Southern Utah, offers 1,960 miles of shoreline interspersed by rugged canyons (96 major ones and hundreds of offshoots).

Lake Powell began to fill in 1963 and "topped out" in 1980. It is surrounded by the nation's greatest concentration of national parks and is now the second

51

most popular overnight stop in the national park system.

The second largest manmade lake on the continent has been called a "Grand Canyon with water." As a gigantic watersports playground in a 78% sunshine belt, open year-round, it is as attractive to employees as to visitors. Says Wood, "There's no other place like it, anywhere!"

A temperate climate, wide-open waterways and broad bays make 186-mile-long Lake Powell a waterskier's delight. The season runs from spring to fall with average water temperatures ranging from 64° (May) to 80° (August) to 69° (October).

Houseboat Instructor, Wahweap Lodge, Lake Powell

Interview by National Parks Trade Journal with Richard Briggs,
Holuseboat Instructor, Wahweap Lodge, Lake Powell

TJ: Rich, why a houseboat instructor?

RB: A lot of people are apprehensive about boating on a lake with 1,960 miles of shoreline. And even veteran sailors need the basics of houseboat operation. Average "check-out" takes 50 minutes--inventory check, fuel, water, toilet, starting motors and other basics. Including a spin around the harbor.

TJ: What are the most commonly asked questions?

RB: Except for operation, which we cover thoroughly, we get questions like, "How far can I go today?" "Where are the best beaches?" and "What happens if I don't get the boat back in time?"

TJ: Do you explain policies to the entire houseboating party?

RB: We've found it best to limit instructions to one or two people. Sometimes it's evident who is the main driver. Sometimes I have to ask, "Who's the captain, here?" When they ask why it makes any difference. I say: "Captains never have to get a drink or cook." That breaks the ice.

TJ: What are your main challenges?

RB: Instilling confidence, covering basic procedures in a quick, efficient manner and keeping it fairly "light".

TJ: What happens if they forget instructions?

RB: They have been provided literature before arrival, instructions when they pay for the boat, and there's an on-board manual that covers every point I do. Don't forget fellow boaters--probably the friendliest fraternity in the world. Somebody's always glad to answer questions.

TJ: Who takes out houseboats on Lake Powell?

RB: Just about anybody. Typical party size is three couples or a family of six. Our biggest boats sleep 12 and sometimes all the bunks and beds are used. And more Europeans are doing it. They used to stay in the lodge and take boat tours but now they rent our powerboats and houseboats.

TJ: Are more people houseboating than ever before?

RB: They are at Lake Powell. Webb marinas have 307 houseboats; for six months they're almost always rented, for three months they're half rented and for the three winter months, we have the time to perform maintenance.

With 1,960 miles of shoreline and 161,000 surface acres of water, Lake Powell provides adventure to this "Grand Canyon with water." Houseboating and boat tours to Rainbow Bridge National Monument are popular ways of exploring some of the lake's 96 major canyons. Wahweap, Bullfrog, Hall's Crossing and Hite are the lakes four full service marinas. Wahweap Resort is Lake Powell's largest facility, with 270 rooms and many restaurants.

TJ: Is houseboating safe?

RB: Our boats sit on huge pontoons, compartmentalized and almost unsinkable. Common sense is all that is needed. Of course, instructors have to be careful.

TJ: What do you mean?

RB: Once when I was showing a customer how to tilt a motor and examine the prop, someone started the motor. Now I take the keys out of the console.

TJ: What about Lake Powell? Is it a new attraction?

RB: Lake Powell didn't fill until 1980, but it's already drawing more than 3 million visitors a year. If I had to describe it I would say it is like a Grand Canyon, with water. It's got 96 major canyons with hundreds of side canyons. It's a great place to boat, fish, ski, hike, photography and just relax.

TJ: I take it you like Lake Powell? What do you do to relax?

RB: I love the lake and my job. I get a big charge out of dealing with people, particularly when they look me up after a trip to tell me it was one of the best experiences of their lives. And Powell fits my hobby -- waterskiing.

TJ: Do you ski a lot?

RB: More than the average. I believe I hold the world record for non-stop slalom skiing--240 miles.

TJ: What is your average day?

RB: Check out small boats until 10 a.m., then switch to houseboats.

TJ: Do you consider Lake Powell a good place to work?

RB: Yes. For two years I worked at the front desk of the lodge. We have boat tours, RV parks, general stores and restaurants. There's lots of opportunities to cross-train. Our company has five marinas on the lake as well as a raft operation in the Grand Canyon.

TJ: Do you operate 12 months a year?

RB: Yes. We do maintenance in the winter, when boats are rented mostly by fishermen. You learn how boats are put together.

TJ: Would you recommend your position to others, including seasonal help?

RB: Without reservations. We have seasonal boat instructors and need them. Lake Powell is a great place to live and work.

Lake Powell, Houseboat Instructor Richard Briggs, Glen Canyon Nat. Rec. Area.

THE SOUTHWEST

IS OUR CLASSROOM

PRESCOTT COLLEGE offers a positive alternative to traditional education. With small classes, extensive field work, and the opportunity for students to design their own educational path, students here become actively involved in the learning process.

Environmental Studies is an essential component of our curriculum. Areas of study include: Field Ecology, Environmental Education, Natural History, American Indian Concepts of Nature, Wildlife Biology, Earth Science, and the Politics and Economics of the Environment.

Students here become part of a warm, yet demanding educational community, which is closely knit in common purpose. Besides studying the environment, they work with an outstanding faculty in such interdisciplinary areas as Southwest Studies, Human Development, Humanities, Outdoor Leadership, and others. Our home is the town of Prescott in the pine-clad mountains of central Arizona. The educational journey here may take you to remote parts of the Grand Canyon, the Sea of Cortez, and to many other parts of the world. It will also take you within yourself, and into the vast world of thought, knowledge, and learning. For more information write to the:

Director of Admissions
PRESCOTT COLLEGE
220-P Grove Avenue
Prescott, Arizona 86301
(602) 778-2090

HOT SPRINGS
NATIONAL PARK
(Arkansas)

MAILING ADDRESS:

Buckstaff Bath House Co.
Hot Springs, Ark 71901

SEASONAL EMPLOYMENT

5	5	5	5
SPRING	**SUMMER**	**FALL**	**WINTER**

BEST TIME TO APPLY: Year-round

GENERAL EMPLOYMENT:

■ Indicates services and facilities with employment opportunities.

☐ Management	☐ Administration	☐ Housekeeping
☐ Gift Shops	☐ Front Desk	☐ Tour Guides
☐ Stables	☐ Maintenance	☐ Grocery/Supplies
☐ Food Service	☐ Security	☐ Garage/Gas Station
☐ Janitorial	☐ Gardening	☐ Transportation
☐ Rental Shops	☐ x-c Skiing	☐ Alpine Skiing
☐ Climbing (Ice/Rock)	☐ Camping	☐ Boating (rafting, canoeing etc.)

ADDITIONAL INFORMATION: Bath house attendant, massage service

EMPLOYER PROVIDED LODGING:

☐ Dorms ☐ Tents ■ Cabins
☐ Other:

LODGING RESTRICTIONS:

■ Pets ☐ Guests
☐ Other:

EMPLOYEE MEAL PROGRAMS:

☐ Yes ■ No

EMPLOYEE COOKING FACILITIES:

☐ Yes ■ No

NEARBY RELIGIOUS SERVICES:

■ Yes ☐ No

NEARBY PRIVATE HOUSING:

■ Yes ☐ No

GROOMING RESTRICTIONS:

☐ Hair ☐ Moustache ■ Beard
■ Other: Neat appearance

OFF SEASON ADDRESS:

Same as above

DUCK DECOY MAGIC !

Eliminate the most disagreeable part of duck hunting . . puttin' out and pickin' up the decoys. Patented QUACKER-PACKER^{TM} does this with nary a drop of icy water touching your hands. No winding or unwinding decoy cords or weights. Each unique QUACKER-PACKER^{TM} easily handles a dozen or more decoys into shallow marshes and ponds. If you store your decoys at the blind, it works even better.

Endorsed by many hunters and duck clubs, the QUACKER-PACKER^{TM} is inexpensive (less than 1/3 the cost of a decoy bag) and is the quickest and driest way to put 'em out and pick 'em up devised. <u>We guarantee it or your money back</u>!! Imagine . . put out 2 dozen decoys in 2 minutes and pick 'em up in 1C minutes. Send $1.00 to: Graybill Co., Dept. 12-A, P.O. Box 1752, Oakland, CA 94604 for details and price.

DEATH VALLEY
NATIONAL MONUMENT
(California)

MAILING ADDRESS:

TW Services, Inc.
451 N. Main
P.O. Box 400
Cedar City, UT 84720

SEASONAL EMPLOYMENT

340	120	340	340
SPRING	**SUMMER**	**FALL**	**WINTER**

BEST TIME TO APPLY: May thru August

GENERAL EMPLOYMENT:

■ Indicates services and facilities with employment opportunities.

☐ Management	■ Administration	■ Housekeeping
■ Gift Shops	■ Front Desk	■ Tour Guides
■ Stables	■ Maintenance	■ Grocery/Supplies
■ Food Service	■ Security	■ Garage/Gas Station
■ Janitorial	■ Gardening	☐ Transportation
■ Rental Shops	☐ x-c Skiing	☐ Alpine Skiing
■ Climbing (Ice/Rock)	■ Camping	☐ Boating (rafting, canoeing etc.)

ADDITIONAL INFORMATION: Tennis & Golf Instructors

EMPLOYER PROVIDED LODGING:

■ Dorms　☐ Tents　■ Cabins
■ Other: Full hook-up for employee
　　　　　trailers provided

EMPLOYEE MEAL PROGRAMS:

■ Yes　☐ No

NEARBY RELIGIOUS SERVICES:

■ Yes　☐ No

GROOMING RESTRICTIONS:

■ Hair　☐ Moustache　■ Beard
☐ Other:

LODGING RESTRICTIONS:

■ Pets　☐ Guests
☐ Other:

EMPLOYEE COOKING FACILITIES:

☐ Yes　■ No

NEARBY PRIVATE HOUSING:

☐ Yes　■ No

OFF SEASON ADDRESS:

Same as above

61

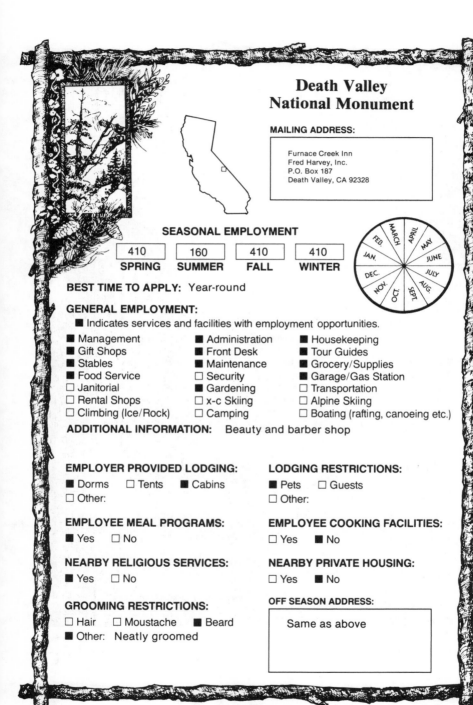

Death Valley
National Monument

MAILING ADDRESS:

Furnace Creek Inn
Fred Harvey, Inc.
P.O. Box 187
Death Valley, CA 92328

SEASONAL EMPLOYMENT

410	160	410	410
SPRING	**SUMMER**	**FALL**	**WINTER**

BEST TIME TO APPLY: Year-round

GENERAL EMPLOYMENT:

■ Indicates services and facilities with employment opportunities.

■ Management	■ Administration	■ Housekeeping
■ Gift Shops	■ Front Desk	■ Tour Guides
■ Stables	■ Maintenance	■ Grocery/Supplies
■ Food Service	□ Security	■ Garage/Gas Station
□ Janitorial	■ Gardening	□ Transportation
□ Rental Shops	□ x-c Skiing	□ Alpine Skiing
□ Climbing (Ice/Rock)	□ Camping	□ Boating (rafting, canoeing etc.)

ADDITIONAL INFORMATION: Beauty and barber shop

EMPLOYER PROVIDED LODGING:

■ Dorms　　□ Tents　　■ Cabins
□ Other:

LODGING RESTRICTIONS:

■ Pets　　□ Guests
□ Other:

EMPLOYEE MEAL PROGRAMS:

■ Yes　　□ No

EMPLOYEE COOKING FACILITIES:

□ Yes　　■ No

NEARBY RELIGIOUS SERVICES:

■ Yes　　□ No

NEARBY PRIVATE HOUSING:

□ Yes　　■ No

GROOMING RESTRICTIONS:

□ Hair　　□ Moustache　　■ Beard
■ Other:　Neatly groomed

OFF SEASON ADDRESS:

Same as above

62

Golfers enjoy a leisurely round on the course at Furnace Creek Ranch.

SAND DUNES AT DEATH VALLEY NATIONAL MONUMENT
A Special Treat in a Basin of Natural Wonders
By J. Emilio Reynoso

Sand dunes are among the most fascinating effects of geomorphosis. They seem in every respect to be vibrant communities of symbiotic life systems-- assuming crescent-shaped ranges with continuous but undulating and sharp crests. Or they turn into domed peaks of swirling mocha mounds in another mood. Or they may do everything that dunes do all at once in the same field.

Diurnal changes at Death Valley National Monument are profound. They range from extremes in ground temperatures of 175 degrees Fahrenheit or more at mid-day, to sub-freezing air temperatures by night. Rains come in torrents, and sand-laden winds blast rock surfaces. These set the stage for highly accelerated erosion, releasing quartz granules from their matrix. Those are the stuff of sand dunes.

J. E. Reynoso

The dunes of Stovepipe Wells and Panamint Valley behave much like those of the great continental arid basins of Africa, Australia and Asia. They are ruled by dominant wind velocity, and their quartz grains are alluvial in origin. Their color and texture, save for parental variation, and age, are much alike. The ratios of wavelength to amplitude follow the same patterns as they move downwind. The threshold wind velocities, which govern granular movement, follow the same set of rules. Their avalanche angle (of repose) on the lee side is 33 degrees. Their base-to-height proportions are the same.

Unlike the great migrating continental dunes which may travel thousands of miles and reach great heights along alleys of trade winds, Death Valley dunes are confined to movement within a small, well defined area, dictated by local winds which move over their basin.

Once quartz has been released from its matrix, dune-forming grains must measure not less than 0.05 nor exceed 2.00 mm in diameter. Anything less and the particle becomes suspended by wind as dust, and heavier grains rest where they lie.

J. E. Reynoso

Sand Dunes confined in Panamint Valley.

The initial motion of grains relative to wind velocity is to roll along the ground for a few meters before they begin to saltate. This bounding motion of granules along flat trajectories within the airstream is associated with small grains. These grains in turn collide with larger grains to move them upslope along the dune.

Two things happen when the airflow travels along the dune crest: air compresses and increases its velocity, thereby tossing over the crest the larger grains which have accumulated at the ridge; or it falters after it has passed the crest, and deposits its load of sand at the lee side of the dune. There the grains rest in a wind eddy, but only until they reach the avalanche angle (of repose) of 33 degrees. Then they fall until another equilibrium is reached. This is why the rules of proportion of base and height vary only negligibly.

At Stovepipe Wells the dunes are called compound because they form in combinations of simple forms. Unlike the Panamint dunes, they are subject to complex wind patterns created by this topography: the irregularly formed Amargosa Range to the east; a fairly clean longitudinal Panamints to the west; a gaping playa to the south; and a downramp of extensive alluvial fan systems to the north.

The Panamint dunes, on the other hand, are simple dunes characterized by common pyramidal forms. They occur as sand catchments at the junction of longitudinal crestal ridges where sand-loaded winds eddy and lose their load. In this case, winds from a transverse direction might also alternately, or simultaneously occur with the prevailing airflow.

As catchment dunes form and grow, they may create their own vortical currents and eddy systems, and so the Panamint dunes do assert their individuality among a common peerage.

Here we do not concern ourselves with transformation in terms of geological time. Nor do we need to extrapolate from a body of wisdom to know what might have been, or what may take place. Sand dunes. We can appreciate them grain for grain in everyday human terms.

J.E. Reynoso

Panamint Dunes

LASSEN VOLCANIC NATIONAL PARK
(California)

MAILING ADDRESS:

Calif. Guest Services, Inc.
2150 Main #7
Red Bluff, CA 96080

SEASONAL EMPLOYMENT

5	40	8	50
SPRING	**SUMMER**	**FALL**	**WINTER**

BEST TIME TO APPLY:

GENERAL EMPLOYMENT:

■ Indicates services and facilities with employment opportunities.

■ Management
■ Gift Shops
■ Stables
■ Food Service
■ Janitorial
■ Rental Shops
□ Climbing (Ice/Rock)

□ Administration
□ Front Desk
■ Maintenance
□ Security
□ Gardening
■ x-c Skiing
■ Camping

■ Housekeeping
□ Tour Guides
■ Grocery/Supplies
■ Garage/Gas Station
□ Transportation
■ Alpine Skiing
□ Boating (rafting, canoeing etc.)

ADDITIONAL INFORMATION:

EMPLOYER PROVIDED LODGING:

■ Dorms   □ Tents   □ Cabins
■ Other: Summer Only

LODGING RESTRICTIONS:

■ Pets   □ Guests
□ Other:

EMPLOYEE MEAL PROGRAMS:

□ Yes   ■ No

EMPLOYEE COOKING FACILITIES:

□ Yes   ■ No

NEARBY RELIGIOUS SERVICES:

□ Yes   ■ No
       1 location only summer

NEARBY PRIVATE HOUSING:

■ Yes   □ No

GROOMING RESTRICTIONS:

□ Hair   □ Moustache   □ Beard
■ Other: Neat, clean appearance

OFF SEASON ADDRESS:

Same as above

SEQUOIA AND KINGS CANYON NATIONAL PARKS

(California)

MAILING ADDRESS:

Guest Services
Personnel
Sequoia Nat'l Park, CA 93262

SEASONAL EMPLOYMENT

130	390	175	115
SPRING	**SUMMER**	**FALL**	**WINTER**

BEST TIME TO APPLY: January thru April

GENERAL EMPLOYMENT:

■ Indicates services and facilities with employment opportunities.

■ Management	☐ Administration	■ Housekeeping
■ Gift Shops	■ Front Desk	■ Tour Guides
☐ Stables	■ Maintenance	■ Grocery/Supplies
■ Food Service	■ Security	■ Garage/Gas Station
■ Janitorial	☐ Gardening	■ Transportation
☐ Rental Shops	■ x-c Skiing	■ Alpine Skiing
☐ Climbing (Ice/Rock)	☐ Camping	☐ Boating (rafting, canoeing etc.)

ADDITIONAL INFORMATION:

EMPLOYER PROVIDED LODGING:

■ Dorms ☐ Tents ■ Cabins
☐ Other:

LODGING RESTRICTIONS:

■ Pets ■ Guests
☐ Other:

EMPLOYEE MEAL PROGRAMS:

■ Yes ☐ No

EMPLOYEE COOKING FACILITIES:

☐ Yes ■ No

NEARBY RELIGIOUS SERVICES:

■ Yes ☐ No

NEARBY PRIVATE HOUSING:

☐ Yes ■ No

GROOMING RESTRICTIONS:

☐ Hair ☐ Moustache ☐ Beard
■ Other: Clean, well groomed

OFF SEASON ADDRESS:

Same as above

WHISKEYTOWN
NATIONAL RECREATION AREA
(California)

MAILING ADDRESS:

Oak Bottom Marina
PO Box 197
Whiskeytown, CA 96095

SEASONAL EMPLOYMENT

25	25	0	0
SPRING	**SUMMER**	**FALL**	**WINTER**

APRIL MAY JUNE JULY AUG. SEPT.

BEST TIME TO APPLY: February and March

GENERAL EMPLOYMENT:

■ Indicates services and facilities with employment opportunities.

☐ Management ☐ Administration ☐ Housekeeping
☐ Gift Shops ☐ Front Desk ☐ Tour Guides
☐ Stables ☐ Maintenance ■ Grocery/Supplies
■ Food Service ☐ Security ☐ Garage/Gas Station
■ Janitorial ☐ Gardening ☐ Transportation
■ Rental Shops ☐ x-c Skiing ☐ Alpine Skiing
☐ Climbing (Ice/Rock) ☐ Camping ☐ Boating (rafting, canoeing etc.)

ADDITIONAL INFORMATION:

EMPLOYER PROVIDED LODGING:

☐ Dorms ☐ Tents ☐ Cabins
■ Other: None

LODGING RESTRICTIONS:

☐ Pets ☐ Guests
■ Other: N/A

EMPLOYEE MEAL PROGRAMS:

■ Yes ☐ No

EMPLOYEE COOKING FACILITIES:

☐ Yes ■ No

NEARBY RELIGIOUS SERVICES:

■ Yes ☐ No

NEARBY PRIVATE HOUSING:

■ Yes ☐ No

GROOMING RESTRICTIONS:

☐ Hair ☐ Moustache ☐ Beard
■ Other: Neat, pleasant personality

OFF SEASON ADDRESS:

Same as above

YOSEMITE
NATIONAL PARK
(California)

MAILING ADDRESS:

Yosemite Park and Curry Co.
Personnel Office
Yosemite Nat'l Pk., CA 95389

SEASONAL EMPLOYMENT

1200	1800	1200	900
SPRING	**SUMMER**	**FALL**	**WINTER**

BEST TIME TO APPLY: January thru March; July

GENERAL EMPLOYMENT:

■ Indicates services and facilities with employment opportunities.

■ Management	■ Administration	■ Housekeeping
■ Gift Shops	■ Front Desk	■ Tour Guides
■ Stables	■ Maintenance	■ Grocery/Supplies
■ Food Service	■ Security	■ Garage/Gas Station
■ Janitorial	■ Gardening	■ Transportation
■ Rental Shops	■ x-c Skiing	■ Alpine Skiing
■ Climbing (Ice/Rock)	□ Camping	□ Boating (rafting, canoeing etc.)

ADDITIONAL INFORMATION: Employee recreation program
includes dances, movies, wellness program, theatre, sports, etc.

EMPLOYER PROVIDED LODGING:
■ Dorms   ■ Tents   □ Cabins
□ Other:

LODGING RESTRICTIONS:
■ Pets   ■ Guests
□ Other:

EMPLOYEE MEAL PROGRAMS:
■ Yes   □ No

EMPLOYEE COOKING FACILITIES:
■ Yes   □ No

NEARBY RELIGIOUS SERVICES:
■ Yes   □ No

NEARBY PRIVATE HOUSING:
□ Yes   ■ No

GROOMING RESTRICTIONS:
■ Hair   ■ Moustache   □ Beard
■ Other: Collar length hair for
for men trimmed moustaches,
no multi-colored hair,
no earrings for men,
conservative image.

OFF SEASON ADDRESS:

Same as above

70

"Half Dome from the Illilouette Ridge."

Yosemite
National Park
(California)

MAILING ADDRESS:

Pinetree Market
P.O. Box 2097
Wawona, CA 95389

SEASONAL EMPLOYMENT

1	3	1	1
SPRING	**SUMMER**	**FALL**	**WINTER**

BEST TIME TO APPLY: Spring

GENERAL EMPLOYMENT:

■ Indicates services and facilities with employment opportunities.

☐ Management ☐ Administration ☐ Housekeeping
☐ Gift Shops ☐ Front Desk ☐ Tour Guides
☐ Stables ☐ Maintenance ■ Grocery/Supplies
☐ Food Service ☐ Security ☐ Garage/Gas Station
☐ Janitorial ☐ Gardening ☐ Transportation
☐ Rental Shops ☐ x-c Skiing ☐ Alpine Skiing
☐ Climbing (Ice/Rock) ☐ Camping ☐ Boating (rafting, canoeing etc.)

ADDITIONAL INFORMATION:

EMPLOYER PROVIDED LODGING:

☐ Dorms ☐ Tents ☐ Cabins
■ Other: Various, depending
            on availability

LODGING RESTRICTIONS:

☐ Pets ☐ Guests
■ Other: N/A

EMPLOYEE MEAL PROGRAMS:

☐ Yes ■ No

EMPLOYEE COOKING FACILITIES:

☐ Yes ■ No

NEARBY RELIGIOUS SERVICES:

■ Yes ☐ No

NEARBY PRIVATE HOUSING:

■ Yes ☐ No

GROOMING RESTRICTIONS:

☐ Hair ☐ Moustache ☐ Beard
■ Other: Well groomed

OFF SEASON ADDRESS:

Same as above

Yosemite
National Park
(California)

MAILING ADDRESS:

The Redwoods
P.O. Box 2085
Wawona, CA 95389

SEASONAL EMPLOYMENT

25	25	25	20
SPRING	**SUMMER**	**FALL**	**WINTER**

BEST TIME TO APPLY:

GENERAL EMPLOYMENT:

■ Indicates services and facilities with employment opportunities.

- ■ Management
- □ Gift Shops
- □ Stables
- □ Food Service
- ■ Janitorial
- □ Rental Shops
- □ Climbing (Ice/Rock)

- ■ Administration
- ■ Front Desk
- ■ Maintenance
- □ Security
- □ Gardening
- □ x-c Skiing
- □ Camping

- ■ Housekeeping
- □ Tour Guides
- □ Grocery/Supplies
- □ Garage/Gas Station
- □ Transportation
- □ Alpine Skiing
- □ Boating (rafting, canoeing etc.)

ADDITIONAL INFORMATION:

EMPLOYER PROVIDED LODGING:

□ Dorms   □ Tents   □ Cabins
■ Other: None

LODGING RESTRICTIONS:

□ Pets   □ Guests
■ Other: N/A

EMPLOYEE MEAL PROGRAMS:

□ Yes   ■ No

EMPLOYEE COOKING FACILITIES:

□ Yes   ■ No

NEARBY RELIGIOUS SERVICES:

■ Yes   □ No

NEARBY PRIVATE HOUSING:

■ Yes   □ No

GROOMING RESTRICTIONS:

□ Hair   □ Moustache   □ Beard
■ Other: Neat, well groomed

OFF SEASON ADDRESS:

Same as above

Yosemite
National Park
(California)

MAILING ADDRESS:

Yosemite Medical Clinic
P.O. Box 547
Yosemite, CA 95389

SEASONAL EMPLOYMENT

22	27	22	22
SPRING	**SUMMER**	**FALL**	**WINTER**

BEST TIME TO APPLY: All year

GENERAL EMPLOYMENT:

■ Indicates services and facilities with employment opportunities.

■ Management	■ Administration	☐ Housekeeping
☐ Gift Shops	☐ Front Desk	☐ Tour Guides
☐ Stables	☐ Maintenance	☐ Grocery/Supplies
☐ Food Service	☐ Security	☐ Garage/Gas Station
■ Janitorial	☐ Gardening	☐ Transportation
☐ Rental Shops	☐ x-c Skiing	☐ Alpine Skiing
☐ Climbing (Ice/Rock)	☐ Camping	☐ Boating (rafting, canoeing etc.)

ADDITIONAL INFORMATION: 8 full time R.N.'s, 3 full time M.D.'s
& 2 full time lab x-ray technicians.
Please send C.V./resume to above address.

EMPLOYER PROVIDED LODGING:

■ Dorms   ☐ Tents   ☐ Cabins
☐ Other: Only for R.N.'s & M.D.'s

LODGING RESTRICTIONS:

☐ Pets   ☐ Guests
■ Other: N/A

EMPLOYEE MEAL PROGRAMS:

☐ Yes   ■ No

EMPLOYEE COOKING FACILITIES:

■ Yes   ☐ No

NEARBY RELIGIOUS SERVICES:

■ Yes   ☐ No

NEARBY PRIVATE HOUSING:

☐ Yes   ■ No

GROOMING RESTRICTIONS:

☐ Hair   ☐ Moustache   ☐ Beard
■ Other: Appropriate for
medical clinic

OFF SEASON ADDRESS:

Same as above

STAR TREK V LANDS IN YOSEMITE

It's not everyday the Starship Enterprise lands in Yosemite. When it did, Dave Anzalone had this exclusive interview with William Shatner of the Star Trek V crew.

Dave Anzalone: Mr. Shatner, why did you choose Yosemite?

William Shatner: Well, Yosemite is the mecca for every climber in the world. We know that anybody who wants to climb granite faces has to come to Yosemite because this is the cathedral that all rock climbers worship in. I'm not a rock climber, but I've admired the sport and admire the people who require such discipline in order to do it in such courage and bravery in face of death, give or take a mistake. So, Yosemite was the natural place to come.

D.A.: I've notice throughout the shooting that many National Park Service, Yosemite Association and Yosemite Park & Curry Co. employees assisted your film crews. Do you have any words for them?

W.S.: Yes. From the very top to the very bottom we've had nothing but the greatest cooperation. They have given us strict rules to abide by in filming. Those strict rules are: nothing is to be hurt, nothing is to be tampered with, take only photos, leave only memories. We have been stringent in our desire to follow all rules because, more than anyone else, we know the value of keeping a wilderness area wild and pristine. So, that in following those rules and abiding by what we've been told, we've had nothing but the greatest cooperation from everyone.

D.A.: What would Captain Kirk's thoughts be of the future of mankind?

W.S.: On the future of mankind?

D.A.: You've already seen it, right?

W.S.: Well, no I haven't. I can't give you Captain Kirk's view because that's from a distance a long way from now. My view, however, of the future of mankind, is if we can maintain areas like Yosemite, wild and natural as nature, if we can increase them, and educate people to understand the need not to destroy, not to defile, not to uproot nature, particularly in the wilderness areas, we do have a future. If we can't educate people into the worship of nature, then we're dead.

D.A.: Do you have any clues for our readers about Star Trek V?

W.S.: We know that early in the film Yosemite appears, O.K.? (Smiles....)

> *"It is the ultimate act of creativity. It's the end result of everything I wanted to do. And to see it all come alive is beyond my ability to verbalize how thrilling it is."*
>
> Actor William Shatner, on directing "Star Trek 5."

75

Dave Anzalone strolling with William Shatner during interview at Glacier Point.

ELLIE HAWKINS SOLOS 2,000-FOOT WALL IN YOSEMITE VALLEY!

By Kim Saunders

In September, petite Ellie Hawkins of Bear Valley, CA, scaled a 2,000-foot wall near El Capitan, solo, in what Bruce Brossman, Director of the Yosemite Mountaineering School, calls a "major, major feat." Only a handful of routes in Yosemite Valley have ever been soloed on a first ascent, but what makes Ellie's climb even more front-page noteworthy is that she suffers from Dyslexia.

Dyslexia is a learning disability that causes one to read or write certain words or letters backwards. In Ellie's case the problem is a little more complicated. She often hears, speaks and perceives things in their mirror image. Undiagnosed until just seven years ago, Ellie saw a PBS program on Dyslexia and realized the problem she'd been aware of since early childhood had a name.

At this point in her life, she and husband Bruce Hawkins were already free climbing, a sport that came easily to her. Advancing to more difficult climbing, with the use of ropes and other aids, however, was more of a problem. She must work in deep concentration during a climb, checking each move carefully many times, to compensate for her Dyslexia. "I become like a machine on the rock," she says.

But, the efforts are well worth it; she may not move as quickly as other climbers, but Ellie Hawkins has become one of the top climbers in the world.

Born in The Dalles, Oregon, in 1949, Ellie started to climb when she was twenty-one. The majority of her climbs have been in Yosemite but she's also climbed in Great Britain, Norway, the Alps, Canada and elsewhere in the Western U.S. In 1984, Ellie climbed the "Direct North Face" route of Half Dome, becoming the first woman to solo the face of Half Dome. Earlier this year, she became the first woman to solo the "Never, Never Land" route of El Capitan.

That September's effort, during which she kept in two-way radio contact with Alan Richmond of YP&CC, a sponsor of the trip, was one of her most difficult challenges. Not previously climbed, the way was covered with debris, forcing Ellie to clean dirt and moss from the cracks. and pound holes for each step she took. Despite the difficulty of the venture, Ellie enjoyed the climb, found time to note the view was "spectacular," and also kept a journal of the adventure.

What drives her to set such goals, accomplish such feats? "Dyslexia's not a thing to be ashamed of. I think it motivates me," she says. It's something

Ellie Hawkins, September 1985 on "Dyslexia" Peak.

people hide, and more and more people I know are hiding it." Her mother, Hazel Knepper of Portland, Oregon, says, "Ellie wants the general public to have a better understanding of children and adults with learning disabilities." She hopes to encourage schools to routinely test children for Dyslexia and to provide special assistance to those children discovered to have the disability.

An estimated one in ten persons is Dyslexic and the mysterious disability occurs in four times as many boys as girls, but some of history's most brilliant and successful people have been Dyslexic - among them Thomas Edison, Albert Einstein, Leonardo da Vinci and Winston Churchill.

Ellie wants Dyslexic children to realize that the same disability that causes them problems in school can be the one that motivates them to strive for higher successes. She visits grade school classes, speaks to children and shows slides of her climbs, as well as gives interviews for television and publications, all in an effort to educate the public regarding the disability from which she suffers.

There are no real cures for Dyslexia; the challenge falls to each individual to develop his or her own way to get things done, according to Marcia Henry, Vice President of the international Orton Dyslexia Society of Baltimore, Maryland, one of the sponsors of Ellie's recent climb.

For Ellie the challenge continues, but this September, she found her own way to conquer the disability, and reaching the top of the mountain, christened her new route "Dyslexia."

CAMP CHILNUALNA is a group of cabins located on private property near the South Fork of the Merced River within **Yosemite National Park.**

The cabins range in size from two bedrom, one or two bath units, or up to four bedroom three bath units.

All have spacious sundecks with barbeque braziers and deck furniture.

The kitchens are fully equipped, including microwave ovens.

All cabins have fireplaces with firewood provided.

During summer, the Merced River provides excellent swimming and fishing.

Golfing and horseback riding are also nearby.

During winter, cross country and downhill skiing are available at Badger Pass, just 17 miles away.

CAMP CHILNUALNA
Box 2095
Wawona, Ca 95389
(209) 375-6295

CHALLENGING YEARS IN
CALIFORNIA'S GREAT OUTDOORS

Reopening streams along the North Coast to salmon and trout migrations... building trails and restoring meadows in Yosemite...fighting forest fires in the Klamath National Forest...renovating a neighborhood center in Long Beach...installing solar panels at state parks...reconstructing the historic Santa Barbara Presidio.

These are just a few of the thousands of ambitious projects the California Conservation Corps and its 2,000 young people have taken on over the years. The CCC, as it is known, was created in 1976 with a dual mission: the protection and enhancement of the state's natural resources, and the employment of young men and women between the ages of 18 and 23.

The pairing of these two important resources -- youth and the environment --has resulted in a 12-year success story for the Corps. The largest and oldest youth conservation program now in operation, the CCC is a model for similar programs worldwide.

In the CCC, young people take on challenging projects and come away with a sense of satisfaction and solid skills that will last them a lifetime. What's more, their efforts are helping to preserve California's heritage, history and natural resources for future generations.

Reopening streams to salmon and trout migrations along California's North Coast.

There are now 40,000 young people who have participated in the CCC, who can look back with pride on the work they've done to enhance California's natural resources. And all of us can share in and enjoy their accomplishments.

Corpsmembers start out making about $740 a month, and right away can work toward a 10 percent pay increase. Benefits include health insurance, vacation and sick leave. There are 17 residential CCC centers located throughout California, and 25 nonresidential satellite locations, where young people live at home and commute to work.

All in a Day's Work

On a typical day, corpsmembers are installing irrigation lines for a demonstration garden designed to showcase water conserving landscapes. They're planting trees in the Klamath, Shasta-Trinity, Stanislaus, and Sequoia national forests, in areas devastated by fire. They're enhancing streams to assist salmon migrations. They're pouring concrete for a park trail that will be accessible to those in wheelchairs. And they're landscaping the median strip on a major thoroughfare in San Francisco.

Along with the physical work, corpsmembers spend several evenings a week in the classroom, taking community college classes, learning about career opportunities, or participating in the CCC's conservation awareness program, designed to promote a greater understanding of conservation principles and the value of natural resources -- the "why" behind their work.

Funded by the State of California, the CCC is a labor force that assists government agencies at all levels in undertaking projects of public benefit.

The CCC is also called in to provide emergency assistance in natural disasters. Corpsmembers fight wildfires, sandbag during floods, and provide cleanup aid following earthquakes.

Yosemite: A Spectacular Worksite

Using their hands, a basic complement of hand tools, granite rock and other native building materials, select members of the CCC spend up to six months each year building and restoring trails in the state's wilderness areas. These crew members do some of the toughest work in the CCC, from the most remote and spectacular worksites. The CCC's Backcountry Trails Project is a cooperative venture between the CCC, the National Park Service, the U.S. Forest Service, and the California Department of Parks and Recreation.

At Yosemite National Park, the Corps has now rebuilt more than 500 miles of park trails at Half Dome, Yosemite Falls, Mirror Lake, Hetch

Hetchy, Waterwheel Falls, among other locations.

Just to get to the worksites each morning, corpsmembers often must hike two to three miles. The work has proved not only to be difficult on the tools but corpsmembers often wear out two pairs of gloves a day on the strenuous work! But they still leave the backcountry at season's end filled with great memories. As one corpsmember so aptly put it, "I survived the Backcountry, sometimes triumphantly, sometimes by the skin of my teeth..."

For More Information

For more information on the CCC or to join, call toll-free 1-800-952-JOBS (for California callers only) or 916-445-0307.

Corpsmember "mopping up" after the fire, making sure to extinguish all the embers.

Constructing a staircase of granite rock at Yosemite.

CALIFORNIA'S UNDERWATER PARKS
A 'SECRET' PART OF THE STATE PARK SYSTEM

There's a little-known part of the California State Park System that's completely under water.

It's the underwater parks program.

The department of Parks and Recreation's underwater parks program was established in 1968 to preserve the best representative examples of California's natural underwater resources found in coastal and inland waters. The program also aims to provide a variety of underwater recreational opportunities, especially in areas near metroplitan centers.

Working with the State Lands Commission, the department and the Advisory Board on Underwater Parks and Reserves identify potential areas for under water parks and determine how they should be managed for both preservation and recreation. Twelve units are currently in operation and many more are in the planning stages.

The underwater parks offer scenic diving and related activities, such as underwater photography and spear fishing.

Ken Collier, Project Manager for the underwater parks program and Executive Secretary for the Board, explained, "The parks are being designed for divers and non-divers, with interpretation for both in visitor centers, kiosks and exhibit boards. Eventually there could be ranger/lifeguarded-led

underwater tours. There are also facilities for day-use activities, such as picnicking.

"In California, you can dive anyplace you have legal access to the water. What we're attempting to do is provide safe, convenient access for divers with a lot of facilities, including fresh water washdown showers and restrooms."

The twelve existing underwater parks include Russian Gulch State Park, MacKerricher State Park, Van Damme State Park, Manchester State Beach, Salt Point State Park, Fort Ross State Historic Park, Sonoma Coast State Beach, Point Lobos State Reserve, Julia Pfeiffer Burns State Park, Lake Perris State Recreation Area, Crystal Cove State Park and Doheny State Beach.

Three of the units are full-operational: Crystal Cove State Park between Newport Beach and Laguna Beach in southern California; Point Lobos State Reserve near Carmel in central California; and Salt Point State Park near Jenner in northern California. Salt Point has optimum facilities, including restrooms/changing rooms, lockers, fresh water washdown showers, drying racks, a catch cleaning station and parking areas. All have safe, convenient access to the water's edge. Air is available for divers in limited locations.

Collier explained, "With our locations, we can provide safer access and egress for divers as well as information on what they can expect once they're underwater. Our areas are so well studied and detailed, we know how to

86

have people enter and exit safely. Divers are often able to enter a quiet cove with no large, breaking waves. The areas will be clearly marked with information about the unit's scenic resources and any necessary precautions that might be needed. Also, in some areas, there are dive teams available to assist with any problems that might be encountered. Point Lobos and Salt point are good examples."

"The parks are designed to provide a threshold experience to divers. When new divers are learning, it's almost a hand-held experience with their instructor. When they 'graduate' and they're on their own it can be frightening. In fact, there's a 80-90% drop-out rate among first-time diving students graduates. We can provide information on what they can expect out there when they dive, making the experience less formidable."

A number of possible locations for new underwater parks are currently under consideration with an optimum system of 30 units along the coast, plus others in inland lakes, reservoirs and rivers.

Ken Collier added, "The potential is there. We need the continued support of the public. There is some volunteer work already being done. For example, at Point Lobos State Reserve volunteers have built - and rebuilt - an access stairway."

As for the future of the underwater parks program, he says, "Watch us grow."

NOTE: A 27 minute VHS-format videotape about the State Park Underwater Parks program, "Parks In The Sea", is available for $19.95 plus taxes, shipping and handling, from:

Publications Office
Department of Parks and Recreation
P.O. Box 942896
Sacramento, CA 94296-0001

For additional information, the phone number of the Publications Office is (916) 322-7000.

"If one advances confidently in the direction of their dreams, and endeavors to live the life which they have imagined, they will meet with success unexpected in common hours."
Henry David Thoreau

KAYAKING FOR THE NATURALIST AND ENTREPRENEUR

By J. Emilio Reynoso

Point Lobos State Wildlife Reserve, Monterey Bay, California

It was a warm summer afternoon and the sun was low above the Pacific horizon. A dense flock of gulls had settled well inside Whaler's Cove, bobbing gently on royal blue water against a backdrop of pine-studded cliffs that have turned crimson with the afternoon light. I paddled with stealth, as only a human in a kayak can, toward a pair of fat spotted seals. Then I began to shoot--not with a harpoon as I might have in times past, but with a thirty-five. The pup on the higher ledge clung stubbornly to his precious nap, but the other nearer the rising tide popped open an eye before he greeted me with a most sonorous and gaping yawn that only the young of any species can muster without shame.

At sea the ground swell had built to ten feet, yet it conveyed its enormous power in a friendly cadence. Along the north edge of the point, an expanse of kelp filters the ocean swells into moving lines of glassy mounds that beckon the child in anyone to glide down their clean faces for that giddy pleasure that is unique to a wave.

Exhausted from so exhilarating a rhythm of pleasure, plunging down peak to trough in a sleek sea-stick on mound upon silky mound, I settled behind small rock islands to find myself in the company of a table-size jelly fish floating in another atmosphere below me. His hues were those of many

rainbows, his tentacles drooping down perhaps 30 feet--their ends just below my ability to see, and he too seemed to have found just the right spot to take in the grace of the sea at this day's end.

South Lake Tahoe, California

We awoke to the giggles of a gaggle of little girls who had likely been making fun of us for some time. It was now mid-morning on a beach near Camp Richardson, and we had slept between our kayaks right on through sunrise and the rattle of Big Ben. Typical tourists, Spencer and I.

We marvelled at the beauty and expanse of the lake, gloated that again we were in that province of unfolding earthly mysteries and spiritual enrichment-the Sierra Nevada. We stood, amazed at the clarity of the water, and the skies, and how much closer points seem in the absence of deceptive dirt.

We paddled on, Spencer his pensive self, and I swinging my paddle to see how it sliced the thin air, and taking in data from the seat of my pants on how my hull design acts in fresh water.

Suddenly Spencer yelled "Wow! God, look, look!" as he pointed a finger underwater, which was invisible to me. Not a Great White, I thought. What could stagger Spencer in this lake? Then I saw. Some eighty feet below, a rock garden of 50-ton granite boulders that were arranged as though some keen giant had indulged himself over many a sundown hour to leave his mark in art for all posterity to enjoy.

Then Spencer said in uncharacteristic excitement--"This is it! People have got to see this. This is it--you've gotta talk to the Park guys and we'll guide people here this summer!"

Who can say no?

90

UPDATE ON KAYAKING:
Nautical Pacific Franchised Kayak Tours And Schools

FRANCHISING. Nautical Pacific has set up prototype franchise operations on the beach at Camp Richardson at South Lake Tahoe. In 1985 Nautical Pacific set out to design, build and distribute kayaks. Its *Nautical Thrill* is a top-ranked regatta performer.

Called *Nautical Pacific Recreational Company*, the new operation deviates in many aspects from "sea kayaking centers" which are found on the Pacific and Atlantic coasts. It rejects that one must master the open sea to enjoy kayaking. Fact is, many more people, including families and inland and mountain-oriented folk, would paddle on a beautiful and friendly lake than those who would challenge the Pacific or Atlantic. And it forgoes retail operations.

A fleet of new kayaks is provided to qualified operators who will be trained by Nautical in instruction and trip leadership, and in accommodating clients with special needs and interests. Training includes full management, marketing, and location guidelines, and on-site management consulting.

During weeks of moonlight at Tahoe we will offer evening paddling tours besides morning and afternoon excursions. Activities center on half-day and overnight guided tours around spectacular Emerald Bay, plus a full range of classes from beginning to expert, instructor training, and guided trip leadership.

Mondays are devoted to public service, teaching economically disadvantaged children of ages 12 to 17, and developmentally handicapped children and young adults.

If you live at or have access to a high-traffic summer lake resort, with extensive experience in guiding and teaching in the outdoors, we may be interested in each other! Mail resume.

Contact Nautical Pacific
Schoonmaker Point
Sausalito, CA 94965

AN INTERVIEW WITH ROYAL ROBBINS

One of America's most notable mountaineers, Royal Robbins has pioneered many impressive rock climbs and river descents both in and outside the national park system. NPTJ editor Robert Frankel was fortunate enough to spend an hour with Royal at his business headquarters in Modesto, California, where Royal talked about ethics, experiences, and the future.

Robert Frankel -- Your story entitled "Fantasia" first appeared in *Advanced Rockcraft* (La Siesta Press, Glendale, Ca. 1985). Tell us about the story.

Royal Robbins -- I wrote "Fantasia" from a personal experience. It's the name of a climb at Lover's Leap which I climbed with Ken Wilson. I changed some things around, like not using his name, because I wanted this to be a story where I could extend fictionally although it's pretty straightforward.

This route was fantastic: so interesting, so different, so special. I was trying to describe it as a climb but more importantly I was trying to describe the values that motivate me as a climber and the things I think about in the course of an ascent. That includes right and wrong, such as what you let yourself do and what you don't do. I tried to show what goes through my mind when I'm trying to climb safely while minimizing the amount of aids I use. Although this is an action story it's meant to be instructional, and that's why it's in *Advanced Rockclimbing*.

R.F. -- In the section of the book called "Values", you mentioned the relationship between technique and technology and you said that ultimately it's up to each climber to decide what to use and when to use it. What are your personal feelings about, for example, battery-operated drills and bolt-routes?

Royal -- I've never had to face that choice. I would do it now. I think it's too bad that these devices are available though they've changed the essence of bolting. They're used by bottom-up climbers who are placing bolts as they go and not using aid, and, that way, it's a quicker way of doing something that was already being done. They really haven't changed the nature of bolting, for the essence of bolting is not whether it's easy or hard to place...it takes skill. Bolting is a substitute for getting past a problem by aid or free climbing, and I'm not the one to make the call because I'm not out there. If I was I'd make the choice based on my idea of keeping the game straight.

The dilemma is similar to the shoe question -- there's no doubt that today's shoes make climbing easier. I'm not suggesting they make it so much easier that it's responsible for the difference in standards, but they do make it incrementally easier just as the shoes we were using were better than those used by the previous generation.

It's too much to ask people to keep the same technology and the same shoes. These advances are natural and right. When I do a route in shoes that was done previously by someone in mountaineering boots, I discount my effort by that much. I realize that if I'm barely scraping up a rock I take my hat off to those who preceded me because I realize I'm not doing the same thing they did.

Using technological advances is not "cheating", but I am concerned about the way in which bolts are used as opposed to how easy it is to place them. When you do place a bolt do a good job, make a good bolt that's going to last a long time. It should be an integral part of the route and it should be there. It shouldn't be a piece of crap, but something other climbers can rely on and therefore be part of the "signature" of the routefinder. A good route is done with as much free climbing as possible; and if you use aid, use as little as possible. The same goes for bolts -- place them well, use them well, keeping the asthetics of the route and keeping with my view of climbing as the creation of a supreme naturalistic expression.

A lot of climbers who have been around for awhile are concerned with some of the new methods which I fear will reduce climbing to a mere physical activity, taking the essential spirit out of it. What's always meant the most to me about climbing is the way one did it, looking up to the great predecessors who paid attention to their way of climbing. Those who didn't go up the easy way, or use pitons, or who didn't place any more bolts than they absolutely had to.

John Salathé was 45 when I started climbing and was doing his greatest routes at that time. When we started climbing his routes as youngsters we had the advantages of youth and the fact that he'd gone before us. We were amazed at the quality of his routes. He'd placed bolts here and there but we had a devil of a time getting from one bolt to the next because of the standards of his climbing. To me, the guiding values of climbing essentially answer the question of how you go about doing it.

That's not all there is to climbing, though. I don't mind bouldering, or climbing routes with bolts every six feet...that's fun, too. What we do should lead towards the kind of climbing that embraces the spirit of attention and awareness...not just exertion.

R.F. - How did you get involved with kayaking?

Royal -- We'd started selling kayaks back in '74 or '75 out of our mountain shops in Modesto and Fresno. Some years later we ran the South Fork of the Merced from Wawona to Hite's Cove. The first day I capsized and hit

93

a rock under the surface, dislocating my shoulder. We hiked out, leaving our boats, and returned a week or so later to finish the trip. It's not a run I recommend, as there were many long, tough portages and plenty of poison oak.

In the late '70's I started to develop arthritis in my wrists and ankles, and for awhile it was pretty bad. I couldn't climb much, but I could kayak. Physically it's easier going downhill, but at the same time it's just as challenging ---you have to keep your act together, you have to evaluate the dangers, and you have to "keep your house in order" or you'll eat it and get in a lot of trouble.

R.F. -- How do you feel about some of these rivers being considered for inclusion in Wild and Scenic preserves?

Royal -- I really don't want those areas bombarded with people, which has happened to some of our parks. Although protection of wild places is becoming increasingly necessary, the increased publicity may lead to increased access and diminish the remoteness and wildness of such areas.

R.F. -- What did you learn from your mountaineering adventures that you have applied to business?

Royal -- Although I often had companions when I was climbing or kayaking, those are essentially solo activities; whereas business is about people. In business we're all on the same rope and everybody has to pull together. On the other hand, my mountaineering adventures taught me an important lesson which I could carry over to business. The lesson is about fear.

While climbing I'd get to a spot where I was afraid to continue. Having lost my confidence I would fall, because in my mind I was certain to fail. By adopting a positive attitude I discovered that it was my fear of failure causing these falls, and not my lack of ability.

Whether we're talking about climbing, kayaking, or running a business, failure will happen. Nobody's perfect. Nevertheless, you can't give in to the fear of failure, for failure is part of how we learn to succeed. It's better to be prepared than to worry about what might happen.

I don't consider my business as being absolutely successful. It hasn't been tested enough. After a few more years, after we've weathered a few storms and pulled through the inevitable hard times that every business goes through, that's when I'll think of our operation as being truly successful.

Photo by Robert Frankel

FANTASIA

Kent hailed from England. He knew the Grit, and Harrison's. He had savored the Rock of the Ben, and been on the Isle of Lundy. He knew North Wales, had done a book on the Black Crag. Sea Cliffs? Gogarth his favorite, but never disdained to grab rock at Swanage or Cornwall. His fingers had stroked the limestone of Avon and the Pennines. And he had more than a nodding acquaintance with the Jewels of the Lake District. He was, in fact, an authority on British climbing, with a book soon coming to prove it.

Kent had come to sample the wonders of the Valley, to taste the climbing, the rocks, the social scene. I lured him from the hot bed of the climbing game, the arena of competition, of mangled hands and knees, exultation and despair, arrogance and sycophancy, where the sun shines So Hot. A tight, noisy place. Actually, most of that rather suited Kent, but he was tempted by my tales of a northern crag, of routes with sufficient character, and beauty, and variety, to please his connoisseur's palate. And maybe a first ascent! He decided to come. There might be a chance for a good copy. Perhaps I would fall.

"What a crag," whooped Kent, as we treaded along the old jeep trail beneath the cliff. "It looks nearly good." Nearly good was Kent's highest praise.

"It's as high as Cloggy," I observed, "though it's not yet got as many routes. Perhaps we'll add one today."

I pointed out the lines. "Corrugation Corner is just there, that dihedral, a super route - steep, makes you think, but not extreme. And just to its left - Travelers - takes that lower pillar, and then up the crack in the face, around to the right, and then, very exciting, back around, and up the edge, straight up. It's called Travelers because of that pink rock there. A subtle name, a period piece of the fifties. And that deep chimney is Eeyore's - had a good day there with Dorworthy last winter, one of the most demanding days I've had. But that seems to happen whenever I climb with Dorworthy." I pointed out Hourglass, Eagle Buttress, Letter Box, and nightmarish Incubus, a savage route. "And there's the Line," I said, pointing to a crack tracing a plumb line up the vertical 300 foot face of the East Wall. "The first pitch is as good as Cenotaph Corner." I knew Kent would appreciate this comparison.

But our objective was further on, nearly to the end of the cliff. "That's Haystack on the left, and over there is Scimitar, put up by Coving, Tun, and

Urb. Our line will go up between them."

"Will it?" said Kent.

"Well, it's meant to. I was suppose to do this route with Rope, but he's off flying. He's always off flying. He's crazy, you know. We're all crazy."

Our proposed route lay up a rounded buttress nearly devoid of vertical cracks. We would have to pick our way up the horizontal striations peculiar to this rock, weaving back and forth to avoid the blank areas. It looked chancy whether it would go. "You might waste your only day here," I said, "but we can have some good fun trying."

"Great, let's go," beamed Kent.

We left the path and in the blue light of mountain shade moved through tough scrub oak, and over rickety, retangular blocks of talus, quickly reaching the rock.

An arch curved up rightwards, I followed it, though I could just as easily have climbed straight up, for the rock is striped with horizontal bands sandwiched between layers of less resistent rock, and forming ledges of varying dimensions, sometimes quite small and brittle. One has, therefore, a sort of natural ladder which sometimes makes the climbing quite easy. But when the angle is steep, and it generally is here, these ledges, while offering a way up, also hold out the danger of luring one into a trap, for runners are sometimes scarce, and it is hard to climb down. It is an area where technical competence combined with "attack", if freed from the chain of prudence, can easily lead to becoming airborne.

At the top of the arch I was 40 feet up without a runner. It was easy. Then it got hard fast. The rock suddenly steepened to overhanging. It was too steep to go straight up, but 15 feet left, above a singular patch of orange lichen the holds appeared to be better. It was strenuous looking. And scary. I took half an hour arranging my runners. Why? I was nearly scared. At the beginning of the traverse there was a small alcove with several cracks. I slotted two chocks and supported them with two pitons slipped gently into fissures from which, I reasoned, the direction of pull could not pluck them. I climbed up, struggling, and got a nut into a higher horizontal crack. Came down, panting and trembling with the effort. After a rest, I started the traverse. It was all on the arms, and when I was halfway there I saw in a flash two things: the overhang at the end of the traverse might not go, and if it didn't, I wouldn't have the strength to climb back, and a 30 foot swinging fall would result. So I geared up and hung on with weakening limbs and fought to secure another chock in the horizontal crack, near the end of the traverse. I struggled and grunted, and gasped, shifting first to one arm then to the other, desperately conserving what little strength I had, while trying to keep cool in the head, to think clearly about getting that chock slotted. Not very elegant, not very cool. Just a thrashing human sorting out his weaknesses and strengths above the rockwork orange.

Finally I got a good big nut secured and, attempting the hand traverse equivalent of stepping smartly, worked my way on weakening arms back to the safety of the alcove. I braced a knee, dropped my arms, and panted.

Kent was enjoying it. "Hey Shann, were you freaked, man, were you freaked?" This came out with great glee and a twist of the word "freaked"; along with a physical seizure which hunched his shoulders, caused his head to shoot forward on a stiff neck, and his eyes to bulge. Kent loved Americanisms. He seemed to have a special fondness for the harsh, grating ones. One of his favorites was "trash", which he could repeat intermittently for hours on end. Adding "can" gave him even more pleasure. Whenever I offered him the rope, or carabiners, or water, or candy, he'd say "No thanks, throw it in the TRASH CAN." And then whisk it from my hands. "Yeah, Shann, you sure looked freaked; were you freaked?"

"Well, Kent," I replied, trying to restrain my thirst for oxygen, "you've got that American slang almost nearly right." This interchange so broke the tension that I burst out in hysterical laughter. Kent stared at me blankly, startled. He was dumbfounded by what tickled my funny bone. A rare occurrence, for Kent isn't often at a loss for words.

Soon the time had come for the big effort. I launched out, scared, but with confidence in the runners. I so wanted it to go, but I was so afraid it wouldn't. What if the holds just weren't there? There were no straight-forward pull-ups, as I had hoped. I didn't have time to work it all out, so I just went, and in several complicated, strenuous moves, was up. "Phew, heavy duty!" I shouted, borrowing a phrase from my friend Mac not Davis. "It's just as good as it looks, a struggle, but it's all there."

"Will it go above the overhang" cried the belayer, looking up. I feebly answered "yes", and slowly crept on up. "We're not out of the woods yet, old boy." And so we weren't. But it was easy for a while. The striae were usable, though one wanted to keep on one's toes to avoid putting weight on the snapable edges.

I climbed 30 feet above the overhang, sans difficulty, sans runners. Then I was stopped by a smooth wall spotted with three grey knobs, like a triple-breasted woman. Things were getting woodier and woodier. A classic problem. Below the blank section was a long, narrow ledge, above it, jugs and safety. But it would take some doing to get from one to the other. Perhaps an all-out effort? Not up here. I was discouraged, but began, without much hope of success, to work it out.

The knob on the left was the highest, and it had a lip which might prevent a runner from slipping off, if the knob itself didn't break. Something about it suggested an inner corruption. Still, for want of anything better I laid on a sling of half-inch webbing. It was a "manky" runner. (As Keng digs Americanisms, so I am fascinated by Anglicisms. "Manky" has just the tone of disdain I felt, and just that implication of sinister unreliability that characterized my "protection.") I had to climb as if free solo, knowing at least, that if I did make a mistake, there was a chance I wouldn't go all the way.

The knob on the right (more of a rounded nubbin, really) was too far away to use. There were a couple of discolorations low on the face. These proved to be tiny bulges, which, though one couldn't stand on them, could nevertheless be used as toe holds and would take some of the weight off the fingers, the tips of which were dug into the lip on top of the left grey knob. I tested the holds, moving up, and carefully back down. Then up again and back down. It was going to be hard, which is to say getting up would require a major effort of creative climbing. I would have to combine a solution to the problem with self-control in working it out and in carrying it through. In short, I was going to have to do a little internal suffering. I didn't relish the prospect, but I did so want to get up.

I moved up again, feet higher, and stretched to feel with my left hand along the edge of a horizontal crack just at the end of my reach. Fingers moved along the edge, feeling, searching for that little ridge, or pocket which would make all the difference. Nothing. I carefully crept back down. After resting, I tried again. And again. There was an edge there, but not enough. Another approach. I moved up with my toes on the grey marks, my fingers biting intensely into the grey knob. Putting my left foot on the highest purchase I would find, I swung my right foot up to the center grey knob, placing the toe just so, and then pulled up with my fingers until my right foot was taking some weight. With the fingers of my left hand gripping the hold like life, I reached with my right hand for the horizontal crack. Ah! The edge was better over here. Distinctly better. It might yet go. And carefully, so carefully, climbed back down, to regain my strength. And consider. Then another try, same result. And again, and again. Each time I went up it was easier. My body was learning the movements. But still I couldn't do it. Each time I reached the apex, and felt the edge with the fingers of my right hand, I dared not let go my left hand, for I would be forced to do a one-arm pull-up onto my right foot. My fingers might slip or my strength might go. It was too chancy. And each time I failed I had to use the greatest precision in climbing down. I couldn't afford the luxury of a moment's carelessness.

There had to be a way. And then I saw it: The problem was that if I attempted to stand up with my foot on the center grey knob, my arm would be bending. It would take strength to pull up, and worse, as I got higher, there would be an outward pull on my fingers, and they might slip. If I could keep my arm straight...I was breathing hard in anticipation of the effort. Soon I was ready. It had to go. I sank my fingers into the grey knob. My toes moved to the smudges below: left foot, right, left, the the right leg arching up and the foot carefully set on the now familiar center knob I pulled forward toward that foot, and up, reaching to my limit, fingers on the edge. I had it. Then...easy...I pivoted a bit, arching my back, getting more weight on the right foot, but keeping my right arm, its fingers gripping the high edge, extended. With a quick movement I took the fingers out of my left hand from their grip and - this was the worst moment - turned my hand around and pressed the heel of it down on the sloping hold. I could then push on my left hand, gaining six critical inches, and could move my other hand up and right to, as I had guessed, a more secure edge. My total being was focused on that right hand, and it pulled me up, up, until I could remove my left hand and replace it with my left foot. Phew, heavy duty! I was trembling with excitement and fear. What if it was harder up here than I anticipated? What if I couldn't get any runners? But not to worry. I searched around, found some good holds, and pulled up, moving with relief to a belay spot amid cracks, flakes, and small ledges. I fixed a couple of nuts, dropped a piton behind a flake, and a looped a runner over a spike. "Come on up, Kent. It's a piece of cake."

My friend armed across the traverse, and was almost armed out, as he pulled past the layered overhang. "Say, that tightens the forearms, doesn't it, Shann ol' boy? No place to hesitate!" He soon reached the grey knobs. He had trouble there, being unfamiliar with those peculiar trunsy, twisty, pushy techniques which one must master in the Valley. He tried, and reached, and fussed, and then got angry, and went for it, determined, and almost slipped, got his feet on the knobs, stood up, smiling happy, and forgetting nearly good, exclaimed, "Hey, this climb is fantastic!"

"Everything in nature contains all the powers of nature.
Everything is made of one hidden stuff."
>   *Ralph Waldo Emerson*

Little did I know I had opened a book that was a door to a world of adventure. I was 15 when I saw that picture of a man on a rock wall. "Hard rock, thin air, a rope," is all the caption said. I grabbed my mother's clothesline and headed for the graffiti-covered sandstone cliffs of the San Fernando Valley.

SKIING YOSEMITE'S WILD SIDE

By Tim Messick

Yosemite in winter can be a cold snowy place, where for over sixty years many skiers have had their peak experiences.

Orland Bartholomew skied to Yosemite from Mt. Whitney, California in the winter of 1928-29. Such accomplishment is remarkable even today. As decades of winter roll by, dedicated skiers have improved and pushed the standards of what can be skied.

Coupling the advancements made on backcountry equipment with emphasis on better skiing technique, modern skiers have every advantage to safely tackle more difficult slopes. Releasable three-pin bindings and self-arrest poles have probably decreased the number of injuries to backcountry skiers by quite a margin. Although skis and skiers keep improving season after season, there is no substitute for using common sense when deciding what to ski.

Yosemite Valley lay blanketed under a cushion of snow during the winter of '89. Loaded with snow, chutes and gullies sent avalanches screaming down towards the Valley floor. Looking up at the natural steep spookiness, I imagined a descent on cross-country skis. Shivering the picture of a death fall out of my mind and replacing that vision with one of precisely linked turns, I smiled, and yearned for the ultimate ski run to the Valley floor.

Le Conte Gully is an impressive drainage ending in a talus slope directly above the Le Conte Memorial in Yosemite Valley. Looking from below, one sees the gully rising 3000 feet towards Glacier Point, and another thousand before opening up it walls to Sentinel Dome. This drainage is hard to miss, and after three days of watching avalanches of snow, rock and ice barrelling down the gully all finally became quiet. It looked ready to be skied.

The next morning at Badger Pass, I knew weaseling my way out of teaching a ski class wouldn't be an easy chore, but by 9:30 I had escaped with fellow skiers Chris Falkenstien, a local pro patroller, and Dave Page, the lift/slope manager. Having our three-pin boots and skis cached near Glacier Point enabled us to blitz out the long ten miles on lightweight skating gear as we skied the perfectly groomed trail on Glacier Pt. Road.

Arriving at our heavier skis we booted up, tightening our laces with the help of extra adrenalin naturally flowing through our bodies. Being at the rim of the Yosemite Valley only two hours after leaving Badger Pass was a different sensation.

Usually we turn around after taking in the view of the high country and laughing at the personified ants circling on the Curry ice rink below. Not this time! Soon we'd be at the ice rink!

We turned towards our goal. The gully was down and left, eternity was at our right. We went left. Skiing wet funky snow into the mouth of the gully we entered carefully, one at a time. Conditions improved as we negotiated one jump-turn after another down the 45-degree slope. Here the snow was well packed from three days of sun, wind, the cold and avalanches. As the morning sun shone across the Valley towards Yosemite Falls, its water turned into a rainbow of colors framed by the walls of the massive gully. We had now committed ourselves to ski.

Focusing on the descent, we began hearing ice fall breaking off from the cliffs above. That unnerving sound, combined with the beeping of our avalanche beacons and the overall acoustics of the chute continued keeping the adrenalin pumping hard.

Luck was on our side, and we reached our halfway mark--Moran Pt. It was a brief island of safety, so we took a break on the crest of the point jutting out from the wall and avalanche danger. This point was the turning spot for the old (and now closed) Ledge Trail, which came up from Curry Village before being wiped out by rockfall.

The steepest, narrowest pitch is in the opposite direction, and it was now at our feet. The snow was harder. Falling could possibly have been fatal. Thankfully there were no falls as we continued the descent to the talus slope. A bit of scary walking over snow-covered talus was involved before remounting our skis for some final turns to the Le Conte Memorial.

Shocked faces stared out the windows at the tired and sweaty skiers who had reached their goal, happy and full of life.

Tim Messick has been a ski instructor and guide with Yosemite Mountaineering School for eight years. He is the author of Cross Contry Skiing in Yosemite, (Chockstone Press, Denver, CO. 80218). He recommends the use of common sense and safety before skiing any slope.

"I saw a delicate flower had grown up two feet high between the horse's feet and the wheel track. An inch more to right or left had sealed its fate, or an inch higher. Yet it lived to flourish, and never knew the danger it incurred. It did not borrow trouble, nor invite an evil fate by apprehending it."
Henry David Thoreau

RIVER OF LIFE

White waters, white waters, flow over me,
Take me back to the deep blue sea,
White water, white water flow over me,
Wash away all my sad memories.

Oh the river is flowing through here
As she marks her passage of time,
Her message so deep
Although it's quite clear
If our minds not too shallow
And our vision too near.

So let us thirst for the river of live,
Be accursed if we don't treat her right,
For she's a gift from above:
Melted snow, pure as the dove,
Praise the River, the River of Life....

Harvey Lee White

This excerpt of Harvey's song, written in Yosemite National Park, is one example of his support of Greenpeace, protection of the rainforests, and all the many integral environmental causes so important to the quality of life on our planet.

Harvey is a romantic dreamer inspired by the awesome beauty of Yosemite, where he has lived for the past thirteen years. His greatest joy is sharing his music at weddings, receptions, and around the campfire.

If you would like him to play at your campfire or special event in or near Yosemite, his permanent address is:

Harvey Lee White
P.O. Box 2204
Wawona Station
Yosemite National Park, CA 95389

Harvey has written and performed many love songs, and would like to share another lyric his romance with nature and particularly with the harmonious lifestyle of the indigenous tribes of the world and our country's Indian heritage:

TURN BACK AGAIN
By Harvey Lee White

You can't trust your fate to the toss of an Indian Head nickel...
Heads: you lose the Indians...
Tails: you lose the Buffalo

Why can't we turn back again, It's so hard to turn back again,
We took the land from those who knew it's beginnings,
We couldn't let it be and we boasted of our winnings,
Our heads held high with false pride, if we could really look
Back we couldn't look an Indian in the eyes,
And that's why we can't turn back again, It's so hard to turn
Back again, But we must turn back again.

Smoke signals are burning so high we can't even see them,
Nobody really cares and no-one wants to read them anymore,
And that's why we must turn back again, It's so hard to turn
Back again, But we must turn back again,

We've gotta get back to them mountains, back to the sea,
Back to the clear blue skies, oh the river of life
She's calling you and me,

All these things I'm saying have been said before,
And all these thoughts I'm putting on you have been sung before,
But I can see they're not listening again, and you know this
Old world needs a friend, so when this song comes around again
Let us all join in,

Can you visualize what this place could be, you and I hand in
Hand by the sea, the wave of time may wash our mistakes,
If we can only see the darkness of our ways,
So we've gotta get back down to it now, back to the real
Nitty gritty yea, can you hear the Whales a wailin',
Back to the sea, oh the river of life is calling you and me

Just save me enough steel for my old guitar strings,
Singing, hummin' and a grinnin', how happy I will be,
I gotta get back down to it now, back to the real
Nitty gritty...

To hell with my guitar strings and all them crazy things,
Just save me some clean mountain air and some fresh
River water to drink, I gotta get back down to it now,
Back to the real nitty gritty yea, no time for joking no more,
Ya can't kill a beaver to save a tree, you can't kill an
Indian to save a buffalo, you can't kill a buffalo to save
A white man, you can't kill the white men to save the earth,
You can't kill the earth to save the universe, and you can't kill
The universe to save my soul, so we've gotta get back to them
Mountains, back to the sea, back to the clear blue skies,
Oh the river of life is calling you and me.

Composer Harvey Lee White

California's High Sierra,

Mammoth/June Ski Resort is a year-round destination recreation resort located on the eastern side of the California Sierra Nevada Mountains. In the winter the Ski Resort hosts well over one million skiers. During the summer over two million visitors enjoy the area's beautiful outdoors. If you have ever thought of living and working in a mountain resort, now is your chance!

Ski Area Operations

Mammoth/June Ski Resort's many departments and facilities provide a wide variety of jobs. Our ski lifts, ticket sales locations, ski rental and repair shops, cafeterias, sport shops, transportation systems, garages and other facilities employ over 1,500 people.

Mammoth Mountain Inn

The Mammoth Mountain Inn is a year-round, full service resort hotel. Our restaurants, cocktail lounges, tour operations, guest services, day care facility and other operations offer many summer and winter jobs.

It's not just a Job,
It's Mammoth!

Job Applications

For more information and a complete Mammoth/June Ski Resort job application packet, fill out & tear off the attached portion of this brochure and drop it in the mail. E.O.E.

Employment Benefits

★ Free Season Ski Pass
★ Free Ski Lessons
★ Free Race Clinics
★ Sport Shop Discounts
★ Food Discounts
★ Flexible Work Hours
★ Employee Housing
★ And Much More

I want to live & work in the High Sierra!

Send me information on employment opportunities at Mammoth/June Ski Resort. Please fill out the following, tear off this bottom portion and drop it in the mail.

Name: _____

Address: _____ Phone:_____

City: _____ State: _____ Zip: _____

Mammoth/June Ski Resort
Personnel Department, Box 24, Mammoth Lakes, CA 93546 (619) 934-2571

110

Ski Resort Employment
Fun . . . Excitement . . . Skiing . . .

SKI RESORT

SEASONAL POSITIONS
Full and part time employees in a full range of service categories — food service and hotel operations to equipment operators and ski instructors.

BENEFIT BY WORKING AT KIRKWOOD
Ski Kirkwood FREE; Courtesy lift tickets for family and friends; cash discounts at the resort; FREE ski lessons; paid holidays; paid time-and-a-half for over eight or over forty hours; low cost medical insurance for full-time employees. Starting hourly wages: $4.75 to $7.75.

Some employee housing on site.

Transportation from South Lake Tahoe available.

KIRKWOOD SKI RESORT
35 miles south of Lake Tahoe on Highway 88
For further information contact:
Personnel: Kirkwood, P.O. Box 1, Kirkwood, CA 95646
(209) 258-6000

Kirkwood Ski Resort offers group and private lessons designed to introduce beginners to the sport and help pros shave points off their downhill time. Located 30 miles south of Lake Tahoe on Highway 88, Kirkwood's 7,800' base elevation assures the area's best snow conditions for learning and enjoyment.

MTN HIGH SKI AREA

Seasonal Employment

45 **45** **75** **700**

Spring Summer Fall Winter

GENERAL EMPLOYMENT OPPORTUNITIES:

Management	Laborers	Heavy Equip Oper
Retail Shops	Parking Atten	Electricians
Rental Shops	Security	Snow Making
Ticket Sales	Food Service	Mechanics
Lift Operators	Ski Instructors	Ski Lift Mech
Janitorial	Ski Patrol	Bldg Maint

Benefits: Discounts on Rental Equipment, Retail Items, Food!!!

FREE SKIING!!! GOOD PAY!!!

For more information: Contact Personnel, Mtn. High Ski Area, P.O. Box 428, Wrightwood, Calif. 92397

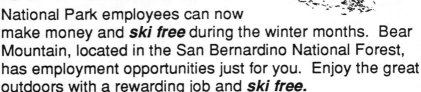

CURECANTI
NATIONAL RECREATION AREA
(Colorado)

MAILING ADDRESS:

Elk Creek Marina
46 Apache Rd.
Cunnison, CO 81230

SEASONAL EMPLOYMENT

0	20	0	0
SPRING	**SUMMER**	**FALL**	**WINTER**

BEST TIME TO APPLY: April

GENERAL EMPLOYMENT:

■ Indicates services and facilities with employment opportunities.

☐ Management
■ Gift Shops
☐ Stables
■ Food Service
☐ Janitorial
■ Rental Shops
☐ Climbing (Ice/Rock)

☐ Administration
■ Front Desk
☐ Maintenance
☐ Security
☐ Gardening
☐ x-c Skiing
☐ Camping

☐ Housekeeping
☐ Tour Guides
■ Grocery/Supplies
■ Garage/Gas Station
☐ Transportation
☐ Alpine Skiing
■ Boating (rafting, canoeing etc.)

ADDITIONAL INFORMATION:

EMPLOYER PROVIDED LODGING:

☐ Dorms   ☐ Tents   ☐ Cabins
■ Other: None

LODGING RESTRICTIONS:

☐ Pets   ☐ Guests
■ Other: N/A

EMPLOYEE MEAL PROGRAMS:

☐ Yes   ■ No

EMPLOYEE COOKING FACILITIES:

☐ Yes   ■ No

NEARBY RELIGIOUS SERVICES:

■ Yes   ☐ No

NEARBY PRIVATE HOUSING:

■ Yes   ☐ No

GROOMING RESTRICTIONS:

☐ Hair   ☐ Moustache   ☐ Beard
■ Other: None

OFF SEASON ADDRESS:

Same as above

MESA VERDE
NATIONAL PARK
(Colorado)

MAILING ADDRESS:

Mesa Verde Co.
Box 277
Mancos, CO 81328

SEASONAL EMPLOYMENT

0	100	100	0
SPRING	**SUMMER**	**FALL**	**WINTER**

BEST TIME TO APPLY: January thru March

GENERAL EMPLOYMENT:
■ Indicates services and facilities with employment opportunities.

- ■ Management
- ■ Gift Shops
- ☐ Stables
- ■ Food Service
- ■ Janitorial
- ☐ Rental Shops
- ☐ Climbing (Ice/Rock)

- ■ Administration
- ■ Front Desk
- ■ Maintenance
- ☐ Security
- ■ Gardening
- ☐ x-c Skiing
- ☐ Camping

- ■ Housekeeping
- ☐ Tour Guides
- ■ Grocery/Supplies
- ■ Garage/Gas Station
- ■ Transportation
- ☐ Alpine Skiing
- ☐ Boating (rafting, canoeing etc.)

ADDITIONAL INFORMATION:

EMPLOYER PROVIDED LODGING:
☐ Dorms   ☐ Tents   ■ Cabins
☐ Other:

LODGING RESTRICTIONS:
■ Pets   ☐ Guests
☐ Other:

EMPLOYEE MEAL PROGRAMS:
■ Yes   ☐ No

EMPLOYEE COOKING FACILITIES:
☐ Yes   ■ No

NEARBY RELIGIOUS SERVICES:
■ Yes   ☐ No

NEARBY PRIVATE HOUSING:
☐ Yes   ■ No

GROOMING RESTRICTIONS:
☐ Hair   ☐ Moustache   ■ Beard
■ Other: Neatly groomed

OFF SEASON ADDRESS:

Same as above

ROCKY MOUNTAIN
NATIONAL PARK

(Colorado)

MAILING ADDRESS:

Rocky Mountain Park Co.
P.O. Box 2680
Estes Park, Colorado 80517

SEASONAL EMPLOYMENT

0	50	50	0
SPRING	**SUMMER**	**FALL**	**WINTER**

BEST TIME TO APPLY:

GENERAL EMPLOYMENT:

■ Indicates services and facilities with employment opportunities.

☐ Management   ☐ Administration   ■ Housekeeping
■ Gift Shops   ■ Front Desk   ☐ Tour Guides
☐ Stables   ☐ Maintenance   ☐ Grocery/Supplies
■ Food Service   ☐ Security   ☐ Garage/Gas Station
☐ Janitorial   ☐ Gardening   ☐ Transportation
☐ Rental Shops   ☐ x-c Skiing   ☐ Alpine Skiing
☐ Climbing (Ice/Rock) ☐ Camping   ☐ Boating (rafting, canoeing etc.)

ADDITIONAL INFORMATION:
          Warehouse, parking attendants

EMPLOYER PROVIDED LODGING: **LODGING RESTRICTIONS:**

■ Dorms   ☐ Tents   ☐ Cabins   ■ Pets   ■ Guests
☐ Other: ☐ Other:

EMPLOYEE MEAL PROGRAMS: **EMPLOYEE COOKING FACILITIES:**

■ Yes   ☐ No   ☐ Yes   ■ No

NEARBY RELIGIOUS SERVICES: **NEARBY PRIVATE HOUSING:**

■ Yes   ☐ No   ☐ Yes   ■ No

GROOMING RESTRICTIONS:

■ Hair   ☐ Moustache   ■ Beard

■ Other: Well groomed

OFF SEASON ADDRESS:

Rocky Mountain Park Co.
PO Box 29041
Phoenix, AZ 85038

ROCKY MOUNTAIN NATIONAL PARK

(Colorado)

MAILING ADDRESS:

Hidden Valley Ski Area
PO Box 98
Estes Park, CO 80517

SEASONAL EMPLOYMENT

0	0	0	55
SPRING	**SUMMER**	**FALL**	**WINTER**

BEST TIME TO APPLY: September and October

GENERAL EMPLOYMENT:

■ Indicates services and facilities with employment opportunities.

☐ Management
■ Gift Shops
☐ Stables
■ Food Service
■ Janitorial
■ Rental Shops
☐ Climbing (Ice/Rock)

☐ Administration
■ Front Desk
☐ Maintenance
☐ Security
☐ Gardening
☐ x-c Skiing
☐ Camping

☐ Housekeeping
☐ Tour Guides
☐ Grocery/Supplies
☐ Garage/Gas Station
☐ Transportation
■ Alpine Skiing
☐ Boating (rafting, canoeing etc.)

ADDITIONAL INFORMATION: Lift operators; maintenance and other ski area workers

EMPLOYER PROVIDED LODGING:

☐ Dorms   ☐ Tents   ☐ Cabins
■ Other: None

LODGING RESTRICTIONS:

☐ Pets   ☐ Guests
■ Other: N/A

EMPLOYEE MEAL PROGRAMS:

☐ Yes   ■ No

EMPLOYEE COOKING FACILITIES:

☐ Yes   ■ No

NEARBY RELIGIOUS SERVICES:

■ Yes   ☐ No

NEARBY PRIVATE HOUSING:

■ Yes   ☐ No

GROOMING RESTRICTIONS:

■ Hair   ☐ Moustache   ☐ Beard
☐ Other:

OFF SEASON ADDRESS:

Same as above

KEYSTONE

MAILING ADDRESS:

> *Keystone Resort
> Box 38
> Keystone, CO 80435

SEASONAL EMPLOYMENT

1000	1000	2000	2000
SPRING	**SUMMER**	**FALL**	**WINTER**

BEST TIME TO APPLY:

GENERAL EMPLOYMENT:

■ Indicates services and facilities with employment opportunities.

■ Management	■ Administration	■ Housekeeping
■ Gift Shops	■ Front Desk	□ Tour Guides
■ Stables	■ Maintenance	■ Grocery/Supplies
■ Food Service	■ Security	■ Garage/Gas Station
■ Janitorial	■ Gardening	■ Transportation
■ Rental Shops	■ x-c Skiing	□ Alpine Skiing
□ Climbing (Ice/Rock)	□ Camping	■ Boating (rafting, canoeing etc.)

ADDITIONAL INFORMATION: Landscape/General Labor

EMPLOYER PROVIDED LODGING:

■ Dorms   □ Tents   □ Cabins
□ Other:

LODGING RESTRICTIONS:

■ Pets   □ Guests
□ Other:

EMPLOYEE MEAL PROGRAMS:

■ Yes   □ No

EMPLOYEE COOKING FACILITIES:

■ Yes   □ No

NEARBY RELIGIOUS SERVICES:

■ Yes   □ No

NEARBY PRIVATE HOUSING:

■ Yes   □ No

GROOMING RESTRICTIONS:

■ Hair   □ Moustache   ■ Beard
■ Other: Neat, clean appearance

OFF SEASON ADDRESS:

> *Same as above

Holiday Inn Resort
P.O. Box 1468
101 S. St. Vrain
Estes Park, CO 80517

SEASONAL EMPLOYMENT

10	55	10	0
SPRING	**SUMMER**	**FALL**	**WINTER**

BEST TIME TO APPLY: January thru June

GENERAL EMPLOYMENT:

■ Indicates services and facilities with employment opportunities.

■ Management	■ Administration	■ Housekeeping
■ Gift Shops	■ Front Desk	☐ Tour Guides
☐ Stables	■ Maintenance	☐ Grocery/Supplies
☐ Food Service	☐ Security	☐ Garage/Gas Station
☐ Janitorial	☐ Gardening	☐ Transportation
☐ Rental Shops	☐ x-c Skiing	☐ Alpine Skiing
☐ Climbing (Ice/Rock)	☐ Camping	☐ Boating (rafting, canoeing etc.)

ADDITIONAL INFORMATION:

EMPLOYER PROVIDED LODGING:

■ Dorms   ☐ Tents   ☐ Cabins
☐ Other:

LODGING RESTRICTIONS:

■ Pets   ☐ Guests
■ Other: No drinking, controlled
visitation.

EMPLOYEE MEAL PROGRAMS:

■ Yes   ☐ No

EMPLOYEE COOKING FACILITIES:

☐ Yes   ■ No

NEARBY RELIGIOUS SERVICES:

■ Yes   ☐ No

NEARBY PRIVATE HOUSING:

■ Yes   ☐ No

GROOMING RESTRICTIONS:

☐ Hair   ☐ Moustache   ☐ Beard
■ Other: Neat, clean appearance,
neatly trimmed moustaches
and beards.

OFF SEASON ADDRESS:

Same as above

122

Holiday Inn®
of Estes Park

CAREER TRAINING IN THE ROCKIES!

By Pam Sweetser

The Rocky Mountain region is known for providing endless opportunities to enjoy your leisure time - downhill and cross-country skiing, backpacking, hiking, fishing, camping, biking, sailing, waterskiing, canoeing, whitewater rafting, and much more - but the Rocky Mountains can offer you more than an endless vacation; you can also spend your time learning valuable career skills that will afford you the opportunity to **stay** in the Rockies as a vital member of the workforce.

In fact, Colorado is again at the threshold of a revolutionary age in advanced technology and professional service, and you can become an active part of this development and growth. The choice is yours, and DIT provides the way to successfully participate in this revolution of career opportunities.

Advanced technology is prevalent in Colorado's industry; Colorado companies are using electronics systems to build aerospace components; hospitals are using laser technology to treat disease; large automotive dealerships are using digital electronics to diagnose engine problems; Computer Assisted Drafting systems are used to develop complex plans in the architecture, engineering, and land development industries; surveyors in Colorado use electronics devices to measure distance and angles in their field; computerized desk-top publishing is a reality in Colorado's graphic arts industry; and the management of information is a vital element in the Rocky Mountain region's growing hospitality service industry.

DIT offers quality, specialized training in each of these highly skilled areas and more. For instance, professional service has become the cornerstone to successful business operations in today's technological world. Skilled technicians and managers must also provide reliable, quality service to meet the needs of clients, colleagues, and customers. Professional development and integrity is part of the learning experience in every DIT program.

DIT invites you to become acquainted with the many opportunities available to ambitious students who want to live and learn in the Rocky Mountain region. Please contact the Admissions Department at 1-800-6163, or in Colorado 1-800-843-6531 for further information, and plan to become an integral part of growing industry in the Rocky Mountain region by providing technical expertise and professional service.

125

▲ ASPEN SKIING COMPANY

ASPEN MOUNTAIN · BUTTERMILK MOUNTAIN · SNOWMASS SKI AREA

Located in the Rocky Mountains, two hundred miles west of Denver, lies the magic of The Aspens. Here in the wilderness of the White River National Forest are the spectacular ski mountains of Aspen, Buttermilk, and Snowmass.

We at the Aspen Skiing Company want to provide our guests with the ultimate skiing experience, an experience that can be shared and enhanced by our employees.

Most of our positions require daily guest contact. We're looking for <u>new</u> employees who like people and know how to show it.

The fall applicant screening held in Aspen mid-October; offers approximately 150 job openings in lift operations, ski school, ticket sales, guest services, hotel and restaurant personnel, ski rentals, trail maintenance, snowmaking, office support staff and ski patrol. A clinic held the first week of December is for people seeking jobs as ski instructors, ski patrollers, and snowmobile patrollers. Because of turn-over during the ski season, Thanksgiving to mid-April, applicants are considered throughout that time who are able to apply in person and secure housing. However, the cost of living can be expensive due to the shortage of available affordable housing. While we are able to provide limited employee housing to new employees for approximately $200 per month, we urge that you look into the situation before you commit to the move. Many guests enjoy spring skiing, and employees are needed to work through the first week in April. This is also a favored time of our employees for making turns in the sun!

In many ways the image of our community is health-oriented. To that end, we offer participation in our health insurance program, discounted rates at our local health clubs, free rides on the employee bus, discounts on nutritious meals while working on the mountains and, not least, unlimited complimentary skiing on The Aspens' 3,134 acres of skiable terrain. We want to show you how great it can be!

To request an employment brochure, write: Personnel Department, Aspen Skiing Company, Box 1248, Aspen, Colorado 81612; or telephone 303/925-9494.

126

PURGATORY

WINTER / SUMMER

Super Location

Spend a season working in Southwest Colorado - it will capture your heart and provide fond memories for the rest of your life. Enjoy a spectacular setting in the majestic San Juan Mountains and our wonderfully mild climate, both summer and winter.

Nearby Durango

Durango is a popular resort town, bustling with cultural history and plenty of outdoor spirit. It's a great place to live. You'll appreciate the abundance of affordable housing and friendly atmosphere of town.

Winter Staff - 750
Summer Staff - 175

Be a part of our happy, well-groomed staff!

Employment Opportunities

- Hotel Operations
- Food Service
- Grounds Maintenance and Parking
- Ski Lift Operations
- Ski Instruction
- Administration, Accounting, Cashiers
- Sports and Rental Shops
- Guest Services

Many other support jobs too numerous to mention.

For More Information About Employment Opportunities Contact:

PURGATORY RESORT
PERSONNEL DEPT.
PO BOX 666
DURANGO, CO 81302
303-247-9000

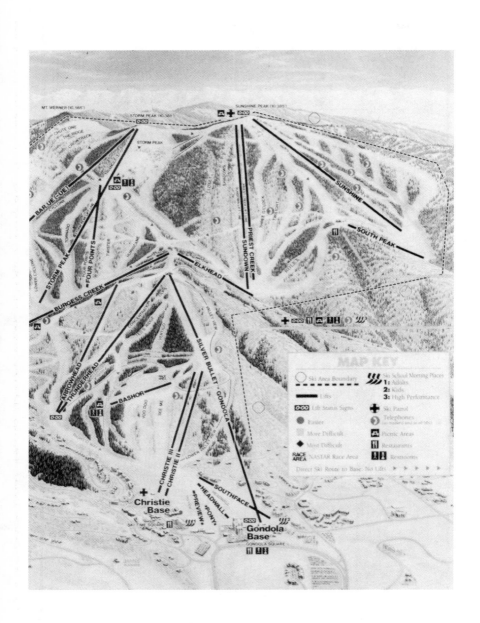

128

Steamboat
ski corporation

COME WORK AND PLAY IN BEAUTIFUL SKI TOWN, USA!

Come spend a winter season in Steamboat Springs, Ski Town,

USA and be a part of the people who make STEAMBOAT Colorado's

most friendly ski resort. We offer you the following:

o Unlimited usage ski pass

o Competitive hourly wage with an end of season bonus

o Health Insurance

o Discounts at company restaurants & shops

o Complimentary ski tickets to give to friends

o An employee assistance program

o Special employee recognition awards

o A positive, friendly and enthusiastic work environment

We will be hiring in the Fall for these positions: lift

operators, cafeteria workers, parking attendants, ticket

sellers, nursery attendants, ski instructors, wait staff,

race/special events staff and snowmakers. If this is you,

contact the STEAMBOAT SKI CORPORATION, 1-(303)879-6111.

An equal opportunity employer.

Steamboat
ski corporation

2305 Mt. Werner Circle
Steamboat Springs, Colorado 80487

129

COPPER MOUNTAIN RESORT
COLORADO

Copper Mountain Resort, nestled in the Colorado Rockies, is known throughout the country for it's award winning trails and is recognized as one of the top ski areas in the United States.

Mailing Address
Copper Mountain Resort
Box 3001
Copper Mountain, CO 80443

Seasonal Employment

1200 +	450	400	1200 +
Spring	Summer	Fall	Winter

Best Time To Apply: Year-Round

Winter Employment: Lift operations, ticket sales, retail/rental shops, janitorial, lodging services, food and beverage operations, ski school, ski patrol, transportation, nursery teachers, administrative/clerical positions.

Summer Employment: Copper Mountain is a year-round Resort offering summer activities as well as our winter activities. These activities include an 18 hole golf course, Racquet and Athletic Club, horseback riding, and scenic chairlift rides. Job opportunities are available in these areas in addition to our lodging services, food and restaurants and sport activities.

Keep in mind that resort communities are known for their high rents and limited seasonal housing.

Additional Benefits: Free season ski pass, ticket discounts at other areas, free transportation, discounted day care, complimentary ski tickets, discounts on ski lessons, ski accessories and food and great friends.

WE WELCOME YOU TO JOIN US FOR AN
UNFORGETTABLE WINTER OF SKIING.
Copper Mountain Resort is an Equal Opportunity Employer.

SHOULDN'T YOU BE GETTING OUTSIDE MORE OFTEN?

Have your own copy of OUTSIDE Magazine delivered each month by subscribing at the low one year introductory rate of $14.95. We'll bill you later—just send your order today to OUTSIDE, Dept. 6NPJ, P.O. Box 54706, Boulder, CO 80322-4706 .

Or call toll-free

1 800-786-8002

(Weekdays 6 a.m. to Midnight, Mountain Time)

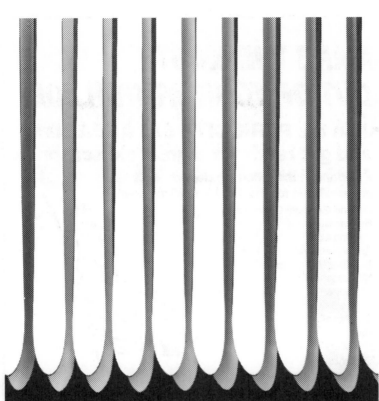

We make 12 pairs of skis a day, except when it snows.

Our priorities are a little different than most ski manufacturers. Somehow we got the idea that quality was more important than quantity.

Evolution combines aerospace technology with the highest grade materials. We handcraft them one at a time. Each pair of skis takes ten hours to complete.

But when it snows... we ski. What better way to insure our skis will perform under any condition.

Available at select ski shops or at Evolutions' new Factory Service Center at 790 West 1700 South Salt Lake City, Utah. We offer complete tuning and repair services on all skis, and feature Montanas' Crystal Glide Finish.

For more information about our handcrafted Alpine and Nordic skis or service center, call (801) 972-1144.

EVOLUTION
S K I   C O M P A N Y

Everglades National Park

MAILING ADDRESS:

T.W. Services, Inc.
P.O. Box 428
Everglades Park Division
Flamingo, FL 33030

SEASONAL EMPLOYMENT

80	20	80	120
SPRING	**SUMMER**	**FALL**	**WINTER**

BEST TIME TO APPLY: October

GENERAL EMPLOYMENT:

■ Indicates services and facilities with employment opportunities.

☐ Management
■ Gift Shops
☐ Stables
■ Food Service
■ Janitorial
☐ Rental Shops
☐ Climbing (Ice/Rock)

☐ Administration
■ Front Desk
■ Maintenance
■ Security
☐ Gardening
☐ x-c Skiing
☐ Camping

■ Housekeeping
■ Tour Guides
■ Grocery/Supplies
■ Garage/Gas Station
☐ Transportation
☐ Alpine Skiing
☐ Boating (rafting, canoeing etc.)

ADDITIONAL INFORMATION:

EMPLOYER PROVIDED LODGING:

☐ Dorms   ☐ Tents   ☐ Cabins
■ Other: Semi-Private
           Lodge Rooms

LODGING RESTRICTIONS:

■ Pets   ☐ Guests
☐ Other:

EMPLOYEE MEAL PROGRAMS:

■ Yes   ☐ No

EMPLOYEE COOKING FACILITIES:

☐ Yes   ■ No

NEARBY RELIGIOUS SERVICES:

■ Yes   ☐ No

NEARBY PRIVATE HOUSING:

☐ Yes   ■ No

GROOMING RESTRICTIONS:

☐ Hair   ☐ Moustache   ☐ Beard
■ Other: Neatly trimmed
          moustaches and beards

OFF SEASON ADDRESS:

Same as above

HAWAII VOLCANOES
NATIONAL PARK
(Hawaii)

MAILING ADDRESS:

Kilauea Volcano House, Inc.
Hawaii Volcanoes Nat'l Park
HI 96718

SEASONAL EMPLOYMENT

30	30	30	30
SPRING	**SUMMER**	**FALL**	**WINTER**

BEST TIME TO APPLY: Year-round

GENERAL EMPLOYMENT:

■ Indicates services and facilities with employment opportunities.

- ■ Management
- ■ Gift Shops
- ☐ Stables
- ■ Food Service
- ☐ Janitorial
- ☐ Rental Shops
- ☐ Climbing (Ice/Rock)

- ■ Administration
- ■ Front Desk
- ■ Maintenance
- ☐ Security
- ■ Gardening
- ☐ x-c Skiing
- ☐ Camping

- ■ Housekeeping
- ☐ Tour Guides
- ☐ Grocery/Supplies
- ☐ Garage/Gas Station
- ☐ Transportation
- ☐ Alpine Skiing
- ☐ Boating (rafting, canoeing etc.)

ADDITIONAL INFORMATION:

EMPLOYER PROVIDED LODGING:
☐ Dorms   ☐ Tents   ☐ Cabins
■ Other: Very limited housing

LODGING RESTRICTIONS:
■ Pets   ☐ Guests
☐ Other:

EMPLOYEE MEAL PROGRAMS:
■ Yes   ☐ No

EMPLOYEE COOKING FACILITIES:
☐ Yes   ■ No

NEARBY RELIGIOUS SERVICES:
■ Yes   ☐ No

NEARBY PRIVATE HOUSING:
■ Yes   ☐ No

GROOMING RESTRICTIONS:
☐ Hair   ☐ Moustache   ☐ Beard
■ Other: Neatly groomed

OFF SEASON ADDRESS:
Same as above

WELL BEING: THE IMPORTANCE OF AEROBIC EXERCISE

By Kim Saunders

Aerobic. You hear the term frequently these days. But, what does it mean and of what importance is it to your health and well being?

The word aerobic is Greek in origin; aero means air, "bic" for bios, meaning life. Aerobic exercise is, therefore, exercise that depends upon air for life.

Although aerobic exercise is just one part of a total fitness program, it is the foundation. Aerobics require a full supply of rich oxygen that enables the muscles and other cells of the body to produce energy. Using the body's largest muscle groups in rhythmic, continuous movements for a sustained period of time, makes you breathe deeply, sending oxygen-rich blood throughout the body.

How effectively your body uses its oxygen supply is the best measure of your overall fitness. The importance of aerobic exercise is to train your heart to work more effectively and thus, less stressfully. As you achieve good condition, your heart will become so efficient that it can pump the amount of blood necessary to your body in fewer beats per minute. Achieving a high level of fitness and maintaining it will affect your life profoundly,

Photo by Harvey White

"Emergency Medical Technician Karen Wood between workouts."

138

both mentally and physically, as the cardiorespiratory system is the "heart" of vitality for the entire body.

To be most effective, aerobic exercise must be:

BRISK. The ideal aerobic workout will get your heart pumping significantly above its resting rate but still below its maximum. Your goal should be about 75% of the maximum number of times your heart beats in a minute; this is your training heart rate. Exercise below 60% will provide little conditioning benefit, and above 85% is not necessary to maintain fitness.

Remember, too, the importance of air...if you exercise so hard that you cannot breathe comfortably your efforts become anareobic, or working without air. Your body needs sufficient oxygen to perform; remember to go longer at a slower pace, for good aerobic benefit. The best way to monitor your heart rate is to check your pulse frequently.

STEADY and SUSTAINED. Dependent upon the type of aerobic exercise you select, a good session should last a minimum of 15-30 minutes. Very brisk exercises, such as running, cross country skiing, stationary biking, uphill hiking, and dancing, will easily push you to your upper range training rate and initially need only be maintained for a minimum of 15 minutes. Mildly brisk exercise, such as walking, swimming, cycling, and calisthenics, don't work your heart as strenuously and should be maintained a minimum of 30 minutes, initially. As your condition improves, these times can be extended, but remember: go longer, not faster.

REGULAR and CONSISTANT. To maintain your fitness level, you should work out aerobically three times weekly; to improve it, up to six times a week. After achieving a good fitness level, you need not extend beyond three times weekly, at 30-60 minutes each session, to maintain it.

As with any fitness program, it is essential to be sensible. If you have special medical circumstances, are overweight, or over 35 and inactive, see your doctor for advice before starting an aerobic exercise program. Of utmost importance to any exercise program is a warm-up period before the exercise and a cooling down period afterwards. Be fair to your body; allow time for both. They are critical to avoid injury and undue physical stress.

And, remember that aerobics are just one factor in fitness. Strengthening and stretching exercises, a balanced diet, and periods of rest are also essential elements of a complete fitness program.

The benefits of a complete fitness program are extensive: a strong, healthy body and mind that work efficiently, more energy, greater alertness, a stronger immune system, a better tolerance to stress, and many others; perhaps most importantly, just feeling good...that sense of well-being!

MAMMOTH CAVE
NATIONAL PARK
(Kentucky)

MAILING ADDRESS:

National Park Concessions, Inc.
Mammoth Cave, KY 42259

SEASONAL EMPLOYMENT

0	50	50	0
SPRING	**SUMMER**	**FALL**	**WINTER**

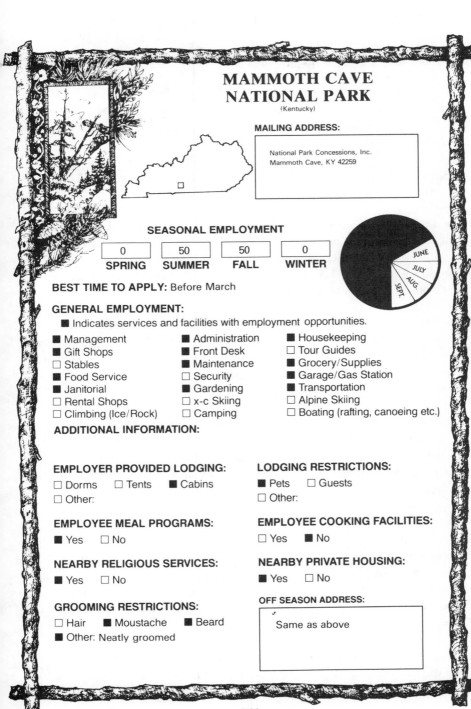

BEST TIME TO APPLY: Before March

GENERAL EMPLOYMENT:

■ Indicates services and facilities with employment opportunities.

■ Management	■ Administration	■ Housekeeping
■ Gift Shops	■ Front Desk	□ Tour Guides
□ Stables	■ Maintenance	■ Grocery/Supplies
■ Food Service	□ Security	■ Garage/Gas Station
■ Janitorial	■ Gardening	■ Transportation
□ Rental Shops	□ x-c Skiing	□ Alpine Skiing
□ Climbing (Ice/Rock)	□ Camping	□ Boating (rafting, canoeing etc.)

ADDITIONAL INFORMATION:

EMPLOYER PROVIDED LODGING:

□ Dorms □ Tents ■ Cabins
□ Other:

LODGING RESTRICTIONS:

■ Pets □ Guests
□ Other:

EMPLOYEE MEAL PROGRAMS:

■ Yes □ No

EMPLOYEE COOKING FACILITIES:

□ Yes ■ No

NEARBY RELIGIOUS SERVICES:

■ Yes □ No

NEARBY PRIVATE HOUSING:

■ Yes □ No

GROOMING RESTRICTIONS:

□ Hair ■ Moustache ■ Beard
■ Other: Neatly groomed

OFF SEASON ADDRESS:

Same as above

REMEMBER ME? I'M THE TRAINEE

By P. Carol Broadwell

As a flight-attendant for a major airline, I'm required to supervise an in-flight staff as well as train them. The Federal Aviation Administration also requires me to be trained at regular intervals. My dual roles as trainer and trainee can be frustrating. As a trainer, I try to follow the involvement and motivation principles I've learned. But then I end up in a training class that violates all of them.

Speaking as a trainee, I'd like to offer trainers a short list of things to remember:

• I'm not Einstein--Don't expect me to have all the answers. We trainees walk into entirely too many classes, especially those in which we are considered "already knowledgeable," and hear things like, "Of course, you already know this, so we'll go on..." As a matter of fact, I often don't already understand that point. Have you forgotten the purpose of our time together?

As trainees, we want to be stimulated. We want to be reminded of the facts and figures we don't use every day on the job. Of course, we also want to learn new things that will help us do our jobs better: What's more motivating than learning something useful--and knowing you've learned it? But start where we are, not where you are.

• But I'm not a kindergartener, either---I don't appreciate being condescended to or treated as if I have nothing to offer. One reason I resist the idea of being trained is that I suspect you're going to behave as if all my knowledge and experience suddenly don't count for anything. Encourage me to share my expertise.

As an instructor, you are rarely able to spend time on the line and get current experience in the so-called "real world." It may be threatening for you to acknowledge that we trainees probably know more than you do about at least some aspects of our jobs. But it's your responsibility to try to understand what it is that we want to learn, need to learn and have a good idea of how to learn. Above all, show us that you respect our ability to understand and apply the learning.

• I'm not as excited about this as you are---I'm used to being on the job five days a week, moving, doing, talking. You, on the other hand, are used to being in the classroom all day, perhaps all week. Give me a break---literally!

You get energy from teaching, motivating and walking around the classroom. Many of us trainees get most of our stimulation from the intake of caffeine in the cafeteria at break time. At the very least, start different portions of the day with an exercise that gets the mind and adrenaline flowing. If calisthentics are out of the question, at least give us a chance to stretch occasionally.

• Give me some "ammo" for my boss back home---It's not hard to convince me that a week away from the old grind is of vital importance to the company, my future in it or even national security. The person who needs convincing is my boss--the one who grudgingly released me from my daily duties to attend this course and is now back at the office juggling schedules to make up for my absence.

So go ahead and teach me the new company policies, but make sure you teach me to do something really useful when I get back home. Give me the ammunition to convince my boss and colleagues that the time and money spent on my training will pay off in the near future.

• Don't try to sell me on the organization---I'm participating in this training exercise so that I can learn what you have to teach me. But I want to be trained, not brainwashed. Sell me on how this will benefit me. Let me know how it will help me do my job better, faster or easier, not how much more production the company can squeeze out of me with this new method. Tell me if there's a possibility I will be in line for promotion, but don't try to convince me how wonderful the company is. While I'm here, let's just have an old-fashioned learning session.

• Let me know you're human, too---How many times do I have to sit in a class and listen to some pretentious poop who would have me believe I am in the presence of omniscience personified? It's alright to make an occasional mistake without trying to cover it up or telling me I misunderstood. I realize that people rarely know everything, so don't be afraid to say you don't know. When you pretend to have all the answers, I can't help wondering, "If you're so smart, how come you're in the training department?"

• Help me be better right now---This stuff you're talking about may be better than yogurt, but just make sure it's something I can use on the job.

143

Don't tell me I'm going to need it someday. If I'm going to need it someday, teach it to me someday--not now. I'm having a tough time just trying to keep up with the demands of my present job. That's where I need help right now.

What? Don't I want to expand my horizons and learn to live with future shock? Sure I do. But I'm going to be evaluated at the end of the year on my performance on my present job, so make sure I can do it well.

Remember these things and, when I get home, I'll remember you as a great trainer.

P. Carol Broadwell is a flight attendant with Eastern Airlines and a consultant with the Center for Management Services Inc. in Decatur, GA.

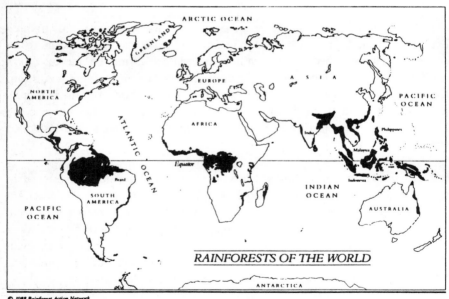

RAINFORESTS OF THE WORLD

© 1988 Rainforest Action Network

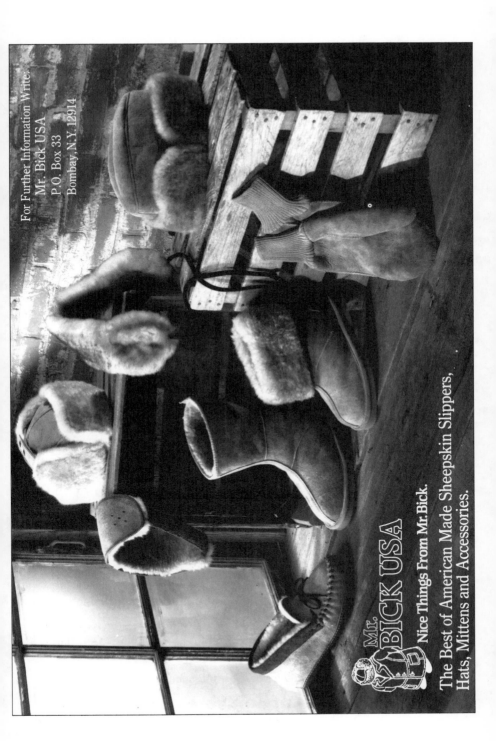

For Further Information Write:
Mr. Bick USA
P.O. Box 33
Bombay, N.Y. 12914

Mr.
BICK USA
Nice Things From Mr. Bick.

The Best of American Made Sheepskin Slippers,
Hats, Mittens and Accessories.

ACADIA
NATIONAL PARK
(Maine)

MAILING ADDRESS:

The Acadia Corporation
Box 24
Bar Harbor, ME 04609

SEASONAL EMPLOYMENT

50	125	100	0
SPRING	**SUMMER**	**FALL**	**WINTER**

BEST TIME TO APPLY: January thru March

GENERAL EMPLOYMENT:

■ Indicates services and facilities with employment opportunities.

■ Management	■ Administration	☐ Housekeeping
■ Gift Shops	☐ Front Desk	☐ Tour Guides
☐ Stables	■ Maintenance	☐ Grocery/Supplies
■ Food Service	☐ Security	☐ Garage/Gas Station
■ Janitorial	☐ Gardening	☐ Transportation
☐ Rental Shops	☐ x-c Skiing	☐ Alpine Skiing
☐ Climbing (Ice/Rock)	☐ Camping	☐ Boating (rafting, canoeing etc.)

ADDITIONAL INFORMATION: Warehouse Positions available

EMPLOYER PROVIDED LODGING:

■ Dorms   ☐ Tents   ☐ Cabins
☐ Other:

LODGING RESTRICTIONS:

■ Pets   ■ Guests
☐ Other:
Couples Housing-not available

EMPLOYEE MEAL PROGRAMS:

■ Yes   ☐ No

EMPLOYEE COOKING FACILITIES:

☐ Yes   ■ No

NEARBY RELIGIOUS SERVICES:

■ Yes   ☐ No

NEARBY PRIVATE HOUSING:

■ Yes   ☐ No

GROOMING RESTRICTIONS:

■ Hair   ■ Moustache   ■ Beard
■ Other: Neat, well groomed

OFF SEASON ADDRESS:

Same as above

The Best Is Here. **Sunday river**
BETHEL, MAINE

We have year-round and seasonal openings in many of our departments. We seek energetic, people-oriented individuals with and without hospitality experience to fill these positions:

☐ Management	☐ Ski Instructors	☐ Cafeteria
☐ Ski Shops	☐ Security	☐ Restaurants
☐ Housekeeping	☐ Reservations	☐ Child Care
☐ Trolley Drivers	☐ Lift Operators	☐ Guest Services
☐ Grocery Shop	☐ Snowmakers	☐ Janitorial
☐ Rental Shops	☐ Ski Patrol	☐ Ticket Sales
☐ Accounting	☐ Receptionists	☐ Front Desk

We invite you to apply and work at New England's Fastest Growing Ski Resort with some of the very best people in the ski industry. Sunday River offers:

- ✿ Competitive Wages
- ✿ Free Skiing
- ✿ Meal Discounts
- ✿ Housing Assistance
- ✿ Rental Discounts
- ✿ Fun And Excitment

Sunday River is located in the beautiful western mountains of Maine. If you'd like to be part of the Sunday River team, send your resume, visit or call our Personnel Department.

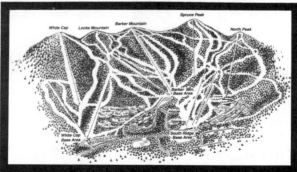

P.O. Box 450, Bethel, Maine 04217
(207) 824-2187
Equal Opportunity Employer

146

THE UNIVERSAL SKI TICKET

UNIVERSAL SKI TICKET

Exchange this ticket at the ticket window of any participating ski area to receive one FREE all day / all lifts ticket.

GOOD THRU

YOUR COMPANY NAME OR LOGO HERE

CORPORATE SKI INCENTIVES, Inc.

Give the fun of skiing with the only flexible sports ticket accepted nationwide!

THE UNIVERSAL SKI TICKET: good for one day of skiing, redeemable at a choice of one of over 170 ski resorts nationwide.

The Ticket's flexibility makes it ideal for use as a premium, sales incentive, product or travel tie-in. With the Universal Ski Ticket, you'll receive some very healthy benefits:

ENHANCED CORPORATE IMAGE through support of a participatory sport that can be enjoyed no matter what the recipient's age or athletic ability.

APPRECIATION for providing the good times in the outdoors that come with skiing.

GREATER PROMOTIONAL IMPACT Skiing—and Universal Ski Tickets—are ideal for sharing with family and friends.

For more information on how you can use the Universal Ski Ticket, contact:
CORPORATE SKI INCENTIVES, INC. BOX 578 · MERRIMACK, NH 03054

**1-800-627-SKIS
1-800-627-7547**

OR 617-229-2916

ISLE ROYALE
NATIONAL PARK
(Michigan)

MAILING ADDRESS:

National Park Concessions, Inc.
Mammoth Cave, KY 42259

SEASONAL EMPLOYMENT

0	55	55	0
SPRING	**SUMMER**	**FALL**	**WINTER**

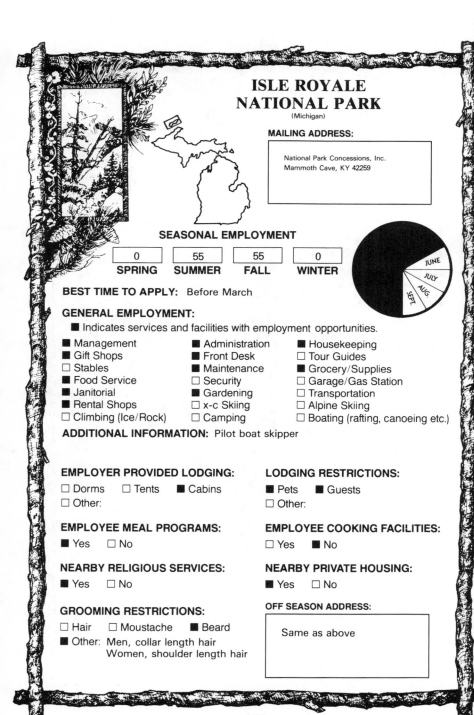

BEST TIME TO APPLY: Before March

GENERAL EMPLOYMENT:

■ Indicates services and facilities with employment opportunities.

■ Management	■ Administration	■ Housekeeping
■ Gift Shops	■ Front Desk	☐ Tour Guides
☐ Stables	■ Maintenance	☐ Grocery/Supplies
■ Food Service	☐ Security	☐ Garage/Gas Station
■ Janitorial	■ Gardening	☐ Transportation
■ Rental Shops	☐ x-c Skiing	☐ Alpine Skiing
☐ Climbing (Ice/Rock)	☐ Camping	☐ Boating (rafting, canoeing etc.)

ADDITIONAL INFORMATION: Pilot boat skipper

EMPLOYER PROVIDED LODGING:

☐ Dorms   ☐ Tents   ■ Cabins
☐ Other:

LODGING RESTRICTIONS:

■ Pets   ■ Guests
☐ Other:

EMPLOYEE MEAL PROGRAMS:

■ Yes   ☐ No

EMPLOYEE COOKING FACILITIES:

☐ Yes   ■ No

NEARBY RELIGIOUS SERVICES:

■ Yes   ☐ No

NEARBY PRIVATE HOUSING:

■ Yes   ☐ No

GROOMING RESTRICTIONS:

☐ Hair   ☐ Moustache   ■ Beard
■ Other: Men, collar length hair
Women, shoulder length hair

OFF SEASON ADDRESS:

Same as above

The Best in the Midwest !

Boyne Mountain

Boyne Highlands

BOYNE USA RESORTS...WHERE THE ACTION IS ALL YEAR LONG.

Boyne Highlands and Boyne Mountain in northern Michigan are the two top destinations in the midwest for skiing, golf, tennis and conventions. The two resorts feature 35 ski slopes, 18 chairlifts, lodges, condominiums, 18 tennis courts, pools and saunas. Their five championship golf courses draw golfers from around the country. Boyne employees share in using the resorts' amenities.

SEASONAL EMPLOYMENT OPPORTUNITIES:

•**Recreational**
Ski, Golf & Tennis Shop Salespeople
Ski, Golf & Tennis Instructors
Ski Rental Staff
Golf Club Runners

•**Restaurant**
Wait & Bus Staff
Host & Hostess/Kitchen Staff
Bartenders/Cocktail Wait Staff
Cafeteria Line Staff

•**Hotels/Condominiums**
Housekeepers
Front Desk Clerks
Reservationists
Convention Crew

•**Outdoor Maintenance**
Summer Landscape Crew
Golf Greens Keepers
Lift Operators
Ticket Checkers
Snowmakers

Boyne USA
RESORTS
BIG SKY ·BOYNE MOUNTAIN · BOYNE HIGHLANDS
BRIGHTON

For further information contact:
Human Resource Manager
Boyne USA Resorts
Boyne Falls, Michigan 49713
☎ 1 (616) 549-2441
  1 (800) GO-BOYNE

VOYAGEURS
NATIONAL PARK
(Minnesota)

MAILING ADDRESS:

Kettle Falls Hotel, Inc.
Ash River Trail
Orr, MN 55771

SEASONAL EMPLOYMENT

12	12	12	0
SPRING	**SUMMER**	**FALL**	**WINTER**

BEST TIME TO APPLY: January and February

GENERAL EMPLOYMENT:

■ Indicates services and facilities with employment opportunities.

☐ Management   ☐ Administration   ■ Housekeeping
☐ Gift Shops   ☐ Front Desk   ☐ Tour Guides
☐ Stables   ■ Maintenance   ☐ Grocery/Supplies
■ Food Service   ☐ Security   ☐ Garage/Gas Station
☐ Janitorial   ☐ Gardening   ☐ Transportation
■ Rental Shops   ☐ x-c Skiing   ☐ Alpine Skiing
☐ Climbing (Ice/Rock)   ☐ Camping   ☐ Boating (rafting, canoeing etc.)

ADDITIONAL INFORMATION: Bartending

EMPLOYER PROVIDED LODGING:
☐ Dorms   ☐ Tents   ■ Cabins
☐ Other:

LODGING RESTRICTIONS:
■ Pets   ■ Guests
☐ Other:

EMPLOYEE MEAL PROGRAMS:
■ Yes   ☐ No

EMPLOYEE COOKING FACILITIES:
☐ Yes   ■ No

NEARBY RELIGIOUS SERVICES:
■ Yes   ☐ No

NEARBY PRIVATE HOUSING:
☐ Yes   ■ No

GROOMING RESTRICTIONS:
☐ Hair   ☐ Moustache   ☐ Beard
■ Other: Well groomed

OFF SEASON ADDRESS:

Kettle Falls Hotel, Inc.
622 12th Ave.
International Falls, MN 56649

OUTDOOR WILDERNESS FABRICS

2511 LATAH NP • NAMPA, IDAHO 83651

Gore-Tex
Ultrex
Versa Tech
Tactel
Taslan
Supplex
Blends
Ballistics
Cordura
Packcloth
Oxford
Ripstop
Tafetta

Polar Plus
Polarguard
Thermo Puf
Thinsulate
Nylon Lock Mesh
No See Um Netting

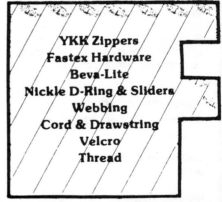

YKK Zippers
Fastex Hardware
Beva-Lite
Nickle D-Ring & Sliders
Webbing
Cord & Drawstring
Velcro
Thread

Small Manufacturer to Home Sewer

Price List Free

VISA/MC

Rolls to Yards

Full Samples - $2.00

Phone 208/466-1602

Glacier National Park

MAILING ADDRESS:

Glacier Park, Inc.
East Glacier Park, MT 59434

SEASONAL EMPLOYMENT

0	100	100	0
SPRING	**SUMMER**	**FALL**	**WINTER**

BEST TIME TO APPLY: January thru April

GENERAL EMPLOYMENT:

■ Indicates services and facilities with employment opportunities.

■ Management	■ Administration	■ Housekeeping
■ Gift Shops	■ Front Desk	☐ Tour Guides
☐ Stables	■ Maintenance	■ Grocery/Supplies
■ Food Service	☐ Security	■ Garage/Gas Station
■ Janitorial	■ Gardening	■ Transportation
■ Rental Shops	☐ x-c Skiing	☐ Alpine Skiing
☐ Climbing (Ice/Rock)	☐ Camping	☐ Boating (rafting, canoeing etc.)

ADDITIONAL INFORMATION:

EMPLOYER PROVIDED LODGING:

■ Dorms   ☐ Tents   ■ Cabins
☐ Other:

LODGING RESTRICTIONS:

■ Pets   ☐ Guests
☐ Other:

EMPLOYEE MEAL PROGRAMS:

■ Yes   ☐ No

EMPLOYEE COOKING FACILITIES:

☐ Yes   ■ No

NEARBY RELIGIOUS SERVICES:

■ Yes   ☐ No

NEARBY PRIVATE HOUSING:

☐ Yes   ■ No

GROOMING RESTRICTIONS:

☐ Hair   ☐ Moustache   ■ Beard
■ Other: Well groomed

OFF SEASON ADDRESS:

Glacier Park Inc.
1735 E. Fort Lowell Rd. #7
Tucson, AZ 95719

THE BIG MOUNTAIN
Ski & Summer Resort
P.O. Box 1400
Whitefish, MT 59937
(406)862-3511

Located in the Northern Rocky Mountains of Montana, The Big Mountain is the largest destination Ski Resort in the State, with over 4,000 acres of skiable terrain and a full service Alpine Village. Seasonable positions available include:

Lift Attendants	Front Desk
Ski Patrol	Parking/Transportation
Grooming Operators	Maintenance
Ticket Cashiers	Housekeeping
Ticket Checkers	Security
Janitorial	Food Service/Bar Service

SEASON DATES

Winter: Thanksgiving - Mid April, Approx. 250 Employees
Summer: Mid May - October 1, Approx. 50 Employees

Best time to apply: July & August for Winter
                      March & April for Summer
Additional information: Nearby private housing available,
                      not provided by The Big Mountain.
Employment benefits: Season Ski Pass.

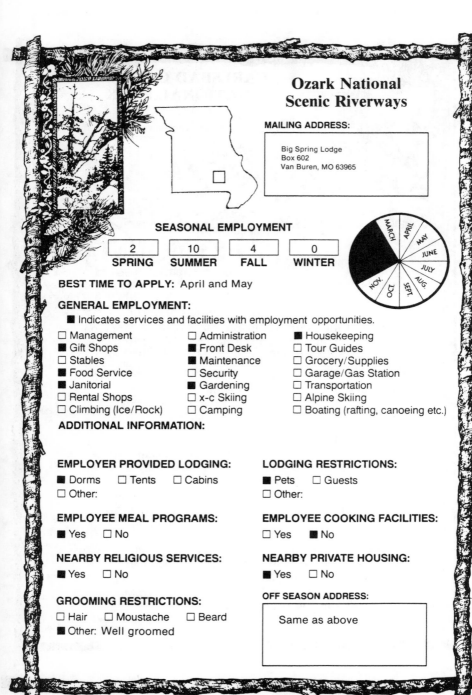

Ozark National
Scenic Riverways

MAILING ADDRESS:

Big Spring Lodge
Box 602
Van Buren, MO 63965

SEASONAL EMPLOYMENT

2	10	4	0
SPRING	**SUMMER**	**FALL**	**WINTER**

BEST TIME TO APPLY: April and May

GENERAL EMPLOYMENT:

■ Indicates services and facilities with employment opportunities.

☐ Management   ☐ Administration   ■ Housekeeping
■ Gift Shops   ■ Front Desk   ☐ Tour Guides
☐ Stables   ■ Maintenance   ☐ Grocery/Supplies
■ Food Service   ☐ Security   ☐ Garage/Gas Station
■ Janitorial   ■ Gardening   ☐ Transportation
☐ Rental Shops   ☐ x-c Skiing   ☐ Alpine Skiing
☐ Climbing (Ice/Rock)   ☐ Camping   ☐ Boating (rafting, canoeing etc.)

ADDITIONAL INFORMATION:

EMPLOYER PROVIDED LODGING:
■ Dorms   ☐ Tents   ☐ Cabins
☐ Other:

LODGING RESTRICTIONS:
■ Pets   ☐ Guests
☐ Other:

EMPLOYEE MEAL PROGRAMS:
■ Yes   ☐ No

EMPLOYEE COOKING FACILITIES:
☐ Yes   ■ No

NEARBY RELIGIOUS SERVICES:
■ Yes   ☐ No

NEARBY PRIVATE HOUSING:
■ Yes   ☐ No

GROOMING RESTRICTIONS:
☐ Hair   ☐ Moustache   ☐ Beard
■ Other: Well groomed

OFF SEASON ADDRESS:

Same as above

CARLSBAD CAVERNS
NATIONAL PARK
(New Mexico)

MAILING ADDRESS:

Carlsbad Supply Co, Inc.
Drawer Y
Carlsbad, NM 88220

SEASONAL EMPLOYMENT

20	20	20	20
SPRING	**SUMMER**	**FALL**	**WINTER**

BEST TIME TO APPLY: Year-round

GENERAL EMPLOYMENT:

■ Indicates services and facilities with employment opportunities.

☐ Management
■ Gift Shops
☐ Stables
■ Food Service
■ Janitorial
☐ Rental Shops
☐ Climbing (Ice/Rock)

☐ Administration
☐ Front Desk
☐ Maintenance
☐ Security
■ Gardening
☐ x-c Skiing
☐ Camping

☐ Housekeeping
☐ Tour Guides
☐ Grocery/Supplies
☐ Garage/Gas Station
☐ Transportation
☐ Alpine Skiing
☐ Boating (rafting, canoeing etc.)

ADDITIONAL INFORMATION: Kennel assistant

EMPLOYER PROVIDED LODGING:

☐ Dorms   ☐ Tents   ■ Cabins
■ Other: Bunkhouse style

LODGING RESTRICTIONS:

■ Pets   ■ Guests
☐ Other:

EMPLOYEE MEAL PROGRAMS:

■ Yes   ☐ No

EMPLOYEE COOKING FACILITIES:

☐ Yes   ■ No

NEARBY RELIGIOUS SERVICES:

■ Yes   ☐ No

NEARBY PRIVATE HOUSING:

■ Yes   ☐ No

GROOMING RESTRICTIONS:

☐ Hair   ☐ Moustache   ■ Beard
■ Other: Neat appearance

OFF SEASON ADDRESS:

Same as above

SHIFTING GEARS TO THE GREAT OUTDOORS
By J. J. Hill

Life is made up of many choices...many of which are in reference to one's search for wealth, happiness, fame, power, etc. Your choice of lifestyle may play the single most important role in your self development. Let's examine the meaning of lifestyle. The American heritage Dictionary defines Life-style as "an internationally consistent way of life or style of living that reflects the attitudes and values of an individual or a culture." Don't we all strive for individuality, the uniqueness of our very being? In this day and age we may sometimes lose sight of who we really are.

When was the last time you sat by a river to feel the flow of your internal self, felt you and only you, surging inside, searching only for direction? Last week? Last month? Last year? Don't let time pass you by -- now is the time to make the choice -- your lifestyle -- your direction -- your choice to be you!

I chose to create my lifestyle in the National Park System. Why? The first part of my decision was based on where I liked to spend my time. Many of my friends lived in urban America -- the fast-paced city life. Day in and day out they challenged themselves, beating the traffic, fighting through lines, battling smog, and searching for the serenity of a moment alone. Seeing their despair I asked what they enjoyed doing in their precious spare time. Surprisingly, the majority of them told me of their adventures to the great outdoors where they found peace and contentment in nature! Interesting!

In my own simple way I thought why live in an area that stresses me out, an area that I find basically unbearable, to make a living that allowed me the occasional weekend in paradise when I could reside in a place of my choice and eliminate the city hassles? I thought of the National Park system.

I can't say when this idea actually hit me, but I do remember realizing the fact that I was in charge of myself and my livestyle. I was no longer willing to accept the way of life my parents had chosen for themselves and their family. I was an individual and had to establish my own goals, my own lifestyle -- Nature was calling and I decided to take time to listen. The great outdoors had always fascinated me, and I decided to do something about it. The best decision of my young life was made when I packed a few clothes and set out for Yosemite National Park!

Where will I live? What job will I have? How will I react to the first bear I see? The questions raced through my mind and yet the answer was always the same: I'm leaving the city behind and starting MY life! I would adapt to this new and exciting lifestyle...AND HOW!! My first summer I backpacked, fished, explored, swam, climbed, and generally had the time of my life in one of natures great wonderlands!

Captain Fortenberry on maneuvers at L. Aloha

Photo by Robert Frankel

NPTJ Staff Photographer in the chute at Kirkwood

Photo by Eric Fortenberry

LAKE MEAD
NATIONAL RECREATION AREA
(Nevada)

MAILING ADDRESS:

Cottonwood Cove Resort and Marina
Box 1000
Cottonwood Cove, NV 89046

SEASONAL EMPLOYMENT

30	50	30	24
SPRING	**SUMMER**	**FALL**	**WINTER**

BEST TIME TO APPLY: February thru April

GENERAL EMPLOYMENT:

■ Indicates services and facilities with employment opportunities.

☐ Management	☐ Administration	■ Housekeeping
☐ Gift Shops	☐ Front Desk	☐ Tour Guides
☐ Stables	■ Maintenance	☐ Grocery/Supplies
■ Food Service	☐ Security	■ Garage/Gas Station
☐ Janitorial	☐ Gardening	☐ Transportation
■ Rental Shops	☐ x-c Skiing	☐ Alpine Skiing
☐ Climbing (Ice/Rock)	☐ Camping	■ Boating (rafting, canoeing etc.)

ADDITIONAL INFORMATION: Air conditioning/refrigeration mechanic, outboard motor mechanic

EMPLOYER PROVIDED LODGING:

☐ Dorms   ☐ Tents   ☐ Cabins

■ Other: Limited housing, Trailer advisable

LODGING RESTRICTIONS:

☐ Pets   ☐ Guests

■ Other: Varies with type of housing

EMPLOYEE MEAL PROGRAMS:

☐ Yes   ■ No

EMPLOYEE COOKING FACILITIES:

■ Yes   ☐ No

NEARBY RELIGIOUS SERVICES:

☐ Yes   ■ No

NEARBY PRIVATE HOUSING:

☐ Yes   ■ No

GROOMING RESTRICTIONS:

■ Hair   ■ Moustache   ■ Beard

■ Other: Trimmed, no long hair

OFF SEASON ADDRESS:

Same as above

158

LAKE MEAD
NATIONAL RECREATION AREA
(Nevada)

MAILING ADDRESS:

Echo Bay Resort
Overton, NV 89040

SEASONAL EMPLOYMENT

80	110	110	80
SPRING	**SUMMER**	**FALL**	**WINTER**

BEST TIME TO APPLY: February and March

GENERAL EMPLOYMENT:

■ Indicates services and facilities with employment opportunities.

■ Management
□ Gift Shops
□ Stables
■ Food Service
■ Janitorial
■ Rental Shops
□ Climbing (Ice/Rock)

■ Administration
■ Front Desk
■ Maintenance
■ Security
■ Gardening
□ x-c Skiing
□ Camping

■ Housekeeping
□ Tour Guides
■ Grocery/Supplies
■ Garage/Gas Station
□ Transportation
□ Alpine Skiing
■ Boating (rafting, canoeing etc.)

ADDITIONAL INFORMATION: Refrigeration / motor boat mechanics, electricians and computer specialists

EMPLOYER PROVIDED LODGING:
□ Dorms   □ Tents   □ Cabins
■ Other: Trailers

LODGING RESTRICTIONS:
■ Pets   ■ Guests
■ Other: Management discretion

EMPLOYEE MEAL PROGRAMS:
■ Yes   □ No

EMPLOYEE COOKING FACILITIES:
■ Yes   □ No

NEARBY RELIGIOUS SERVICES:
■ Yes   □ No

NEARBY PRIVATE HOUSING:
■ Yes   □ No

GROOMING RESTRICTIONS:
□ Hair   □ Moustache   □ Beard
■ Other: Trimmed and neat

OFF SEASON ADDRESS:

Same as above

159

LAKE MEAD
NATIONAL RECREATION AREA
(Nevada)

MAILING ADDRESS:

Lake Mohave Resort and Marina
Katherine Landing
Bullhead City, AZ 86430

SEASONAL EMPLOYMENT

60	100	40	40
SPRING	**SUMMER**	**FALL**	**WINTER**

BEST TIME TO APPLY: April, July and September

GENERAL EMPLOYMENT:

■ Indicates services and facilities with employment opportunities.

- ■ Management
- ■ Gift Shops
- ☐ Stables
- ■ Food Service
- ■ Janitorial
- ■ Rental Shops
- ☐ Climbing (Ice/Rock)

- ■ Administration
- ■ Front Desk
- ■ Maintenance
- ■ Security
- ■ Gardening
- ☐ x-c Skiing
- ☐ Camping

- ■ Housekeeping
- ☐ Tour Guides
- ■ Grocery/Supplies
- ■ Garage/Gas Station
- ☐ Transportation
- ☐ Alpine Skiing
- ■ Boating (rafting, canoeing etc.)

ADDITIONAL INFORMATION: Inboard/outboard motor mechanics

EMPLOYER PROVIDED LODGING:

☐ Dorms ☐ Tents ☐ Cabins
■ Other: Limited Trailers available

LODGING RESTRICTIONS:

☐ Pets ☐ Guests
■ Other: Pets must be leashed

EMPLOYEE MEAL PROGRAMS:

■ Yes ☐ No

EMPLOYEE COOKING FACILITIES:

■ Yes ☐ No

NEARBY RELIGIOUS SERVICES:

■ Yes ☐ No

NEARBY PRIVATE HOUSING:

■ Yes ☐ No

GROOMING RESTRICTIONS:

■ Hair ☐ Moustache ■ Beard
■ Other: Neat, clean appearance

OFF SEASON ADDRESS:

Same as above

160

LAKE MEAD
NATIONAL RECREATION AREA
(Nevada)

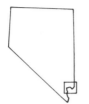

MAILING ADDRESS:

Temple Bar Resort
Temple Bar, AZ 86443

SEASONAL EMPLOYMENT

SPRING	SUMMER	FALL	WINTER
35	41	30	26

BEST TIME TO APPLY: February and March

GENERAL EMPLOYMENT:

■ Indicates services and facilities with employment opportunities.

■ Management	■ Administration	■ Housekeeping
□ Gift Shops	■ Front Desk	□ Tour Guides
□ Stables	■ Maintenance	■ Grocery/Supplies
■ Food Service	□ Security	■ Garage/Gas Station
■ Janitorial	■ Gardening	■ Transportation
■ Rental Shops	□ x-c Skiing	□ Alpine Skiing
□ Climbing (Ice/Rock)	□ Camping	■ Boating (rafting, canoeing etc.)

ADDITIONAL INFORMATION: Inboard/outboard certified mechanics; refrigeration

EMPLOYER PROVIDED LODGING:

□ Dorms   □ Tents   □ Cabins
■ Other: Trailers

LODGING RESTRICTIONS:

□ Pets   □ Guests
■ Other: Pets on leash

EMPLOYEE MEAL PROGRAMS:

■ Yes   □ No

EMPLOYEE COOKING FACILITIES:

■ Yes   □ No

NEARBY RELIGIOUS SERVICES:

□ Yes   ■ No

NEARBY PRIVATE HOUSING:

□ Yes   ■ No

GROOMING RESTRICTIONS:

□ Hair   □ Moustache   □ Beard
■ Other: Neat, clean appearance

OFF SEASON ADDRESS:

Same as above

LAKE MEAD
NATIONAL RECREATION AREA
(Nevada)

MAILING ADDRESS:

Lake Mead Resort Marina
322 Lakeshore Rd.
Boulder City, NV 89005

SEASONAL EMPLOYMENT

70	75	69	50
SPRING	**SUMMER**	**FALL**	**WINTER**

BEST TIME TO APPLY: February and March

GENERAL EMPLOYMENT:

■ Indicates services and facilities with employment opportunities.

■ Management	■ Administration	■ Housekeeping
■ Gift Shops	■ Front Desk	☐ Tour Guides
☐ Stables	■ Maintenance	■ Grocery/Supplies
■ Food Service	■ Security	■ Garage/Gas Station
■ Janitorial	■ Gardening	☐ Transportation
■ Rental Shops	☐ x-c Skiing	■ Alpine Skiing
☐ Climbing (Ice/Rock)	☐ Camping	■ Boating (rafting, canoeing etc.)

ADDITIONAL INFORMATION: Inboard / outboard mechanics
and refrigeration mechanics

EMPLOYER PROVIDED LODGING:

☐ Dorms   ☐ Tents   ☐ Cabins
■ Other: None

LODGING RESTRICTIONS:

☐ Pets   ☐ Guests
■ Other: N/A

EMPLOYEE MEAL PROGRAMS:

■ Yes   ☐ No

EMPLOYEE COOKING FACILITIES:

☐ Yes   ■ No

NEARBY RELIGIOUS SERVICES:

■ Yes   ☐ No

NEARBY PRIVATE HOUSING:

■ Yes   ☐ No

GROOMING RESTRICTIONS:

☐ Hair   ☐ Moustache   ☐ Beard
■ Other: Neat, clean appearance

OFF SEASON ADDRESS:

Same as above

162

Lake Mead
National Recreation Area
(Nevada)

MAILING ADDRESS:

Seven Crown Resorts
Personnel Dept.
688 Wells Rd. Suite A
Boulder City, NV 89005

SEASONAL EMPLOYMENT

675	725	500	400
SPRING	**SUMMER**	**FALL**	**WINTER**

BEST TIME TO APPLY:

GENERAL EMPLOYMENT:

■ Indicates services and facilities with employment opportunities.

■ Management
■ Gift Shops
☐ Stables
■ Food Service
■ Janitorial
■ Rental Shops
☐ Climbing (Ice/Rock)

■ Administration
■ Front Desk
■ Maintenance
■ Security
■ Gardening
☐ x-c Skiing
☐ Camping

■ Housekeeping
☐ Tour Guides
■ Grocery/Supplies
■ Garage/Gas Station
☐ Transportation
☐ Alpine Skiing
■ Boating (rafting, canoeing etc.)

ADDITIONAL INFORMATION:

EMPLOYER PROVIDED LODGING:

☐ Dorms   ☐ Tents   ☐ Cabins
■ Other: Limited

LODGING RESTRICTIONS:

☐ Pets   ☐ Guests
■ Other: Pets must be leashed

EMPLOYEE MEAL PROGRAMS:

■ Yes   ☐ No

EMPLOYEE COOKING FACILITIES:

■ Yes   ☐ No

NEARBY RELIGIOUS SERVICES:

■ Yes   ☐ No

NEARBY PRIVATE HOUSING:

■ Yes   ☐ No

GROOMING RESTRICTIONS:

■ Hair   ■ Moustache   ■ Beard
■ Other: Clean Appearance

OFF SEASON ADDRESS:

Same as above

SIERRA NEVADA COLLEGE-LAKE TAHOE
HIGHER LEARNING IN THE HIGH SIERRA

Despite its prominent location, Sierra Nevada College-Lake Tahoe has been well hidden up to now. A small four-year independent college on the north shore of the largest high mountain freshwater lake in the United States, 20-year-old SNC was recently called by a leading college authority "the best kept secret in the state of Nevada." Judging from the phenomenal growth in enrollment over the last five years, from under 100 to nearly 500 students, it's not likely to stay hidden for long. Nor is there any mystery why college-bound high school seniors and transfer students are sending applications to SNC in greater and greater numbers.

For one thing, this lucky school is located amid one of the most photographed scenes on earth. At 6,700 feet above sea level in the Sierra Nevada range, the Tahoe Basin is a self-contained alpine ecosystem featuring a 191 square-mile azure-blue lake of transcendent beauty. Besides the scenic advantages, the locale affords unequaled academic opportunities for the college's student body.

Like other bachelor's degree programs at the the college, SNC's Science Department echoes the school's mission statement by combining features of

a traditional liberal arts education with practical, modern career preparation in Environmental Science or Recreation Management. For instance, most students serve at least once as an intern in a public or private organization, such as federal and state agencies in Nevada and California and the world-renowned Tahoe Research Group. Even regularly scheduled classes at the college frequently meet in the field, where the school's neighborhood doubles as one of the most photogenic laboratories in academia.

Internships flower into full-time careers for some students. Senior Kim Kauffman found work with the California Department of Parks as the assistant to a Resource Ecologist working on revegetation of flooded stream zones. She intends to continue after graduation. "I'm putting my classes to work," she says, "learning about the forest as a living ecosystem." Graduate Mark Miler turned his internship with the state of Nevada into a job implementing energy conservation measures throughout the state. His only regret, he reports, is having to leave Tahoe for the more subtle beauties of the Las Vegas area.

For undergraduates on campus, looking out classroom windows at the Sierra landscape, participation in small seminar-style discussions means gaining valuable skills in critical thinking and speaking while establishing close personal relationships with friendly, accessible faculty--a clear departure from the ivory-towered image of many similar schools. Another dictum of the mission statement printed in the college's general catalogue decrees that both full-time and adjunct faculty be professionally as well as academically qualified.

Such a focus on real-world success has put several of the college's departments, such as Fine Arts and Ski Business Management, on the cutting edge of their disciplines. The political and social circumstances of the Tahoe region insure that this distinction applies to Environmental Science as well.

Before he joined the SNC faculty as Director of Natural Sciences, Dartmouth Ph.D. and freshwater ecologist Chuck Levitan worked with the Tahoe Research Group to research the intricate chemical and biological processes involved in the fragile Tahoe ecosystem. His voluminous publications on these topics are a series of small steps to clarify the web of factors that are often blamed for a slow but measured decrease in the lake's fabled clarity. Commonly seen as besieged by the area's economic interests, the Tahoe environmnet studied by Levitan and others provides an arena for understanding the necessary compromises between conservation, recreation, and habitation.

SNC Trustee Steve Brandt, a former director of the environmentalist League to Save Lake Tahoe, Senior Lecturer in Management at Stanford University and a frequent contributor to the Sierra Club bulletin, thinks the relationship between economics and environment is one of interdependence rather than conflict. "The question is not whether business has a place at Tahoe," Brandt has said, "But what kinds of businesses are better for the longer run. I used to have a bumper sticker on my old jeep--the one I drove 75,000 miles around Tahoe to agency meetings. It read 'For Recreation--Against Overpopulation.' We can't encourage construction on virgin land any more; we'll only consume our asset, our recreational calling card. We need to emphasize use, not consumption."

The Science degree program at SNC is divided into four areas of emphasis. Two of these are "Environmental Science and Ecology" and "Recreation Management." Environmental Science and Ecology offers an interdisciplinary program that tries to answer these emerging questions by balancing courses in science and technology with studies in the liberal arts. Students learn to approach complex issues of land use, pollution, wildlife management, and tourism from an informed perspective, developing analytical skills sought by a wide variety of businesses and agencies.

Students also obtain a technical perspective by focusing on the biological, chemical and physical interactions which structure ecosystems. Faculty expertise in aquatic ecology takes advantage of the region's wide variety of ponds, high-altitude marshes, streams, reservoirs, and lakes. Students become familiar with the field work and research methods which form a major part of graduate studies and employment in this division of discipline.

The Tahoe Basin provides many resources for the study of Recreation Management. Nearby are National Forests, National Parks, state parks in two states, and many other protected areas. Here again, a wealth of internships abound for students in the program.

The general run of Sierra Nevada College students, whether they're studying science or another discipline, cannot be easily categorized. They run the gamut from 18-year-olds to transfer students from larger schools and men and women in their 30's and 40's embarking on new career paths.

"If there's one common denominator among the student body, it's a love of the outdoors," says Director of Student Services David Fenimore. "Around this campus there's always some activity like skiing, sailing, trekking, rock climbing, bicycling, tennis, golf, softball or suchlike to distract even the worst grade-grubber."

For a location so close to major wilderness areas and trail systems, the school is also convenient to civilized amenities; it's just 45 minutes from Reno, Nevada, and four hours from San Francisco and the Pacific Ocean. Moderate annual snowfall, mild winter temperatures, low humidity and an average of 288 annual days of sunshine provide an ideal climate for maximizing one's outdoor potential.

At the same time, Sierra Nevada College is dedicated to maximizing academic, social, and career potential in every student. Although growing, the school is still small enough to provide each student with the chance to take a leadership role in and out of the classroom.

For collegians whose idea of heaven on earth is a small community in a spectacular place, Sierra Nevada College-Lake Tahoe certainly seems to fit the bill.

THE LATEST CONCEPT IN MOBILE HOMES...

BLUE RIDGE PARKWAY
(North Carolina)

MAILING ADDRESS:

Pisgah Inn
PO Drawer 749
Waynesville, NC 28786

SEASONAL EMPLOYMENT

SPRING	SUMMER	FALL	WINTER
75	75	75	0

BEST TIME TO APPLY: January thru March

GENERAL EMPLOYMENT:
■ Indicates services and facilities with employment opportunities.

☐ Management	☐ Administration	■ Housekeeping
■ Gift Shops	■ Front Desk	☐ Tour Guides
☐ Stables	■ Maintenance	☐ Grocery/Supplies
■ Food Service	■ Security	☐ Garage/Gas Station
■ Janitorial	■ Gardening	☐ Transportation
☐ Rental Shops	☐ x-c Skiing	☐ Alpine Skiing
☐ Climbing (Ice/Rock)	☐ Camping	☐ Boating (rafting, canoeing etc.)

ADDITIONAL INFORMATION:

EMPLOYER PROVIDED LODGING:
☐ Dorms   ☐ Tents   ■ Cabins
☐ Other:

LODGING RESTRICTIONS:
■ Pets   ☐ Guests
☐ Other:

EMPLOYEE MEAL PROGRAMS:
■ Yes   ☐ No

EMPLOYEE COOKING FACILITIES:
☐ Yes   ■ No

NEARBY RELIGIOUS SERVICES:
■ Yes   ☐ No

NEARBY PRIVATE HOUSING:
☐ Yes   ■ No

GROOMING RESTRICTIONS:
■ Hair   ☐ Moustache   ■ Beard
■ Other: Well groomed

OFF SEASON ADDRESS:

Same as above

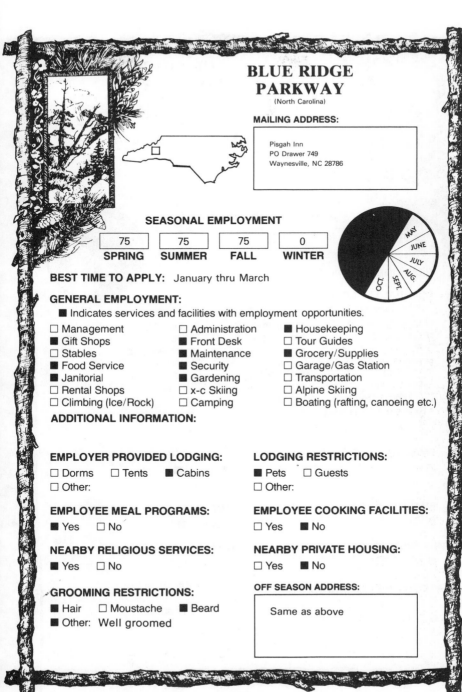

BLUE RIDGE
PARKWAY
(North Carolina)

MAILING ADDRESS:

National Park Concessions, Inc.
Mammoth Cave, KY 42259

SEASONAL EMPLOYMENT

15	20	15	0
SPRING	**SUMMER**	**FALL**	**WINTER**

BEST TIME TO APPLY: Before February 28th

GENERAL EMPLOYMENT:

■ Indicates services and facilities with employment opportunities.

■ Management	■ Administration	■ Housekeeping
■ Gift Shops	■ Front Desk	☐ Tour Guides
☐ Stables	■ Maintenance	☐ Grocery/Supplies
■ Food Service	☐ Security	■ Garage/Gas Station
■ Janitorial	■ Gardening	☐ Transportation
☐ Rental Shops	☐ x-c Skiing	☐ Alpine Skiing
☐ Climbing (Ice/Rock)	☐ Camping	☐ Boating (rafting, canoeing etc.)

ADDITIONAL INFORMATION:

EMPLOYER PROVIDED LODGING:

☐ Dorms ☐ Tents ■ Cabins
☐ Other:

LODGING RESTRICTIONS:

■ Pets ■ Guests
☐ Other:

EMPLOYEE MEAL PROGRAMS:

■ Yes ☐ No

EMPLOYEE COOKING FACILITIES:

☐ Yes ■ No

NEARBY RELIGIOUS SERVICES:

■ Yes ☐ No

NEARBY PRIVATE HOUSING:

■ Yes ☐ No

GROOMING RESTRICTIONS:

☐ Hair ■ Moustache ■ Beard
■ Other: Well groomed

OFF SEASON ADDRESS:

Same as above

THEODORE ROOSEVELT
NATIONAL PARK
(North Dakota)

MAILING ADDRESS:

Tescher Trail Rides, Inc.
Medora, ND 58645

SEASONAL EMPLOYMENT

0	6	0	0
SPRING	**SUMMER**	**FALL**	**WINTER**

JUNE
JULY
AUG.

BEST TIME TO APPLY: March thru May

GENERAL EMPLOYMENT:

■ Indicates services and facilities with employment opportunities.

☐ Management   ☐ Administration   ☐ Housekeeping
☐ Gift Shops   ☐ Front Desk   ■ Tour Guides
■ Stables   ☐ Maintenance   ☐ Grocery/Supplies
☐ Food Service   ☐ Security   ☐ Garage/Gas Station
☐ Janitorial   ☐ Gardening   ☐ Transportation
☐ Rental Shops   ☐ x-c Skiing   ☐ Alpine Skiing
☐ Climbing (Ice/Rock)   ☐ Camping   ☐ Boating (rafting, canoeing etc.)

ADDITIONAL INFORMATION: Horseshoer and trail guide

EMPLOYER PROVIDED LODGING:

☐ Dorms   ☐ Tents   ☐ Cabins
■ Other: Bunkhouse

LODGING RESTRICTIONS:

■ Pets   ■ Guests
■ Other: No smoking or drinking

EMPLOYEE MEAL PROGRAMS:

■ Yes   ☐ No

EMPLOYEE COOKING FACILITIES:

☐ Yes   ■ No

NEARBY RELIGIOUS SERVICES:

■ Yes   ☐ No

NEARBY PRIVATE HOUSING:

☐ Yes   ■ No

GROOMING RESTRICTIONS:

■ Hair   ☐ Moustache   ■ Beard
■ Other: Neat shave and hair cut;
        western wear

OFF SEASON ADDRESS:

Tescher Trail Rides
Rt. 2, Box 139
Beach, ND 58621

CRATER LAKE
NATIONAL PARK
(Oregon)

MAILING ADDRESS:

Crater Lake Lodge
Crater Lake, OR 97604

SEASONAL EMPLOYMENT

0	120	90	0
SPRING	**SUMMER**	**FALL**	**WINTER**

JUNE
JULY
AUG.
SEPT.

BEST TIME TO APPLY: January thru April

GENERAL EMPLOYMENT:

■ Indicates services and facilities with employment opportunities.

- ■ Management
- ■ Gift Shops
- □ Stables
- ■ Food Service
- ■ Janitorial
- □ Rental Shops
- □ Climbing (Ice/Rock)

- ■ Administration
- ■ Front Desk
- ■ Maintenance
- □ Security
- ■ Gardening
- □ x-c Skiing
- □ Camping

- ■ Housekeeping
- □ Tour Guides
- ■ Grocery/Supplies
- ■ Garage/Gas Station
- ■ Transportation
- □ Alpine Skiing
- □ Boating (rafting, canoeing etc.)

ADDITIONAL INFORMATION: Personal interview required

EMPLOYER PROVIDED LODGING:

■ Dorms   □ Tents   □ Cabins
■ Other: Bunkhouse style

LODGING RESTRICTIONS:

■ Pets   □ Guests
□ Other:

EMPLOYEE MEAL PROGRAMS:

■ Yes   □ No

EMPLOYEE COOKING FACILITIES:

□ Yes   ■ No

NEARBY RELIGIOUS SERVICES:

■ Yes   □ No

NEARBY PRIVATE HOUSING:

□ Yes   ■ No

GROOMING RESTRICTIONS:

□ Hair   □ Moustache   ■ Beard
■ Other: Neat appearance

OFF SEASON ADDRESS:

Same as above

174

OREGON CAVES
NATIONAL MONUMENT
(Oregon)

MAILING ADDRESS:

Oregon Caves Chateau
PO Box 128
Cave Junction, OR 97523

SEASONAL EMPLOYMENT

0	65	65	0
SPRING	**SUMMER**	**FALL**	**WINTER**

BEST TIME TO APPLY: January and February

GENERAL EMPLOYMENT:

■ Indicates services and facilities with employment opportunities.

- ☐ Management
- ■ Gift Shops
- ☐ Stables
- ■ Food Service
- ■ Janitorial
- ☐ Rental Shops
- ☐ Climbing (Ice/Rock)
- ☐ Administration
- ■ Front Desk
- ■ Maintenance
- ■ Security
- ☐ Gardening
- ☐ x-c Skiing
- ☐ Camping
- ■ Housekeeping
- ■ Tour Guides
- ☐ Grocery/Supplies
- ☐ Garage/Gas Station
- ☐ Transportation
- ☐ Alpine Skiing
- ☐ Boating (rafting, canoeing etc.)

ADDITIONAL INFORMATION:

EMPLOYER PROVIDED LODGING:
■ Dorms   ☐ Tents   ☐ Cabins
☐ Other:

LODGING RESTRICTIONS:
■ Pets   ☐ Guests
☐ Other:

EMPLOYEE MEAL PROGRAMS:
■ Yes   ☐ No

EMPLOYEE COOKING FACILITIES:
☐ Yes   ■ No

NEARBY RELIGIOUS SERVICES:
■ Yes   ☐ No

NEARBY PRIVATE HOUSING:
☐ Yes   ■ No

GROOMING RESTRICTIONS:
■ Hair   ☐ Moustache   ■ Beard
☐ Other:

OFF SEASON ADDRESS:

Oregon Caves Chateau
1439 NE 6th St. #2
Grants Pass, OR 97526

"Between forty and fifty percent of all types of living things—as many as 5 million species of plants, animals and insects—live in tropical rainforests, though these forests cover only two percent of the globe. Within these ancient forests, evolution has rolled on uninterrupted for sixty million years, making them the oldest and most diverse biological communities on earth."

Earth First!

"The Forest. . .a peculiar organism of unlimited kindness and benevolence that makes no demands for its sustenance and extends generously the products of its life activity; it affords protection to all beings, offering shade even to the axeman who destroys it."

The Buddha as cited in the IUCN Buletin (International Union for Conservation of Nature and Natural Resources)

"It has been said that we know more about some areas of the moon than we do about tropical rainforests. Yet what we have learned about them so far has revolutionized our view of all life on this planet."

Catherine Caufield, Environmental Journalist

Photo by Chris Mitchell

BADLANDS
NATIONAL PARK
(South Dakota)

MAILING ADDRESS:

Joan Davis
PO Box 5
Interior, SD 57750

SEASONAL EMPLOYMENT

10	10	10	0
SPRING	**SUMMER**	**FALL**	**WINTER**

BEST TIME TO APPLY: January-February

GENERAL EMPLOYMENT:

■ Indicates services and facilities with employment opportunities.

☐ Management	☐ Administration	■ Housekeeping
■ Gift Shops	■ Front Desk	☐ Tour Guides
☐ Stables	☐ Maintenance	☐ Grocery/Supplies
■ Food Service	☐ Security	☐ Garage/Gas Station
■ Janitorial	☐ Gardening	☐ Transportation
☐ Rental Shops	☐ x-c Skiing	☐ Alpine Skiing
☐ Climbing (Ice/Rock)	☐ Camping	☐ Boating (rafting, canoeing etc.)

ADDITIONAL INFORMATION:

EMPLOYER PROVIDED LODGING:

☐ Dorms   ☐ Tents   ☐ Cabins
■ Other: None

LODGING RESTRICTIONS:

☐ Pets   ☐ Guests
■ Other: N/A

EMPLOYEE MEAL PROGRAMS:

■ Yes   ☐ No

EMPLOYEE COOKING FACILITIES:

☐ Yes   ■ No

NEARBY RELIGIOUS SERVICES:

■ Yes   ☐ No

NEARBY PRIVATE HOUSING:

■ Yes   ☐ No

GROOMING RESTRICTIONS:

☐ Hair   ☐ Moustache   ■ Beard
■ Other: Neatly groomed

OFF SEASON ADDRESS:

Same as above

WIND CAVE
NATIONAL PARK
(South Dakota)

MAILING ADDRESS:

Wind Cave Concession
Box 310
Hot Springs, SD 57747

SEASONAL EMPLOYMENT

0	10	0	0
SPRING	**SUMMER**	**FALL**	**WINTER**

BEST TIME TO APPLY: March and April

GENERAL EMPLOYMENT:

■ Indicates services and facilities with employment opportunities.

☐ Management
■ Gift Shops
☐ Stables
■ Food Service
■ Janitorial
☐ Rental Shops
☐ Climbing (Ice/Rock)

☐ Administration
☐ Front Desk
☐ Maintenance
☐ Security
☐ Gardening
☐ x-c Skiing
☐ Camping

☐ Housekeeping
☐ Tour Guides
☐ Grocery/Supplies
☐ Garage/Gas Station
☐ Transportation
☐ Alpine Skiing
☐ Boating (rafting, canoeing etc.)

ADDITIONAL INFORMATION:

EMPLOYER PROVIDED LODGING:

☐ Dorms   ☐ Tents   ☐ Cabins
■ Other: None

LODGING RESTRICTIONS:

☐ Pets   ☐ Guests
■ Other: N/A

EMPLOYEE MEAL PROGRAMS:

■ Yes   ☐ No

EMPLOYEE COOKING FACILITIES:

☐ Yes   ■ No

NEARBY RELIGIOUS SERVICES:

■ Yes   ☐ No

NEARBY PRIVATE HOUSING:

■ Yes   ☐ No

GROOMING RESTRICTIONS:

☐ Hair   ☐ Moustache   ☐ Beard
■ Other: Neatly groomed

OFF SEASON ADDRESS:

Same as above

179

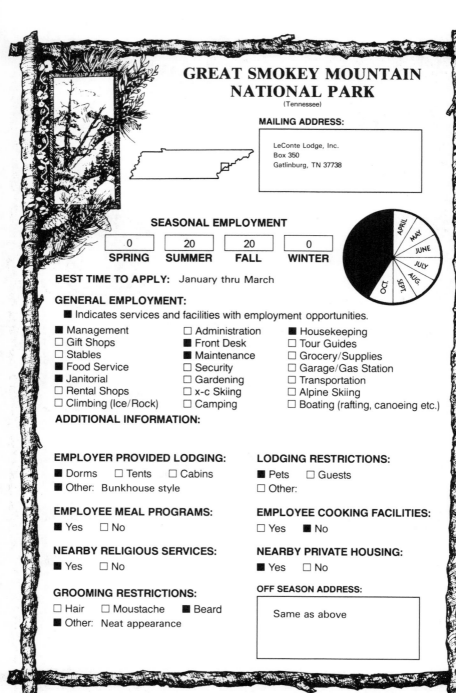

GREAT SMOKEY MOUNTAIN
NATIONAL PARK
(Tennessee)

MAILING ADDRESS:

LeConte Lodge, Inc.
Box 350
Gatlinburg, TN 37738

SEASONAL EMPLOYMENT

0	20	20	0
SPRING	**SUMMER**	**FALL**	**WINTER**

BEST TIME TO APPLY: January thru March

GENERAL EMPLOYMENT:

■ Indicates services and facilities with employment opportunities.

■ Management	□ Administration	■ Housekeeping
□ Gift Shops	■ Front Desk	□ Tour Guides
□ Stables	■ Maintenance	□ Grocery/Supplies
■ Food Service	□ Security	□ Garage/Gas Station
■ Janitorial	□ Gardening	□ Transportation
□ Rental Shops	□ x-c Skiing	□ Alpine Skiing
□ Climbing (Ice/Rock)	□ Camping	□ Boating (rafting, canoeing etc.)

ADDITIONAL INFORMATION:

EMPLOYER PROVIDED LODGING:

■ Dorms   □ Tents   □ Cabins
■ Other: Bunkhouse style

LODGING RESTRICTIONS:

■ Pets   □ Guests
□ Other:

EMPLOYEE MEAL PROGRAMS:

■ Yes   □ No

EMPLOYEE COOKING FACILITIES:

□ Yes   ■ No

NEARBY RELIGIOUS SERVICES:

■ Yes   □ No

NEARBY PRIVATE HOUSING:

■ Yes   □ No

GROOMING RESTRICTIONS:

□ Hair   □ Moustache   ■ Beard
■ Other: Neat appearance

OFF SEASON ADDRESS:

Same as above

BIG BEND
NATIONAL PARK
(Texas)

MAILING ADDRESS:

Chisos Remuda
Big Bend Nat'l Pk.
TX 79834

SEASONAL EMPLOYMENT

3	6	3	3
SPRING	**SUMMER**	**FALL**	**WINTER**

BEST TIME TO APPLY: Year-round

GENERAL EMPLOYMENT:

■ Indicates services and facilities with employment opportunities.

☐ Management
☐ Gift Shops
■ Stables
☐ Food Service
☐ Janitorial
☐ Rental Shops
☐ Climbing (Ice/Rock)

☐ Administration
☐ Front Desk
☐ Maintenance
☐ Security
☐ Gardening
☐ x-c Skiing
☐ Camping

☐ Housekeeping
☐ Tour Guides
☐ Grocery/Supplies
☐ Garage/Gas Station
☐ Transportation
☐ Alpine Skiing
☐ Boating (rafting, canoeing etc.)

ADDITIONAL INFORMATION:

EMPLOYER PROVIDED LODGING:

■ Dorms   ☐ Tents   ☐ Cabins
☐ Other:

LODGING RESTRICTIONS:

■ Pets   ■ Guests
☐ Other:

EMPLOYEE MEAL PROGRAMS:

■ Yes   ☐ No

EMPLOYEE COOKING FACILITIES:

☐ Yes   ■ No

NEARBY RELIGIOUS SERVICES:

■ Yes   ☐ No

NEARBY PRIVATE HOUSING:

☐ Yes   ■ No

GROOMING RESTRICTIONS:

■ Hair   ■ Moustache   ■ Beard
■ Other: Neat appearance

OFF SEASON ADDRESS:

Same as above

181

BIG BEND
NATIONAL PARK
(Texas)

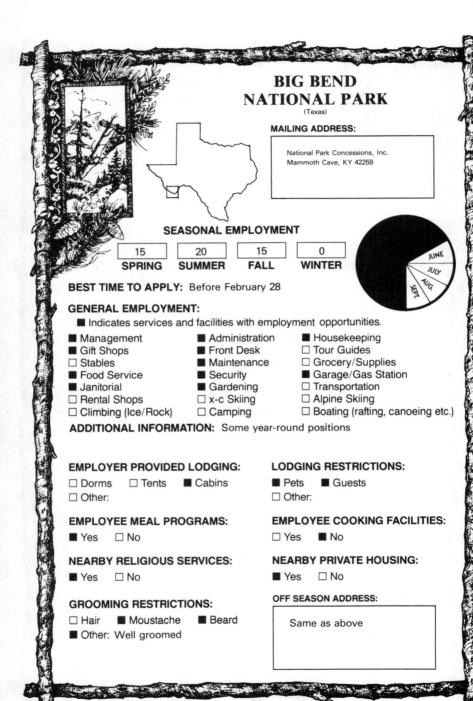

MAILING ADDRESS:

National Park Concessions, Inc.
Mammoth Cave, KY 42259

SEASONAL EMPLOYMENT

15	20	15	0
SPRING	**SUMMER**	**FALL**	**WINTER**

BEST TIME TO APPLY: Before February 28

GENERAL EMPLOYMENT:

■ Indicates services and facilities with employment opportunities.

■ Management	■ Administration	■ Housekeeping
■ Gift Shops	■ Front Desk	□ Tour Guides
□ Stables	■ Maintenance	□ Grocery/Supplies
■ Food Service	■ Security	■ Garage/Gas Station
■ Janitorial	■ Gardening	□ Transportation
□ Rental Shops	□ x-c Skiing	□ Alpine Skiing
□ Climbing (Ice/Rock)	□ Camping	□ Boating (rafting, canoeing etc.)

ADDITIONAL INFORMATION: Some year-round positions

EMPLOYER PROVIDED LODGING:
□ Dorms   □ Tents   ■ Cabins
□ Other:

LODGING RESTRICTIONS:
■ Pets   ■ Guests
□ Other:

EMPLOYEE MEAL PROGRAMS:
■ Yes   □ No

EMPLOYEE COOKING FACILITIES:
□ Yes   ■ No

NEARBY RELIGIOUS SERVICES:
■ Yes   □ No

NEARBY PRIVATE HOUSING:
■ Yes   □ No

GROOMING RESTRICTIONS:
□ Hair   ■ Moustache   ■ Beard
■ Other: Well groomed

OFF SEASON ADDRESS:

Same as above

BRYCE CANYON
NATIONAL PARK
(Utah)

MAILING ADDRESS:

Bryce-Zion Trail Rides
Tropic, UT 84776

SEASONAL EMPLOYMENT

9	15	15	0
SPRING	**SUMMER**	**FALL**	**WINTER**

BEST TIME TO APPLY: February

GENERAL EMPLOYMENT:

■ Indicates services and facilities with employment opportunities.

☐ Management ☐ Administration ☐ Housekeeping
☐ Gift Shops ☐ Front Desk ■ Tour Guides
■ Stables ☐ Maintenance ☐ Grocery/Supplies
☐ Food Service ☐ Security ☐ Garage/Gas Station
☐ Janitorial ☐ Gardening ☐ Transportation
☐ Rental Shops ☐ x-c Skiing ☐ Alpine Skiing
☐ Climbing (Ice/Rock) ☐ Camping ☐ Boating (rafting, canoeing etc.)

ADDITIONAL INFORMATION: Horsemanship very important

EMPLOYER PROVIDED LODGING:

☐ Dorms ■ Tents ☐ Cabins
☐ Other:

LODGING RESTRICTIONS:

■ Pets ☐ Guests
☐ Other:

EMPLOYEE MEAL PROGRAMS:

■ Yes ☐ No

EMPLOYEE COOKING FACILITIES:

■ Yes ☐ No

NEARBY RELIGIOUS SERVICES:

■ Yes ☐ No

NEARBY PRIVATE HOUSING:

☐ Yes ■ No

GROOMING RESTRICTIONS:

■ Hair ☐ Moustache ☐ Beard
☐ Other:

OFF SEASON ADDRESS:

Same as above

183

BRYCE CANYON
NATIONAL PARK
(Utah)

MAILING ADDRESS:

TW Services, Inc.
451 N. Main
P.O. Box 400
Cedar City, UT 84720

SEASONAL EMPLOYMENT

0	225	150	0
SPRING	**SUMMER**	**FALL**	**WINTER**

BEST TIME TO APPLY: January thru April

GENERAL EMPLOYMENT:

■ Indicates services and facilities with employment opportunities.

■ Management	■ Administration	■ Housekeeping
■ Gift Shops	■ Front Desk	■ Tour Guides
□ Stables	■ Maintenance	■ Grocery/Supplies
■ Food Service	■ Security	■ Garage/Gas Station
■ Janitorial	■ Gardening	■ Transportation
□ Rental Shops	□ x-c Skiing	□ Alpine Skiing
□ Climbing (Ice/Rock)	□ Camping	□ Boating (rafting, canoeing etc.)

ADDITIONAL INFORMATION:

EMPLOYER PROVIDED LODGING:

■ Dorms   □ Tents   ■ Cabins
■ Other: Bunkhouse style

LODGING RESTRICTIONS:

■ Pets   □ Guests
□ Other:

EMPLOYEE MEAL PROGRAMS:

■ Yes   □ No

EMPLOYEE COOKING FACILITIES:

□ Yes   ■ No

NEARBY RELIGIOUS SERVICES:

■ Yes   □ No

NEARBY PRIVATE HOUSING:

□ Yes   ■ No

GROOMING RESTRICTIONS:

□ Hair   □ Moustache   ■ Beard
■ Other: Neatly groomed

OFF SEASON ADDRESS:

Same as above

184

CANYONLANDS
NATIONAL PARK
(Utah)

MAILING ADDRESS:

Colorado River and
Trail Expeditions, Inc.
5058 S. 300 West
Salt Lake City, UT 84107

SEASONAL EMPLOYMENT

10	10	4	0
SPRING	**SUMMER**	**FALL**	**WINTER**

BEST TIME TO APPLY: December thru March

GENERAL EMPLOYMENT:

■ Indicates services and facilities with employment opportunities.

☐ Management	☐ Administration	☐ Housekeeping
☐ Gift Shops	☐ Front Desk	■ Tour Guides
☐ Stables	☐ Maintenance	☐ Grocery/Supplies
☐ Food Service	☐ Security	☐ Garage/Gas Station
☐ Janitorial	☐ Gardening	☐ Transportation
☐ Rental Shops	☐ x-c Skiing	☐ Alpine Skiing
☐ Climbing (Ice/Rock)	☐ Camping	■ Boating (rafting, canoeing etc.)

ADDITIONAL INFORMATION:

EMPLOYER PROVIDED LODGING:

☐ Dorms   ☐ Tents   ☐ Cabins
■ Other: Warehouse when not working

LODGING RESTRICTIONS:

■ Pets   ■ Guests
☐ Other:

EMPLOYEE MEAL PROGRAMS:

■ Yes   ☐ No

EMPLOYEE COOKING FACILITIES:

■ Yes   ☐ No

NEARBY RELIGIOUS SERVICES:

■ Yes   ☐ No

NEARBY PRIVATE HOUSING:

■ Yes   ☐ No

GROOMING RESTRICTIONS:

☐ Hair   ☐ Moustache   ☐ Beard
■ Other: None

OFF SEASON ADDRESS:

Same as above

185

CANYONLANDS
NATIONAL PARK
(Utah)

MAILING ADDRESS:

Outlaw Trails, Inc.
Box 336
Green River, UT 84525

SEASONAL EMPLOYMENT

5	15	5	3
SPRING	**SUMMER**	**FALL**	**WINTER**

BEST TIME TO APPLY: January and February

GENERAL EMPLOYMENT:

■ Indicates services and facilities with employment opportunities.

☐ Management	☐ Administration	☐ Housekeeping
☐ Gift Shops	☐ Front Desk	■ Tour Guides
☐ Stables	☐ Maintenance	☐ Grocery/Supplies
☐ Food Service	☐ Security	☐ Garage/Gas Station
☐ Janitorial	☐ Gardening	☐ Transportation
☐ Rental Shops	☐ x-c Skiing	☐ Alpine Skiing
■ Climbing (Ice/Rock)	■ Camping	■ Boating (rafting, canoeing etc.)

ADDITIONAL INFORMATION:

EMPLOYER PROVIDED LODGING:

☐ Dorms   ☐ Tents   ☐ Cabins
■ Other: Live on the river

LODGING RESTRICTIONS:

☐ Pets   ☐ Guests
■ Other: N/A

EMPLOYEE MEAL PROGRAMS:

■ Yes   ☐ No

EMPLOYEE COOKING FACILITIES:

■ Yes   ☐ No

NEARBY RELIGIOUS SERVICES:

■ Yes   ☐ No

NEARBY PRIVATE HOUSING:

■ Yes   ☐ No

GROOMING RESTRICTIONS:

☐ Hair   ☐ Moustache   ☐ Beard
■ Other: None

OFF SEASON ADDRESS:

Same as above

186

CANYONLANDS
NATIONAL PARKS
(Utah)

MAILING ADDRESS:

Tex's River Expeditions
PO Box 67
Moab, UT 84532

SEASONAL EMPLOYMENT

6	6	6	1
SPRING	**SUMMER**	**FALL**	**WINTER**

BEST TIME TO APPLY: Year-round

GENERAL EMPLOYMENT:
■ Indicates services and facilities with employment opportunities.

☐ Management	☐ Administration	☐ Housekeeping
☐ Gift Shops	■ Front Desk	■ Tour Guides
☐ Stables	☐ Maintenance	☐ Grocery/Supplies
☐ Food Service	☐ Security	☐ Garage/Gas Station
☐ Janitorial	☐ Gardening	☐ Transportation
☐ Rental Shops	☐ x-c Skiing	☐ Alpine Skiing
☐ Climbing (Ice/Rock)	☐ Camping	■ Boating (rafting, canoeing etc.)

ADDITIONAL INFORMATION: Automotive mechanic

EMPLOYER PROVIDED LODGING:
☐ Dorms   ☐ Tents   ☐ Cabins
■ Other: Trailers

LODGING RESTRICTIONS:
■ Pets   ☐ Guests
☐ Other:

EMPLOYEE MEAL PROGRAMS:
■ Yes   ☐ No

EMPLOYEE COOKING FACILITIES:
■ Yes   ☐ No

NEARBY RELIGIOUS SERVICES:
■ Yes   ☐ No

NEARBY PRIVATE HOUSING:
■ Yes   ☐ No

GROOMING RESTRICTIONS:
☐ Hair   ☐ Moustache   ☐ Beard
■ Other: Casual but professional

OFF SEASON ADDRESS:

Same as above

CAPITOL REEF
NATIONAL PARK
(Utah)

MAILING ADDRESS:

Rim Rock Motel & Tours
Torrey, UT 84775

SEASONAL EMPLOYMENT

10	10	10	0
SPRING	**SUMMER**	**FALL**	**WINTER**

BEST TIME TO APPLY: March

GENERAL EMPLOYMENT:

■ Indicates services and facilities with employment opportunities.

- ■ Management
- □ Gift Shops
- ■ Stables
- ■ Food Service
- □ Janitorial
- □ Rental Shops
- □ Climbing (Ice/Rock)
- ■ Administration
- ■ Front Desk
- ■ Maintenance
- □ Security
- □ Gardening
- □ x-c Skiing
- □ Camping
- ■ Housekeeping
- ■ Tour Guides
- □ Grocery/Supplies
- □ Garage/Gas Station
- ■ Transportation
- □ Alpine Skiing
- □ Boating (rafting, canoeing etc.)

ADDITIONAL INFORMATION:

EMPLOYER PROVIDED LODGING:

■ Dorms   □ Tents   □ Cabins
■ Other: Very limited

LODGING RESTRICTIONS:

■ Pets   □ Guests
□ Other:

EMPLOYEE MEAL PROGRAMS:

■ Yes   □ No

EMPLOYEE COOKING FACILITIES:

■ Yes   □ No

NEARBY RELIGIOUS SERVICES:

■ Yes   □ No

NEARBY PRIVATE HOUSING:

■ Yes   □ No

GROOMING RESTRICTIONS:

□ Hair   □ Moustache   □ Beard
■ Other: None

OFF SEASON ADDRESS:

Same as above

188

GLEN CANYON
NATIONAL RECREATION AREA
(Utah)

MAILING ADDRESS:

Bullfrog Resort
P.O. Box 4055
Lake Powell, UT 84533

SEASONAL EMPLOYMENT

50	115	50	0
SPRING	**SUMMER**	**FALL**	**WINTER**

BEST TIME TO APPLY: February thru June

GENERAL EMPLOYMENT:

■ Indicates services and facilities with employment opportunities.

- ■ Management
- ■ Gift Shops
- ☐ Stables
- ■ Food Service
- ■ Janitorial
- ■ Rental Shops
- ☐ Climbing (Ice/Rock)

- ■ Administration
- ■ Front Desk
- ■ Maintenance
- ■ Security
- ■ Gardening
- ☐ x-c Skiing
- ☐ Camping

- ■ Housekeeping
- ☐ Tour Guides
- ■ Grocery/Supplies
- ■ Garage/Gas Station
- ☐ Transportation
- ☐ Alpine Skiing
- ■ Boating (rafting, canoeing etc.)

ADDITIONAL INFORMATION:

EMPLOYER PROVIDED LODGING:

■ Dorms ☐ Tents ☐ Cabins

■ Other: Trailers

LODGING RESTRICTIONS:

■ Pets ☐ Guests

☐ Other:

EMPLOYEE MEAL PROGRAMS:

■ Yes ☐ No

EMPLOYEE COOKING FACILITIES:

■ Yes ☐ No

NEARBY RELIGIOUS SERVICES:

■ Yes ☐ No

NEARBY PRIVATE HOUSING:

☐ Yes ■ No

GROOMING RESTRICTIONS:

☐ Hair ☐ Moustache ☐ Beard

■ Other: Neatly groomed

OFF SEASON ADDRESS:

Same as above

189

GLEN CANYON
NATIONAL RECREATION AREA
(Utah)

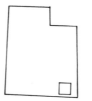

MAILING ADDRESS:

Hall's Crossing
P.O. Box 5101
Lake Powell, UT 84533

SEASONAL EMPLOYMENT

25	65	25	0
SPRING	**SUMMER**	**FALL**	**WINTER**

BEST TIME TO APPLY: February thru June

GENERAL EMPLOYMENT:

■ Indicates services and facilities with employment opportunities.

■ Management	■ Administration	■ Housekeeping
■ Gift Shops	☐ Front Desk	☐ Tour Guides
☐ Stables	■ Maintenance	■ Grocery/Supplies
☐ Food Service	☐ Security	■ Garage/Gas Station
☐ Janitorial	☐ Gardening	☐ Transportation
■ Rental Shops	☐ x-c Skiing	☐ Alpine Skiing
☐ Climbing (Ice/Rock)	☐ Camping	■ Boating (rafting, canoeing etc.)

ADDITIONAL INFORMATION:

EMPLOYER PROVIDED LODGING:

■ Dorms   ☐ Tents   ☐ Cabins
■ Other: Trailers

LODGING RESTRICTIONS:

■ Pets   ☐ Guests
☐ Other:

EMPLOYEE MEAL PROGRAMS:

■ Yes   ☐ No

EMPLOYEE COOKING FACILITIES:

■ Yes   ☐ No

NEARBY RELIGIOUS SERVICES:

■ Yes   ☐ No

NEARBY PRIVATE HOUSING:

☐ Yes   ■ No

GROOMING RESTRICTIONS:

☐ Hair   ☐ Moustache   ☐ Beard
■ Other: Neatly groomed

OFF SEASON ADDRESS:

Same as above

Glen Canyon
National Recreation Area
(Utah)

MAILING ADDRESS:

Hite Marina
P.O. Box 501
Lake Powell, UT 84533

SEASONAL EMPLOYMENT

5	15	5	
SPRING	**SUMMER**	**FALL**	**WINTER**

BEST TIME TO APPLY: February thru June

GENERAL EMPLOYMENT:

■ Indicates services and facilities with employment opportunities.

☐ Management	☐ Administration	■ Housekeeping
☐ Gift Shops	☐ Front Desk	☐ Tour Guides
☐ Stables	■ Maintenance	■ Grocery/Supplies
☐ Food Service	☐ Security	■ Garage/Gas Station
■ Janitorial	☐ Gardening	☐ Transportation
☐ Rental Shops	☐ x-c Skiing	☐ Alpine Skiing
☐ Climbing (Ice/Rock)	☐ Camping	■ Boating (rafting, canoeing etc.)

ADDITIONAL INFORMATION:

EMPLOYER PROVIDED LODGING:

☐ Dorms ☐ Tents ☐ Cabins
■ Other: Trailers

LODGING RESTRICTIONS:

■ Pets ☐ Guests
☐ Other:

EMPLOYEE MEAL PROGRAMS:

☐ Yes ■ No

EMPLOYEE COOKING FACILITIES:

■ Yes ☐ No

NEARBY RELIGIOUS SERVICES:

☐ Yes ■ No

NEARBY PRIVATE HOUSING:

☐ Yes ■ No

GROOMING RESTRICTIONS:

☐ Hair ☐ Moustache ☐ Beard
■ Other: Neatly groomed

OFF SEASON ADDRESS:

Same as above

191

ZION
NATIONAL PARK
(Utah)

MAILING ADDRESS:

TW Services, Inc.
451 N. Main
PO Box 400
Cedar City, UT 84720

SEASONAL EMPLOYMENT

0	200	200	0
SPRING	**SUMMER**	**FALL**	**WINTER**

BEST TIME TO APPLY: January thru April

GENERAL EMPLOYMENT:

■ Indicates services and facilities with employment opportunities.

- ■ Management
- ■ Gift Shops
- ☐ Stables
- ■ Food Service
- ■ Janitorial
- ☐ Rental Shops
- ☐ Climbing (Ice/Rock)

- ■ Administration
- ■ Front Desk
- ■ Maintenance
- ■ Security
- ■ Gardening
- ☐ x-c Skiing
- ☐ Camping

- ■ Housekeeping
- ■ Tour Guides
- ■ Grocery/Supplies
- ■ Garage/Gas Station
- ■ Transportation
- ☐ Alpine Skiing
- ☐ Boating (rafting, canoeing etc.)

ADDITIONAL INFORMATION:

EMPLOYER PROVIDED LODGING:

■ Dorms ☐ Tents ■ Cabins
☐ Other:

LODGING RESTRICTIONS:

■ Pets ☐ Guests
☐ Other:

EMPLOYEE MEAL PROGRAMS:

■ Yes ☐ No

EMPLOYEE COOKING FACILITIES:

☐ Yes ■ No

NEARBY RELIGIOUS SERVICES:

■ Yes ☐ No

NEARBY PRIVATE HOUSING:

☐ Yes ■ No

GROOMING RESTRICTIONS:

☐ Hair ☐ Moustache ■ Beard
■ Other: Neatly groomed

OFF SEASON ADDRESS:

Same as above

192

DEER VALLEY POWDER

THE DEER VALLEY WORK EXPERIENCE WILL WORK FOR YOU!

Deer Valley Ski Resort knows our employees are responsible for our success. And, in return, our employees gain valuable work experience and a notable resume inclusion that will serve them well for a lifetime.

WHAT DOES DEER VALLEY OFFER?
Winter seasonal employment opportunities generally last from mid-November to mid-April, with a competitive wage and benefit package. All employees enjoy free ski privileges, in addition to working in a beautiful mountain environment with magnificent facilities.

WHAT JOBS ARE AVAILABLE?

COOKS	SKI PATROL	CUSTOMER SERVICE ATTENDANTS
STEWARDS	TICKET SALES	RENTAL SHOP TECHNICIANS
WAITPERSON	SKI SCHOOL SALES	RESTAURANT ATTENDANTS
BUSPERSON	LODGE ATTENDANTS	SKI INSTRUCTORS
CASHIERS	RESERVATIONISTS	SNOWCAT OPERATORS
HOST	ACCOUNTING CLERKS	CHILDCARE ATTENDANTS

WHERE DO EMPLOYEES LIVE?
Although we do not offer employee housing, there are rental properties available in Park City (1 mile from our base lodge), as well as Salt Lake City just 35 short interstate minutes away. There is free public transportation in Park City as well.

HOW CAN I FIND OUT MORE?
If you are interested in joining the team that has been internationally acclaimed for its dedication to hospitality and service, please contact us today!

DEER VALLEY SKI RESORT
PERSONNEL DEPARTMENT
P.O.BOX 889
PARK CITY,UT 84060
(801) 649-1000 EXT. 1619

Hot Dog On Your Lunch Break

This winter, work at one of America's greatest ski resorts and ski free while gaining valuable experience in the growing resort industry. We're currently offering exceptional opportunities for people who seek full or part time employment.

Benefits include:

- Family Ski Privileges
- Ski Lessons
- Ski Rentals
- Competitive Wages
- Reduced Day Care Rates
- Retail Discounts
- Food and Beverage Discounts

Please Reply To:
Personnel Manager
Mount Mansfield Resort
RR1, Box 1310
Stowe, VT 05672
(802) 253-7311, ext. 2239

2 WORLD CLASS SKI RESORTS

Killington

&

Mount Snow

SEVERAL HUNDRED JOBS AVAILABLE EACH SKI SEASON !

The best time to apply: September – January

General employment includes some of the following:

CLERICAL * RETAIL * FOOD SERVICE * JANITORIAL
* SKI RENTAL / REPAIR * HOUSEKEEPING *
* LIFT , SNOWMAKING , GROOMING OPERATIONS *
* FRONT DESK * RESERVATIONS *
* CUSTOMER SERVICE * SKI INSTRUCTING *
* CHILDREN'S CENTER AND MUCH MORE !!!

FOR MORE EMPLOYMENT INFORMATION
CALL OR WRITE TO THE FOLLOWING

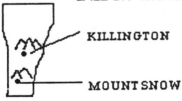

KILLINGTON

MOUNT SNOW

VERMONT

KILLINGTON LTD.
KILLINGTON , VT 05751
ATTN. PERSONNEL
802-422-3333

MOUNT SNOW
MOUNT SNOW, VT 05356
ATTN. PERSONNEL
802-464-3333

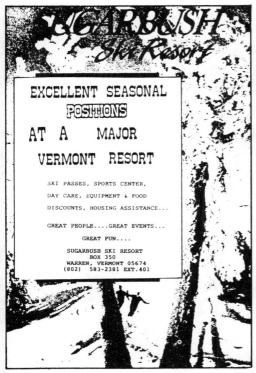

SUGARBUSH
Ski Resort

EXCELLENT SEASONAL
POSITIONS
AT A MAJOR
VERMONT RESORT

SKI PASSES, SPORTS CENTER,
DAY CARE, EQUIPMENT & FOOD
DISCOUNTS, HOUSING ASSISTANCE...

GREAT PEOPLE....GREAT EVENTS...

GREAT FUN....

SUGARBUSH SKI RESORT
BOX 350
WARREN, VERMONT 05674
(802) 583-2381 EXT.401

Photo by Robert Frankel

Photo by Z.J.I.L

SHENANDOAH
NATIONAL PARK
(Virginia)

MAILING ADDRESS:

ARA Virginia Sky-Line Co, Inc.
Box 727
Luray, VA 22835

SEASONAL EMPLOYMENT

150	250	200	0
SPRING	**SUMMER**	**FALL**	**WINTER**

BEST TIME TO APPLY: March thru June

GENERAL EMPLOYMENT:

■ Indicates services and facilities with employment opportunities.

☐ Management
■ Gift Shops
■ Stables
■ Food Service
■ Janitorial
☐ Rental Shops
☐ Climbing (Ice/Rock)

☐ Administration
■ Front Desk
☐ Maintenance
☐ Security
■ Gardening
☐ x-c Skiing
☐ Camping

■ Housekeeping
☐ Tour Guides
■ Grocery/Supplies
☐ Garage/Gas Station
☐ Transportation
☐ Alpine Skiing
☐ Boating (rafting, canoeing etc.)

ADDITIONAL INFORMATION:

EMPLOYER PROVIDED LODGING:

■ Dorms   ☐ Tents   ☐ Cabins
☐ Other:

LODGING RESTRICTIONS:

■ Pets   ■ Guests
☐ Other:

EMPLOYEE MEAL PROGRAMS:

■ Yes   ☐ No

EMPLOYEE COOKING FACILITIES:

☐ Yes   ■ No

NEARBY RELIGIOUS SERVICES:

■ Yes   ☐ No

NEARBY PRIVATE HOUSING:

■ Yes   ☐ No

GROOMING RESTRICTIONS:

■ Hair   ☐ Moustache   ☐ Beard
☐ Other:

OFF SEASON ADDRESS:

Same as above

198

Virgin Islands National Park

MAILING ADDRESS:

Cinnamon Bay Campground
Box 120 Cruz Bay
St. John, U.S.
Virgin Islands 00830

SEASONAL EMPLOYMENT

35	25	25	35
SPRING	**SUMMER**	**FALL**	**WINTER**

BEST TIME TO APPLY: Year-round

GENERAL EMPLOYMENT:

■ Indicates services and facilities with employment opportunities.

☐ Management	☐ Administration	■ Housekeeping
☐ Gift Shops	■ Front Desk	☐ Tour Guides
☐ Stables	■ Maintenance	■ Grocery/Supplies
■ Food Service	☐ Security	☐ Garage/Gas Station
■ Janitorial	■ Gardening	☐ Transportation
☐ Rental Shops	☐ x-c Skiing	☐ Alpine Skiing
☐ Climbing (Ice/Rock)	☐ Camping	☐ Boating (rafting, canoeing etc.)

ADDITIONAL INFORMATION: Summer grounds work; Construction

EMPLOYER PROVIDED LODGING:

☐ Dorms   ☐ Tents   ☐ Cabins
■ Other: None

LODGING RESTRICTIONS:

☐ Pets   ☐ Guests
■ Other: N/A

EMPLOYEE MEAL PROGRAMS:

■ Yes   ☐ No

EMPLOYEE COOKING FACILITIES:

☐ Yes   ■ No

NEARBY RELIGIOUS SERVICES:

■ Yes   ☐ No

NEARBY PRIVATE HOUSING:

■ Yes   ☐ No

GROOMING RESTRICTIONS:

☐ Hair   ☐ Moustache   ☐ Beard
■ Other: Well groomed

OFF SEASON ADDRESS:

Same as above

MOUNT RAINIER NATIONAL PARK
(Washington)

MAILING ADDRESS:

Mt. Rainier Guest Serv.
P.O. Box 108
Ashford, WA 98304

SEASONAL EMPLOYMENT

50	210	175	25
SPRING	**SUMMER**	**FALL**	**WINTER**

BEST TIME TO APPLY: December thru May
or "Drop in"

GENERAL EMPLOYMENT:

■ Indicates services and facilities with employment opportunities.

■ Management	☐ Administration	■ Housekeeping
■ Gift Shops	■ Front Desk	☐ Tour Guides
☐ Stables	■ Maintenance	☐ Grocery/Supplies
■ Food Service	■ Security	■ Garage/Gas Station
■ Janitorial	☐ Gardening	☐ Transportation
■ Rental Shops	■ x-c Skiing	☐ Alpine Skiing
☐ Climbing (Ice/Rock)	☐ Camping	☐ Boating (rafting, canoeing etc.)

ADDITIONAL INFORMATION:

EMPLOYER PROVIDED LODGING:

■ Dorms   ☐ Tents   ☐ Cabins
■ Other: 2 RV spaces
Limited married housing

LODGING RESTRICTIONS:

■ Pets   ■ Guests
☐ Other:

EMPLOYEE MEAL PROGRAMS:

■ Yes   ☐ No

EMPLOYEE COOKING FACILITIES:

☐ Yes   ■ No

NEARBY RELIGIOUS SERVICES:

■ Yes   ☐ No

NEARBY PRIVATE HOUSING:

☐ Yes   ■ No

GROOMING RESTRICTIONS:

☐ Hair   ☐ Moustache   ■ Beard
■ Other: Neat, Clean Appearance
for front-of-house

OFF SEASON ADDRESS:

Same as above

NORTH CASCADES
NATIONAL PARK
(Washington)

MAILING ADDRESS:

Diablo Lake Resort
Rockport, WA 98282

SEASONAL EMPLOYMENT

0	60	60	0
SPRING	**SUMMER**	**FALL**	**WINTER**

BEST TIME TO APPLY: January thru March

GENERAL EMPLOYMENT:
■ Indicates services and facilities with employment opportunities.

■ Management   ■ Administration   ■ Housekeeping
□ Gift Shops   ■ Front Desk   □ Tour Guides
□ Stables   ■ Maintenance   ■ Grocery/Supplies
■ Food Service   □ Security   ■ Garage/Gas Station
■ Janitorial   ■ Gardening   □ Transportation
■ Rental Shops   □ x-c Skiing   □ Alpine Skiing
□ Climbing (Ice/Rock)   □ Camping   □ Boating (rafting, canoeing etc.)

ADDITIONAL INFORMATION:

EMPLOYER PROVIDED LODGING:
□ Dorms   □ Tents   ■ Cabins
□ Other:

LODGING RESTRICTIONS:
■ Pets   □ Guests
□ Other:

EMPLOYEE MEAL PROGRAMS:
■ Yes   □ No

EMPLOYEE COOKING FACILITIES:
□ Yes   ■ No

NEARBY RELIGIOUS SERVICES:
■ Yes   □ No

NEARBY PRIVATE HOUSING:
■ Yes   □ No

GROOMING RESTRICTIONS:
□ Hair   □ Moustache   ■ Beard
■ Other: Neatly groomed

OFF SEASON ADDRESS:

Same as above

NORTH CASCADES
NATIONAL PARK
(Washington)

MAILING ADDRESS:

Ranier Mountaineering, Inc.
201 St. Helens
Tacoma, WA 98402

SEASONAL EMPLOYMENT

0	45	0	0
SPRING	**SUMMER**	**FALL**	**WINTER**

BEST TIME TO APPLY: April

GENERAL EMPLOYMENT:

■ Indicates services and facilities with employment opportunities.

☐ Management   ■ Administration   ☐ Housekeeping
☐ Gift Shops   ☐ Front Desk   ■ Tour Guides
☐ Stables   ☐ Maintenance   ☐ Grocery/Supplies
☐ Food Service   ☐ Security   ☐ Garage/Gas Station
☐ Janitorial   ☐ Gardening   ☐ Transportation
☐ Rental Shops   ☐ x-c Skiing   ☐ Alpine Skiing
■ Climbing (Ice/Rock) ☐ Camping   ☐ Boating (rafting, canoeing etc.)

ADDITIONAL INFORMATION: Mountain guides

EMPLOYER PROVIDED LODGING:

☐ Dorms   ☐ Tents   ■ Cabins
☐ Other:

LODGING RESTRICTIONS:

■ Pets   ■ Guests
☐ Other:

EMPLOYEE MEAL PROGRAMS:

■ Yes   ☐ No

EMPLOYEE COOKING FACILITIES:

■ Yes   ☐ No

NEARBY RELIGIOUS SERVICES:

■ Yes   ☐ No

NEARBY PRIVATE HOUSING:

■ Yes   ☐ No

GROOMING RESTRICTIONS:

■ Hair   ☐ Moustache   ☐ Beard
☐ Other:

OFF SEASON ADDRESS:

Same as above

OLYMPIC
NATIONAL PARK
(Washington)

MAILING ADDRESS:

Kalaloch Lodge
HC 80 Box 1100
Forks, WA 98331

SEASONAL EMPLOYMENT

60	80	50	40
SPRING	**SUMMER**	**FALL**	**WINTER**

BEST TIME TO APPLY: Fall or Spring

GENERAL EMPLOYMENT:

■ Indicates services and facilities with employment opportunities.

☐ Management ☐ Administration ■ Housekeeping
■ Gift Shops ■ Front Desk ☐ Tour Guides
☐ Stables ■ Maintenance ■ Grocery/Supplies
■ Food Service ■ Security ☐ Garage/Gas Station
■ Janitorial ■ Gardening ☐ Transportation
☐ Rental Shops ☐ x-c Skiing ☐ Alpine Skiing
☐ Climbing (Ice/Rock) ☐ Camping ☐ Boating (rafting, canoeing etc.)

ADDITIONAL INFORMATION:

EMPLOYER PROVIDED LODGING:

■ Dorms ☐ Tents ☐ Cabins
■ Other: Bunkhouse style

LODGING RESTRICTIONS:

■ Pets ☐ Guests
☐ Other:

EMPLOYEE MEAL PROGRAMS:

■ Yes ☐ No

EMPLOYEE COOKING FACILITIES:

■ Yes ☐ No

NEARBY RELIGIOUS SERVICES:

■ Yes ☐ No

NEARBY PRIVATE HOUSING:

☐ Yes ■ No
Restricted

GROOMING RESTRICTIONS:

OFF SEASON ADDRESS:

Same as above

☐ Hair ☐ Moustache ☐ Beard
■ Other: Well groomed, clean

OLYMPIC
NATIONAL PARK
(Washington)

MAILING ADDRESS:

Log Cabin Resort
6540 E. Beach Rd.
Port Angeles, WA 98362

SEASONAL EMPLOYMENT

0	45	0	0
SPRING	**SUMMER**	**FALL**	**WINTER**

BEST TIME TO APPLY: January thru April

GENERAL EMPLOYMENT:

■ Indicates services and facilities with employment opportunities.

- ■ Management
- ■ Gift Shops
- ☐ Stables
- ■ Food Service
- ■ Janitorial
- ■ Rental Shops
- ☐ Climbing (Ice/Rock)

- ☐ Administration
- ■ Front Desk
- ■ Maintenance
- ☐ Security
- ■ Gardening
- ☐ x-c Skiing
- ☐ Camping

- ■ Housekeeping
- ☐ Tour Guides
- ■ Grocery/Supplies
- ■ Garage/Gas Station
- ☐ Transportation
- ☐ Alpine Skiing
- ■ Boating (rafting, canoeing etc.)

ADDITIONAL INFORMATION:

EMPLOYER PROVIDED LODGING:

☐ Dorms ☐ Tents ☐ Cabins
■ Other: None

LODGING RESTRICTIONS:

☐ Pets ☐ Guests
■ Other: N/A

EMPLOYEE MEAL PROGRAMS:

☐ Yes ■ No

EMPLOYEE COOKING FACILITIES:

☐ Yes ■ No

NEARBY RELIGIOUS SERVICES:

■ Yes ☐ No

NEARBY PRIVATE HOUSING:

■ Yes ☐ No

GROOMING RESTRICTIONS:

☐ Hair ☐ Moustache ☐ Beard
■ Other: Dress code

OFF SEASON ADDRESS:

Same as above

OLYMPIC
NATIONAL PARK
(Washington)

MAILING ADDRESS:

National Parks Concessions, Inc.
Mammoth Cave, KY 42259

SEASONAL EMPLOYMENT

0	45	30	0
SPRING	**SUMMER**	**FALL**	**WINTER**

BEST TIME TO APPLY: Before March

GENERAL EMPLOYMENT:

■ Indicates services and facilities with employment opportunities.

■ Management	■ Administration	■ Housekeeping
■ Gift Shops	■ Front Desk	☐ Tour Guides
☐ Stables	■ Maintenance	■ Grocery/Supplies
■ Food Service	☐ Security	☐ Garage/Gas Station
■ Janitorial	■ Gardening	☐ Transportation
■ Rental Shops	☐ x-c Skiing	☐ Alpine Skiing
☐ Climbing (Ice/Rock)	☐ Camping	☐ Boating (rafting, canoeing etc.)

ADDITIONAL INFORMATION:

EMPLOYER PROVIDED LODGING:
☐ Dorms ☐ Tents ■ Cabins
☐ Other:

LODGING RESTRICTIONS:
■ Pets ■ Guests
☐ Other:

EMPLOYEE MEAL PROGRAMS:
■ Yes ☐ No

EMPLOYEE COOKING FACILITIES:
☐ Yes ■ No

NEARBY RELIGIOUS SERVICES:
■ Yes ☐ No

NEARBY PRIVATE HOUSING:
■ Yes ☐ No

GROOMING RESTRICTIONS:
☐ Hair ■ Moustache ■ Beard
■ Other: Well groomed

OFF SEASON ADDRESS:

Same as above

OLYMPIC
NATIONAL PARK
(Washington)

MAILING ADDRESS:

Sol Duc Hot Springs Resort
P.O. Box 2169
Port Angeles, WA 98362

SEASONAL EMPLOYMENT

35	45	35	0
SPRING	**SUMMER**	**FALL**	**WINTER**

BEST TIME TO APPLY: March thru July

GENERAL EMPLOYMENT:

■ Indicates services and facilities with employment opportunities.

☐ Management	☐ Administration	■ Housekeeping
■ Gift Shops	■ Front Desk	☐ Tour Guides
☐ Stables	■ Maintenance	■ Grocery/Supplies
■ Food Service	☐ Security	☐ Garage/Gas Station
■ Janitorial	■ Gardening	☐ Transportation
☐ Rental Shops	☐ x-c Skiing	☐ Alpine Skiing
☐ Climbing (Ice/Rock)	■ Camping	☐ Boating (rafting, canoeing etc.)

ADDITIONAL INFORMATION: Bartender and life guards

EMPLOYER PROVIDED LODGING:

■ Dorms   ☐ Tents   ☐ Cabins
■ Other: Bunkhouse style

LODGING RESTRICTIONS:

■ Pets   ■ Guests
☐ Other:

EMPLOYEE MEAL PROGRAMS:

■ Yes   ☐ No

EMPLOYEE COOKING FACILITIES:

☐ Yes   ■ No

NEARBY RELIGIOUS SERVICES:

■ Yes   ☐ No

NEARBY PRIVATE HOUSING:

☐ Yes   ■ No

GROOMING RESTRICTIONS:

☐ Hair   ☐ Moustache   ☐ Beard
■ Other: Neat and well trimmed

OFF SEASON ADDRESS:

Same as above

GRAND TETON
NATIONAL PARK
(Wyoming)

MAILING ADDRESS:

Grand Teton Lodge Co.
Moran, WY 83013

SEASONAL EMPLOYMENT

0	850	850	0
SPRING	**SUMMER**	**FALL**	**WINTER**

BEST TIME TO APPLY:

GENERAL EMPLOYMENT:

■ Indicates services and facilities with employment opportunities.

■ Management	□ Administration	■ Housekeeping
■ Gift Shops	■ Front Desk	□ Tour Guides
■ Stables	■ Maintenance	■ Grocery/Supplies
■ Food Service	■ Security	■ Garage/Gas Station
■ Janitorial	■ Gardening	■ Transportation
□ Rental Shops	□ x-c Skiing	□ Alpine Skiing
□ Climbing (Ice/Rock)	□ Camping	□ Boating (rafting, canoeing etc.)

ADDITIONAL INFORMATION: Employees should be available
through mid-Sept. Housing is provided free of charge,
with mandatory meal deduction.

EMPLOYER PROVIDED LODGING:

■ Dorms □ Tents □ Cabins
■ Other: RV Park available

LODGING RESTRICTIONS:

■ Pets ■ Guests
■ Other: No overnight guests

EMPLOYEE MEAL PROGRAMS:

■ Yes □ No

EMPLOYEE COOKING FACILITIES:

□ Yes ■ No

NEARBY RELIGIOUS SERVICES:

■ Yes □ No

NEARBY PRIVATE HOUSING:

□ Yes ■ No

GROOMING RESTRICTIONS:

■ Hair □ Moustache ■ Beard
■ Other: Trim moustaches, no beards

OFF SEASON ADDRESS:

Same as above

Cathedral Group Grand Teton National Park, Wyoming.

Photo by Jim Burnside

208

GRAND TETON NATIONAL PARK
(Wyoming)

MAILING ADDRESS:

Signal Mountain Lodge
P.O. Box 50
Dept: NPTJ
Moran, WY 83013

SEASONAL EMPLOYMENT

75	115	115	0
SPRING	**SUMMER**	**FALL**	**WINTER**

BEST TIME TO APPLY: January and February
(We accept applications through April).

GENERAL EMPLOYMENT:

■ Indicates services and facilities with employment opportunities.

■ Management	□ Administration	■ Housekeeping
■ Gift Shops	■ Front Desk	□ Tour Guides
□ Stables	■ Maintenance	■ Grocery/Supplies
■ Food Service	□ Security	■ Garage/Gas Station
□ Janitorial	□ Gardening	□ Transportation
□ Rental Shops	□ x-c Skiing	□ Alpine Skiing
□ Climbing (Ice/Rock)	□ Camping	■ Boating (rafting, canoeing etc.)

ADDITIONAL INFORMATION: Marina and Accounting positions also available. All employees must be able to stay at least through Labor Day. Lengthening your availability is a plus.

EMPLOYER PROVIDED LODGING:

■ Dorms ☐ Tents ☐ Cabins
☐ Other:

LODGING RESTRICTIONS:

■ Pets ☐ Guests
☐ Other:

EMPLOYEE MEAL PROGRAMS:

■ Yes ☐ No

EMPLOYEE COOKING FACILITIES:

☐ Yes ■ No

NEARBY RELIGIOUS SERVICES:

■ Yes ☐ No

NEARBY PRIVATE HOUSING:

☐ Yes ■ No

GROOMING RESTRICTIONS:

■ Hair ☐ Moustache ■ Beard
■ Other: Neat appearance

OFF SEASON ADDRESS:

Same as above

209

GRAND TETON
NATIONAL PARK
(Wyoming)

MAILING ADDRESS:

☐

Flagg Ranch
P.O. Box 187
Moran, WY 83013

SEASONAL EMPLOYMENT

10	90	50	20
SPRING	**SUMMER**	**FALL**	**WINTER**

BEST TIME TO APPLY: Year-round

GENERAL EMPLOYMENT:

■ Indicates services and facilities with employment opportunities.

■ Management	☐ Administration	■ Housekeeping
■ Gift Shops	■ Front Desk	☐ Tour Guides
☐ Stables	■ Maintenance	■ Grocery/Supplies
■ Food Service	☐ Security	■ Garage/Gas Station
■ Janitorial	☐ Gardening	☐ Transportation
☐ Rental Shops	☐ x-c Skiing	☐ Alpine Skiing
☐ Climbing (Ice/Rock)	☐ Camping	☐ Boating (rafting, canoeing etc.)

ADDITIONAL INFORMATION:

EMPLOYER PROVIDED LODGING:

■ Dorms   ☐ Tents   ■ Cabins
☐ Other:

LODGING RESTRICTIONS:

■ Pets   ■ Guests
☐ Other:

EMPLOYEE MEAL PROGRAMS:

■ Yes   ☐ No

EMPLOYEE COOKING FACILITIES:

☐ Yes   ■ No

NEARBY RELIGIOUS SERVICES:

■ Yes   ☐ No

NEARBY PRIVATE HOUSING:

☐ Yes   ■ No

GROOMING RESTRICTIONS:

■ Hair   ☐ Moustache   ■ Beard
■ Other: Neat general appearance

OFF SEASON ADDRESS:

Same as above

210

GRAND TETON
NATIONAL PARK
(Wyoming)

MAILING ADDRESS:

☐

Parklands Expeditions, Inc.
Box 371
Jackson, WY 83001

SEASONAL EMPLOYMENT

0	30	30	0
SPRING	**SUMMER**	**FALL**	**WINTER**

BEST TIME TO APPLY: January

GENERAL EMPLOYMENT:

■ Indicates services and facilities with employment opportunities.

☐ Management   ☐ Administration   ☐ Housekeeping
☐ Gift Shops   ☐ Front Desk   ☐ Tour Guides
☐ Stables   ☐ Maintenance   ☐ Grocery/Supplies
■ Food Service   ☐ Security   ☐ Garage/Gas Station
☐ Janitorial   ☐ Gardening   ☐ Transportation
☐ Rental Shops   ☐ x-c Skiing   ☐ Alpine Skiing
☐ Climbing (Ice/Rock) ■ Camping   ■ Boating (rafting, canoeing etc.)

ADDITIONAL INFORMATION: River rafting, backpacking
and horseback guides

EMPLOYER PROVIDED LODGING:

☐ Dorms   ☐ Tents   ☐ Cabins
■ Other: None

LODGING RESTRICTIONS:

☐ Pets   ☐ Guests
■ Other: N/A

EMPLOYEE MEAL PROGRAMS:

■ Yes   ☐ No

EMPLOYEE COOKING FACILITIES:

☐ Yes   ■ No

NEARBY RELIGIOUS SERVICES:

■ Yes   ☐ No

NEARBY PRIVATE HOUSING:

■ Yes   ☐ No

GROOMING RESTRICTIONS:

☐ Hair   ☐ Moustache   ☐ Beard
■ Other: Must be neat

OFF SEASON ADDRESS:

Parklands Expeditions, Inc.
930 Nob Hill Rd.
Redwood City, CA 94061

211

YELLOWSTONE
NATIONAL PARK
(Wyoming)

MAILING ADDRESS:

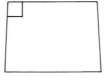

Hamilton Stores, Inc.
PO Box 250
West Yellowstone, MT 59758

SEASONAL EMPLOYMENT

191	700	150	0
SPRING	**SUMMER**	**FALL**	**WINTER**

BEST TIME TO APPLY: January thru August 1

GENERAL EMPLOYMENT:

■ Indicates services and facilities with employment opportunities.

☐ Management	☐ Administration	■ Housekeeping
■ Gift Shops	☐ Front Desk	☐ Tour Guides
☐ Stables	■ Maintenance	■ Grocery/Supplies
■ Food Service	■ Security	☐ Garage/Gas Station
■ Janitorial	☐ Gardening	☐ Transportation
☐ Rental Shops	☐ x-c Skiing	☐ Alpine Skiing
☐ Climbing (Ice/Rock)	☐ Camping	☐ Boating (rafting, canoeing etc.)

ADDITIONAL INFORMATION: Warehouse, auditors and computer operators

EMPLOYER PROVIDED LODGING:

■ Dorms   ☐ Tents   ☐ Cabins
■ Other: Trailer sites

LODGING RESTRICTIONS:

■ Pets   ■ Guests
☐ Other:

EMPLOYEE MEAL PROGRAMS:

■ Yes   ☐ No

EMPLOYEE COOKING FACILITIES:

☐ Yes   ■ No

NEARBY RELIGIOUS SERVICES:

■ Yes   ☐ No

NEARBY PRIVATE HOUSING:

☐ Yes   ■ No

GROOMING RESTRICTIONS:

■ Hair   ■ Moustache   ■ Beard
■ Other: Well groomed

OFF SEASON ADDRESS:

Hamilton Stores, Inc.
PO Box 2700
Santa Barbara, CA 93120

212

YELLOWSTONE NATIONAL PARK

(Wyoming)

MAILING ADDRESS:

T.W. Recreational Services, Inc.
Human Resources Department
Yellowstone Nat'l Park, WY 82190

SEASONAL EMPLOYMENT

0	2300	300	300
SPRING	**SUMMER**	**FALL**	**WINTER**

BEST TIME TO APPLY: November thru March

GENERAL EMPLOYMENT:

■ Indicates services and facilities with employment opportunities.

■ Management	■ Administration	■ Housekeeping
■ Gift Shops	■ Front Desk	■ Tour Guides
■ Stables	■ Maintenance	☐ Grocery/Supplies
■ Food Service	■ Security	☐ Garage/Gas Station
■ Janitorial	■ Gardening	■ Transportation
■ Rental Shops	☐ x-c Skiing	☐ Alpine Skiing
☐ Climbing (Ice/Rock)	☐ Camping	☐ Boating (rafting, canoeing etc.)

ADDITIONAL INFORMATION: Bartender, Laundry Help, & Personnel Position - Letters of reference reccommended - Internships available.

EMPLOYER PROVIDED LODGING:

■ Dorms   ☐ Tents   ■ Cabins
■ Other: Limited trailer sites

LODGING RESTRICTIONS:

■ Pets   ■ Guests
■ Other: Quiet/courtesy Hours

EMPLOYEE MEAL PROGRAMS:

■ Yes   ☐ No

EMPLOYEE COOKING FACILITIES:

☐ Yes   ■ No

NEARBY RELIGIOUS SERVICES:

■ Yes   ☐ No

NEARBY PRIVATE HOUSING:

☐ Yes   ■ No

GROOMING RESTRICTIONS:

■ Hair   ☐ Moustache   ■ Beard
■ Other: Application has more information

OFF SEASON ADDRESS:

Same as above

213

Yellowstone
National Park

MAILING ADDRESS:

Yellowstone Park
Medical Services
707 Sheridan Ave.
Cody, WY 82414

SEASONAL EMPLOYMENT

0	35	0	0
SPRING	SUMMER	FALL	WINTER

BEST TIME TO APPLY: December thru April

GENERAL EMPLOYMENT:

■ Indicates services and facilities with employment opportunities.

☐ Management	☐ Administration	■ Housekeeping
☐ Gift Shops	■ Front Desk	☐ Tour Guides
☐ Stables	■ Maintenance	☐ Grocery/Supplies
■ Food Service	☐ Security	☐ Garage/Gas Station
■ Janitorial	☐ Gardening	☐ Transportation
☐ Rental Shops	☐ x-c Skiing	☐ Alpine Skiing
☐ Climbing (Ice/Rock)	☐ Camping	☐ Boating (rafting, canoeing etc.)

ADDITIONAL INFORMATION: R.N 's, pharmacists, x-ray, and lab positions available

EMPLOYER PROVIDED LODGING:

■ Dorms   ☐ Tents   ☐ Cabins
■ Other: One trailer site

LODGING RESTRICTIONS:

■ Pets   ☐ Guests
☐ Other:

EMPLOYEE MEAL PROGRAMS:

■ Yes   ☐ No

EMPLOYEE COOKING FACILITIES:

■ Yes   ☐ No

NEARBY RELIGIOUS SERVICES:

■ Yes   ☐ No

NEARBY PRIVATE HOUSING:

☐ Yes   ■ No

GROOMING RESTRICTIONS:

☐ Hair   ☐ Moustache   ☐ Beard
■ Other: Well groomed, clean

OFF SEASON ADDRESS:

Same as above

214

YELLOWSTONE
NATIONAL PARK
(Wyoming)

MAILING ADDRESS:

Yellowstone Park Service Stations
Section NPTJ
P.O. Box 11
Gardiner, MT 59030-0011

SEASONAL EMPLOYMENT

25	100	25	0
SPRING	**SUMMER**	**FALL**	**WINTER**

BEST TIME TO APPLY: December thru April

GENERAL EMPLOYMENT:

■ Indicates services and facilities with employment opportunities.

■ Management
□ Gift Shops
□ Stables
□ Food Service
□ Janitorial
□ Rental Shops
□ Climbing (Ice/Rock)

■ Administration
□ Front Desk
■ Maintenance
□ Security
□ Gardening
□ x-c Skiing
□ Camping

□ Housekeeping
□ Tour Guides
□ Grocery/Supplies
■ Garage/Gas Station
□ Transportation
□ Alpine Skiing
□ Boating (rafting, canoeing etc.)

ADDITIONAL INFORMATION: Automobile mechanics, Tow Truck operators, accounting/office staff

EMPLOYER PROVIDED LODGING:

■ Dorms □ Tents ■ Cabins
□ Other:

LODGING RESTRICTIONS:

■ Pets □ Guests
□ Other:

EMPLOYEE MEAL PROGRAMS:

■ Yes □ No

EMPLOYEE COOKING FACILITIES:

□ Yes ■ No

NEARBY RELIGIOUS SERVICES:

■ Yes □ No

NEARBY PRIVATE HOUSING:

□ Yes ■ No

GROOMING RESTRICTIONS:

■ Hair □ Moustache ■ Beard
■ Other: Well groomed

OFF SEASON ADDRESS:

Same as above

215

WINTER PATROL ON JACKSON LAKE
By Doyle Nelson

When the temperatures drop well below zero, and the snow begins to pile deep in the high mountains, the summer crowds have all disappeared. Now the winter quiet is broken only by the sounds of the ice fishermen's snowplanes and snowmobiles. The lure of catching a mess of lake trout, and maybe even getting a "big one" of twenty-five or thirty pounds brings a score or more fisherman to the lake on most winter days.

Jackson Lake doesn't always freeze solid. Warm springs on the lake bottom create areas of open water. Heavy snows on top of shallow ice layers, coupled with fluctuating water levels, push the ice down, causing flooding across the surface that results in frozen slush. So, the net result is layers of ice, snow, or slush in various combinations, usually about six feet deep. Part of the ranger's job is to patrol the lake with an ice auger, take regular measurements of the ice/snow/slush layers, and post a bulletin to warn the visiting public of potential hazards. The safest way to get around the uncertain lake surface is to use a snowplane.

The snowplane was developed in the 1930's. It was the only reliable over-snow vehicle in this area before the development of the snowmobile. In fact, a special version of the snowplane was used to deliver the mail in the days before the roads were plowed. Basically, the snowplane is an aircraft engine, mounted behind a tiny closed cockpit, that sits on three big skis. The propeller pushes the plane over the snow and ice, and when conditions are right, it can attain speeds up to fifty mph. Unfortunately, when conditions are bad, the planes can bog down easily, so it takes an experienced driver with lots of lake sense to manuever them. The hazards aren't always easily seen. The snowplane can keep going over the slush where a snowmobile would bog down and sink. And, the "old hands" tell of incidents where showplanes have been driven over stretches of open water up to thirty feet across. So, even though their design is archaic, and they can be obstinate to get started and to manuever, the ranger's choice of oversnow vehicle for Jackson Lake is the reliable old snowplane.

Sometimes winter patrol of the lake requires that the rangers go into the water. To assist the Wyoming Game and Fish Department in a study they were conducting on trout reproduction, it was recently necessary to recover some of their equipment from the lake bottom during the middle of February. Winter diving when the air temperatures are below zero requires some careful

preparation. First, a four by four hole was cut through the ice, then a tent was erected nearby with a propane heater inside. This gave the divers an almost warm place to change into their dry suits. Once the regulators got wet, they would immediately freeze when exposed to the air, making them inoperable. So, a five-gallon insulated container with hot water was kept nearby. The regulators were kept in the hot water until the diver was in the lake, then quickly attached before they could freeze up. Once in the lake, the diver had to keep the regulator under the water surface to keep it working properly. Two divers worked together in the search for the equipment, while a third diver stayed poised at the hole to provide a safety back-up. The searching pair was always connected with a fourth person at the hole with a rope. In the event of an emergency the divers could be pulled back to their only access to the surface.

Due to the extreme cold of the water, the divers could only stay in for about thirty minutes at a time, then they would have to come out and get re-warmed. Fortunately, the biologists had fairly closely pinpointed their equipment's location, so only two full dives were required to locate and recover it. In addition to providing assistance to the Game and Fish Department, these dives provide good winter search and rescue training for the Park Service.

It's always cold, and sometimes a little scary, but when duty calls, you'll find the rangers on winter patrol of Jackson Lake.

"Love your life, poor as it is. You may perhaps have some pleasant, thrilling, glorious hours, even in a poorhouse. The setting sun is reflected from the windows of the almshouse as brightly as from the rich man's abode."
Henry David Thoreau

"I went to the woods because I wished to live deliberately, to front only the essential facts of life, and see if I could not learn what it had to teach, and not, when I came to die, discover that I had not lived."
Henry David Thoreau

A MISSION IN GOD'S COUNTRY

Reverend from Moose, WY has a ministry in National Parks

By Todd Wilkinson

The Reverend Warren W. Ost of Moose enjoys telling a story of how the real harmonic convergence took place.

Thirteen centuries ago, the bones of St. James purportedly washed ashore near Santiago, Spain. Thounsands of Christians, upon hearing of the miraculous discovery, made a pilgrimage to the coastal city to view the artifact. At that monent, a trend was born linking tourism and organized religion.

A clergyman made for the 1980's, Ost is himself on a mission to places where even heathens stand in awe. Call them what you will...vast tracts of wilderness or urban neighborhoods...his sanctuaries are the National Park System of the United States.

His grassroots organization, "A Christian Ministry In The National Parks," has undergone a slow metamorphisis in the four decades since its birth. Ost says, "This is a structure built from the bottom up, rather than from the top down." He adds, "Our services are inter-denominational, not non-denominational. We believe everyone must be able to do their own thing."

Each summer, 300 seminary students representing some 34 different denominations from across the globe are enlisted to lead worship in 65 national parks. The three-month tour of duty is officially sanctioned by the National Park Service.

As a consultant to the Vatican, Ost, a Presbyterian minister, says Americans today continue to make religious journeys, inspired by the divine creation of nature.

For that reason, the Rome-based Pontifical Commission on Migration and Tourism recognizes the relationship between pleasure travel and a need for spirituality.

Although the Teton mountains or the Yellowstone geysers do not promise religious artifacts, they do hold spiritual power, Ost says, an ethereal presence that often stirs ineffable responses in tourists.

"Here God's hand is so creatively manifest it plays a tremendous role for me," Ost says from his home on Antelope Flats. "Here, in this part of the world, if you're not aware of something much greater than you are, you're not alive."

Two hundred million people travel annually to 354 American national parks and monuments. For those who need to mix wonder with reverence, Ost's mobile ministry provides an outlet. To meet those demands, Ost's life is one of constant travel. Sixty percent of his time is spent away from Jackson Hole as he annually logs between 75,000-100,000 air miles promoting the ministry.

"We're not putting on religious talent shows for tourists but trying to stimulate religion into which the Christian community is invited to share," Ost says. "It's not a canned Protestant program but Catholic in it's best sense. We've fought against turning our services in the national parks into some sort of cult."

In the beginning, it was his pocketbook not the ministry that called Ost to Yellowstone, which he considers his home park. Like hundreds of other college students at this time, "The best way for me to earn my way through college was to work as a bellhop," he said. "I started at the Old Faithful Inn in 1946."

Perhaps a bit precocious in his early years, Ost noticed that no formal religious guidance was offered to park employees or seasonal workers. He remembered his childhood when a Sunday School teacher in New York Mills, Minn., told the preacher, "We send them to Sunday School all during the winter and then in the summer, we let them go to hell."

Ost took his concern to the Yellowstone superintendent, who turned him loose on an ecumenical odyssey.

Ost's dream began to take shape in 1951 when a survey of all the parks in the U.S. revealed that religious services already existed in Yosemite, Sequoia and Grand Canyon national parks. By 1953, the Reverend had pushed to establish regular worship in more than a dozen federal areas.

Although for 34 years Ost and His wife Nancy have remained dedicated to extending their spiritual outreach in the nations premiere wildlife and historical sanctuaries, they are reluctant to take credit for the rapid growth of worship programs.

"When we began, they said it would never work. But it's been something that has developed very easily and very naturally," Ost says. "There were groups of religious people in the early days who practiced on their own in the parks. All we did was find them."

"The real heroes of our ministry are the hundreds of people who did this before us, who did it for their families and sometimes for the public," he added.

Because all of the youth volunteers also work full-time jobs with park service or local concessionaires, Ost says the ministry is threatened by modern economics. "I think kids today are as capable and dedicated as they've ever been," he said. "But the costs of education are greater than ever. Our experience lately in the national parks is there's not as many people available. I'm optimistic. We'll just have to make better use of the student resources we have.''

From the crags of Mt. Rainier in Wahsington State to the shadows of the Statue of Liberty in New York City, Ost has preached a brand of religion that is not designed to be overbearing. His message, he says, is meant to help visitors reflect upon their encounters with the great natural and man-made monuments of the world.

Wyoming Travel Commission Photograph

Lower Falls - Yellowstone Distance

The thundering wonder of the Lower Falls of the Yellowstone River is the major scenic attraction of the world's first and largest national park - Wyoming's Yellowstone. The Falls measure an abrupt 308 feet and are still growing as the big river continues to erode the soft rhyolite material of an old seyser basin - material containing the distinct yellow-red color that inspired the name Yellowstone.

FIRES ADD MORE SPICE TO YELLOWSTONE

The release of nutrients back into the greater Yellowstone ecosystem along with increased light penetration will benefit many plants, large and small animals, and fishes. Overall diversity--the spice of life--is expected to dramatically increase in burned areas of Yellowstone National Park.

Scientifically, a high diversity of plants and animals living in a particular area is thought to indicate a more stable, healthier ecosystem. Generally, fire tends to produce a mosaic of ground cover and tree patterns which benefit a tremendous variety of inter-related wildlife species.

While many travelers this summer will stand back and marvel at the incredible forces of nature which affected nearly half the Park, others will be on their hands and knees photographing the profusion of wildflowers in a carpet of green grass expected this spring and summer. This past winter's snowfall will provide plenty of water to insure a burst of color this spring.

Big game such as deer, elk, bear, moose, beaver, cougar, and buffalo historically increase in numbers after fires--a result of an abundance of lush, nutritive forage. Some species, such as pine marten and wolverine, which are dependent on late stages of plant community development--thick forests--may be displaced.

Increased sunlight to the forest floor and vast diverse plant growth should attract and increase the number and variety of birds. Large birds of prey will find easier hunting and more rodents available. Birds which nest in tree cavities such as mountain bluebirds and the endagnered three-toed woodpecker will find life easier after the fires.

Yellowston's blue-ribbon trophy trout fisheries will also benefit from the wild fires. While siltation may be a short-term problem this spring, the positive effects of these nutirents in the soil and water will directly lead to more, bigger and healthier fish--and more success for fishermen!

Yellowstone this spring and summer will be alive with colorful wildflowers, soaring eagles, grazing elk and buffalo, and hard fighting native cutthroat trout. The fires of 1988 released huge amounts of nutrients--before bound up in inedible trees--which will find their way to more plants and animals than ever before.

The fires of 1988 will result in a more diverse, healthier ecosystem.

224

ULTIMATE TE®

DIRECTION

HIGH PERFORMANCE EQUIPMENT FOR ENDURANCE SPORTS

RESURGENT PEACE CORPS
CHALLENGES A NEW GENERATION

Three loud cracks of the ruler on the desk finally bring the classroom to order. Seventy students rise in unison. "Good morning teacher", they echo. Twenty-five mathematics books are distributed around the class. Despite the lack of materials it is clear what must be done. The lesson begins.

It is the start of a new day for the students of a remote village, and one American who has just begun Peace Corps volunteer service. Approximately ten weeks of training has ended and the long anticipated journey to the new place that is now home, no longer a dream.

Starting a new job has never been more challenging. There is much to adjust to. The climate, food, dress codes, culture and language are all different and exhilarating to the point of exhaustion. In the beginning there is little privacy as the community muses over the new guest that has arrived.

For the 5,500 Americans currently living and working in 65 countries around the world in Africa, Asia, the Caribbean, Latin America and the Pacific, the challenge of Peace Corps service is similar. And like the 130,000 volunteers who have served before them, today's volunteers live at a level equivalent to professionals with comparable skills in their country of service. Their housing conditions vary from an adobe dwelling with no running water or electricity in a rural village, to a modern apartment located in a bustling capital city. They speak languages as familiar as English and as foreign as Swahili. Every day comes alive with new discoveries and newly made friendships. Despite the adventure and excitement of living in another culture there also exists occasional longings for familiar settings. Once in country, the popular Peace Corps slogan "The toughest job you'll ever love," takes on a new and more personal meaning.

Born out of the idealism of the 60's and the vision of a young and vibrant president, John F. Kennedy - the Peace Corps maintains its mission-to achieve a peaceful world free of poverty. And while the original goals remain the same--to help the people of interested countries meet their needs for trained men and women; to help promote a better understanding of the American people on the part of the people served; and to promote a better understanding of other people on the part of the American people--organizationally the Peace Corps has experienced some changes.

In it's twenty-eighth year of existence, the Peace Corps has matured. This is not only appart in the quality of programs, but also in the average age and experience of the volunteers now serving. Today's volunteer is about 30 years old in comparison to 23 during the Kennedy era. Now, 10 percent

Peace Corps/Honduras/Bartlett/May 1984

Peace Corps Volunteer, Jeanette Lorene Dickson ("Dixie") here works with school children at the John F. Kennedy School in the village of Las Quebradas, teaching students how to prepare the soil for planting. She also teaches classes in sanitation, health, and nutrition, works with the women of the village and gives classes in English and cooking. The volunteer from Baton Rouge, Louisiana, has a BA degree in education from Central State and attended graduate school at Louisiana State University. She previously taught for 10 years in Anuco, Venezuela.

Peace Corps/Ecuador/Freeman Nov., 1980

PCV Clay G. Young, of Los Angeles, California, is assigned to Guayaguil as a graphic artist, teaching design for graphic arts and photo mechanics. Here, he works with a group of children at a vocational school. Young is a 1973 graduate of Antioch West in California and holds a bachelor's degree in art.

of all volunteers who serve, are age 50 years or older which is especially attractive to host countries where age is respected and the experience of older volunteers considered an asset. Peace Corps director Loret Miller Ruppe sees the increase in the average age of volunteers as advantageous for the both, the organization and the overseas communities volunteers serve. ''Today we are seeing more and more people who have three to five years of work experience, joining the Peace Corps. Our senior volunteers are valued by the host countries. They have a lot to offer in terms of life experience.'' she said.

Since its inception volunteers have normally worked two years in their country of service. Today the Peace Corps has instituted a one year program called the Associate Volunteer Program (AVP). This alternative form of volunteer service allows professionals to volunteer for tours of 3 to 15 months. Individuals with five or more years of experience in teacher training, veterinary science, financial management and farming skills are being recruited under this program. School systems and various companies around the country have joined in their support of individuals who are seeking to share their expertise in a developing nation by extending leaves-of-absences in lieu of **Peace Corps** service.

Nepal/Bartlett/1983

PCV Jeff McCaskey teaches his TEFL students of Class 7, a group of students aged 12-18, in the Sri Chulachuli Secondary School. He has a number of agriculture-related projects as secondary projects. McCaskey, from Shaker Heights, Ohio, received his BA in history and political science from Hampshire College.

While the Peace Corps continues to recruit people with backgrounds in education, agriculture, health, business, community development and the skilled trades, there is a growing need for highly skilled individuals in these areas. One way the organization is trying to meet this demand is by re-establishing ties with American universities and colleges. In the past year, joint Peace Corps/university programs have been announced with Boston University, The University of Alabama at Birmingham, Colorado State University at Fort Collins, Yale, Rutgers, Harvard and the University of South Carolina at Columbia. These programs will allow individuals to pursue a master's degree in public health, forestry, special education and public policy while at the same time gaining international work experience in those areas through Peace Corps volunteer service. There is still, however, a need for individuals with liberal arts backgrounds. Nearly 40 percent of the volunteer work force is made up of people with liberal arts degrees.

In a growing mode for the first time in several years, the Peace Corps hopes to have 10,000 volunteers working overseas by 1992. As a result of this growth the Peace Corps has been able to begin work in four new countries in need of development assistance. The first volunteers ever to work in Cape Verde, Equatorial Guinea, Guinea and the Comoros are contributing to these nations' development in the areas of education, and cooperative and community development projects.

Peace Corps/Belize/Graves July 1974

PCV John A. Frederick, 29, of Sylmar, California is assigned to Belize as a marine biologist studing the sexual maturity and reproductive habits of the queen conch shellfish in Belize, Central America. The conch, a member of the mollusk family, is a valuable export item for Belize. Its yellowish spiraling shell is used in manufacturing cameos and the meat inside is a popular dish fried or stewed. Here he is shown going out on a fishing boat to examine the methods the fishermen use to catch conchs. Frederick is a 1972 graduate of the California State University with a bachelor's degree in biology. He is the son of Mary K. Frederick of 15445 Colbalt, Sylmar, and Alfred A. Frederick of 933 W. Olive, Burbank, California.

Peace Corps/Honduras/Bartlett/May 1984

Peace Corps Volunteer Kevin Mapp, who works in community services and youth development in Tegucigalpa, works at a school for older orphaned boys where they learn trades. he has many roles at the school but is mainly someone who listens. Here he talks with one of the students who is training to be a mechanic. The volunteer from Branford, Ct., has a degree in social work form Adelphi University with a minor in Spanish, and was an Intern with a Hispanic Counseling Center.

Photo by Pickerell

Left to right - Peace Corps Volunteers Ralph Lowen, John Uminski, Richard Lockett, and Neil Brown, work on surveying and laying the reinforceing rods for the foundation of a new school in Lyndiane, Senegal.

229

Photo by Hammond

PCV Jeff J. Kanne, 23, of Carroll, Iowa is assigned to a rural development project located in Khudia, a poor village in the southeastern part of Senegal. Jeff's primary responsibility is to mobilize village energy in developing garden plots and building latrines. Jeff is a 1976 graduate of the University of Iowa with a B.A. degree in History. Here Jeff is shown with Senegalese women who are retrieving water from the well.

John Kennedy's dream that returned Peace Corps volunteers would choose careers in foreign affairs has become reality. Returned volunteers make up 10 percent of each foreign service class and over 1,000 are now working for the State Department and the United States Agency for International Development. They are leaders in government, business, the arts, and education. 130,000 strong they become an important link in internationalizing the way Americans think.

Through a unique program called the Peace Corps Partnership Program, volunteers overseas are establishing cross-cultural relationships between the communities they serve and communities in the United States that have sponsored their project. "The Peace Corps Partnership Program is a fantastic example of how a group in the United States can provide direct assistance to those in need in a developing country while at the same time helping to create an appreciation of other cultures around the worls," said Martha Saldinger, manager of the Peace Corps Partnership Program.

Peace Corps volunteers come from small towns, large cities and rural areas all across America and represent a variety of ethnic backgrounds. In order to make Peace Corps service a viable option for all, the organization has instituted new policies that provide partial forgiveness and deferments for certain student loans in lieu of Peace Corps service. Volunteers also receive a monthly stipend plus a $4,800 readjustment allowance upon completion of their two-year assignment. All medical and dental expenses are also covered while volunteers are in service.

If you would like more information about how you can become a Peace Corps volunteer call toll-free (800) 424-8580.

We need someone with the confidence of a surgeon, the dedication of a marathoner and the courage of an explorer.

We have a unique opportunity for someone very special.

A chance to spend two years in another country. To live and work in another culture. To learn a new language and acquire new skills.

The person we're looking for might be a farmer, a forester, or a retired nurse. Or maybe a teacher, a mechanic, or a recent college graduate.

We need someone to join over 5,000 people already working in 60 developing countries around the world. To help people live better lives.

We need someone special. And we ask a lot. But only because so much is needed. If this sounds interesting to you, maybe you're the person we're looking for. A Peace Corps volunteer. Find out. Call us at **1-800-424-8580, Ext. 93.**

Peace Corps.
The toughest job you'll ever love.

When famine ravaged Ethiopia in 1984, the American people responded with an over-whelming generosity. This American Red Cross delegate is accounting for American grain destined for a food center.

THE ABCs OF RED CROSS VOLUNTEERISM
By James Cassell

The American Red Cross is the largest volunteer organization in the country. To provide its services it relies on an ethnically diverse volunteer force of about 1.2 million people.

When a flood strikes a community, Red Cross volunteers take time off from the office to work as caseworkers in a shelter. Red cross volunteers are nurses who travel on bloodmobiles collecting blood for hospitals; they are managers in companies who give up an evening or two a week to teach Red Cross first aid and CPR so that others may save lives; they are teens who spend their summers teaching safety in aquatics; they are retirees who transport the homebound to doctors' appointments, bring meals to the homeless, and care for those suffering from AIDS; and they are the disabled who manage emergency communications from their homes. In short, the volunteer is the heart and soul of the American Red Cross.

These are among the more visible services performed by Red Cross volunteers. As a highly decentralized organization, our 2,800 chapters, 56 regional blood centers and 300 SAF&V (Service to Members of the Armed **Forces, Veterans, and Their Families) stations use volunteers in hundreds**

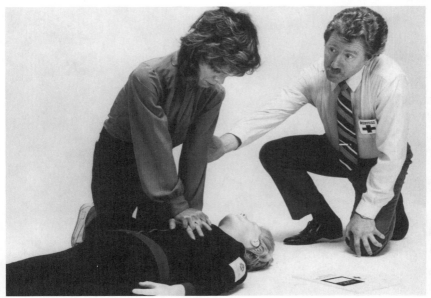

Many people owe their lives to friends or total strangers who have taken Red Cross CPR. The Red Cross issued 2,460,928 certificates in 1987 to people trained in the most effective CPR methods.

Although nothing can take away the pain of losing one's home and possessions to fire, Red Cross disaster volunteers arrive on the scene and provide food, shelter and financial assistance and facilitate the transition away from despair to regaining control of one's life.

When floods devestate homes along rivers, volunteers in Red Cross Disaster Services move in to provide food, shelter and financial assistance. They often remain long afterwards helping people get back on their feet and into permanent housing.

of different programs and roles in their communities. Most of these activities involve health and safety, blood services, disaster services and services to military families. But others are unique, conceived and developed by volunteers who saw a particular unmet need in their community and thought of the Red Cross as the agency that could respond to that need. For example, some of these services may include "latchkey" programs for children whose parents work, or "safe ride" programs that provide a safe ride home to teens at parties who have had too much to drink.

It would be misleading to imply that volunteers only carry out the work that paid staff direct. Volunteers also make the decisions that guide the organization and change it when changes are required. The position of Chairman of the American Red Cross is voluntary as is the position of National Chairman of Volunteers. The 50-member Board of Governors, the organization's supreme policy-making body, is made up exclusively of volunteers, often people who have previous experience as chapter chairmen or chapter managers or who have a high profile as volunteer leaders in their communities. And the boards of the local chapters are all-volunteer.

In an increasingly complex and competitive environment for non-profit organizations (In 1989, United Way will fund 37,000 health and human agencies in the United States, including 4,695 new agencies funded since 1983), many Red Cross chapters have seen fit to seek the volunteer assistance of corporate executives, financial developers and fund raisers to enhance or expand their financial underpinnings.

> *"Great are they who see that spiritual is stronger than any material force; that thoughts rule the world."*
> *Ralph Waldo Emerson*

> *"A friend is a person with whom I may be sincere. Before him, I may think aloud."*
> *Ralph Waldo Emerson*

In communities around the country with large populations of the needy, the Red Cross works to find the homeless housing and to feed the hungry.

Like the other 146 Red Cross and Red Crescent societies around the world, the American Red Cross is part of the international Red Cross movement that was founded a century and a quarter ago; it is committed to the same international principles and to the Geneva Conventions. When war flares up, when an earthquake strikes Armenia, when famine spreads its grip throughout Africa, when floods destroy villages in Bangladesh, the Red Cross movement, consisting of all the Red Cross societies, the Geneva-based League of Red Cross and Red Crescent Societies and the International Committee of the Red Cross, responds by sending doctors, nurses, nutritionists and logistical experts as well as food, medicine and other needed supplies to the stricken areas. All of this is made possible through public contributions.

An effective worldwide Red Cross response to disaster depends on volunteers willing to give of their time to neighbors on the next block or in another part of the world. In recent years, American Red Cross delegates have assisted victims of the Armenian earthquake, the Mexican earthquake, the Salvadoran earthquake, African famine and other global disasters. They are present in many Third World countries helping to set up health programs and assisting in the construction of housing.

People interested in volunteering for the Red Cross in their community should contact their nearest chapter. For those who wish to be considered for possible duty as Red Cross delegates in other parts of the world, solid chapter volunteer service is normally the main prerequisite.

Few organizations provide the number and kinds of volunteer opportunities offered by the American Red Cross. Those who volunteer for the Red Cross enrich not only others less fortunate but, by reaching out, they also enrich themselves.

236

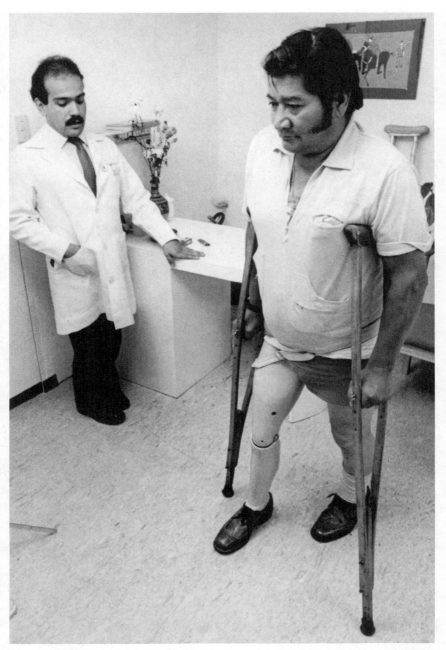

Many who were lucky to survive the Mexican earthquake lost arms or legs. Because of Red Cross prosthesis programs, they are able to walk again and live normal lives.

Somewhere
a child lies crying

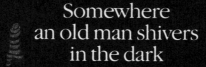

Somewhere
an old man shivers
in the dark

Somewhere
a family's dreams
burn to the ground

Somewhere
somebody needs help.

Please support your
local chapter.

**American
Red Cross**

Because somewhere
is closer than you think.

238

TREKKING IN NEW ZEALAND

By Jeff Grandy

I've worked in Yosemite National Park for most of the last ten years. I didn't believe when someone first told me that living and working here was possible, for to me Yosemite was an Eden, a majestic dream garden seen only on vacations too short and remembered in pictures too small for the vastness of the experience. I'm glad I was wrong, and that ten years later the wonder of this valley has never worn off.

One unique aspect of life in a national park is the constant opportunity to speak with people from other countries. Also the employees themselves tend to be a well-traveled bunch, and the two elements combined creates strong curiosity and an urge to see other places.

I'm a photographer, and although other cultures interest me, it was stories of the ever varied and beautiful landscapes that really grabbed me. Eventually I was on my first overseas trip to New Zealand, and it was superb!

New Zealand represented an easy and painless entry into the overseas travel scene. English is the main language and the people are friendly and helpful. The country is small but so packed with beauty that I never spent much time getting from place to palce. The two main islands of New Zealand comprise an area roughly two-thirds the size of California, with only roughly three million inhabitants. Crowds were never a problem.

Photo by Jeff Grandy

239

New Zealand has eleven national parks, and it always seemed that one was just up the road. Along with Sarah and Jeff, my two friends from Yosemite, I decided to head straight for the closest one.

Mt. Egmont, Mt. Tongariro, and Urewera are the three parks located on the North Island. The south Island includes Abel Tasman, Arthur's Pass, Nelson Lakes, Pancake Rocks, Mt. Cook, Westland, Fiordland, and Mt. Aspiring. We first visited Mt. Egmont, originally named Mt. Taranaki by the native Maoris. This stately cone-shaped old volcano on the west coast of the North Island commands the view and the weather for miles around. Nearby are numerous black sand beaches that contrast wonderfully with the snowy peak. A foggy shroud often forms around the base of the mountain, adding to the spectacle. On this first stop I was already wondering if forty rolls of film were enough for the trip!

Mt. Tongariro, inland and east of Mt. Egmont, is a more recently active volcanic area, and looks it. Always steaming, the large main cone called Mt. Ngauruhoe last erupted in 1975. On a wild day of 25 degree (F.) temperatures with winds of forty-five miles per hour I stood, watching the grey-black cone, while snow fell as steam rose from the ground all around me.

Walking farther, I crested a ridge and saw Emerald Lakes, which are named appropriately. Nearby volcanic activity gives these small lakes unusual chemical contents, creating their very intense green color. Altogether, this is an area of raw beauty, tense with power just under the surface and the certain knowledge that another eruption of natural enthusiasm could occur again at any time. I highly recommend this park.

On the Northwest corner of the South Island is Abel Tasman National Park. The coastal track, best known and well travelled in this area, was an easy hike with enough pristine beaches to please any beach bum. Here the swimming areas were great, while many such areas further south along the coast weren't swimmable due to severe undercurrents. Although we saw many a prize strip of coast, we could only sit and watch the surf.

I should mention that, in most of the parks, we stayed in huts maintained by the National Park Service. These hostels on the trail range from old stone cabins sleeping four people to newly-built, modern huts sleeping forty. A reasonable fee is charged to stay the night. Some huts have radios for safety, and at a certain time each night a head count is taken from hut to hut to ensure everyone's safe arrival. The hut system for the most part was begun in the 1930's to house hunters which the government hired to hunt deer. The deer, an introduced species, has no natural predator in New Zealand. The resulting severe overpopulation damaged the environment. Attempted eradication by the bullet method didn't work out very well, and

the huts were later pressed into service by today's hikers. Many huts are maintained by private hiking clubs, while deer raising for meat and hides is a growing business!

Heading south we stopped at Westland National Park. The Franz Josef and Fox glaciers are two of the main attractions here. Each is about eight miles long and in a period of recession. They are the only glaciers in the world to descend to the rain forest. We hiked the Copeland track along the beautiful glacial-blue Copeland River. Near the Welcome Flat hut we soaked in some fine hot springs, truly a rare delight at the end of a long walk.

The next day we walked from the lush forest to the subalpine border of Mt. Cook National Park. Fully one-third of this park is permanently covered with snow and/or glacier ice. We had lunch next to a blue lake while watching the hanging Copeland Glacier break off in huge chunks, noisily cascading down the mountain like a snowy waterfall. It was one of the great lunch breaks!

I could go on for many more pages about the beauty of New Zealand's national parks. The endless swinging suspension bridges we found spanning many of the creeks, rivers and streams fascinated me. The Ke, a large, loud, curious parrot gave me a few laughs, except when he poked holes in my tent. I'm sure it was an act of revenge for teasing him with food I never gave him. I reminisce of the many glow-worm grottos, where curious tiny creatures light up the dark with pinpoints of fluorescent glow; the snorting wild pigs in the bush at night; and the lush, mossy forests with huge silver ferns and vines like an African jungle.

The parks we visited in New Zealand were as fine as any we had ever seen. The scenes were as diverse and striking as I could have hoped for, and the people we met who worked in and around the national parks were friendly, helpful and ultimately very proud of their park system. They should be. I'll remember them and their parks strongly for a long time.

NATIONAL PARKS AND THE SIERRA CLUB

By Edgar Wayburn, M.D.

The early years of the Sierra Club, John Muir, and the founding of the National Park Service are inextricably tied together. In 1889, Muir and Robert Underwood Johnson, an editor for Century Magazine, planned a campaign for a large Yosemite National Park surrounding the small state park which had been set aside by President Lincoln in 1864. Muir's idea of a single national park was essentially ecological, since it began with the preservation of the complete watersheds of the Merced and Tuolumne Rivers. In 1890, Yosemite National Park was establbished by Congress. In 1892, the Sierra Club was founded, with Muir as its first president.

Although the Sierra Club occasionally ventured outside of California during its first half century, it remained essentially a California organization. All this changed after World War II, in the late 1940's and early 1950's, when the Club entered the campaign for the upper Colorado River project. The Bureau of Reclamation had proposed two dams in Dinosaur National Monument--Echo Park and Split Mountain. The Club rose to protect the integrity of the National Park System. The Club's leaders realized that in order to be able to protect the national parks, the Club would have to go national and to grow in size. Between 1952 and 1989 the membership has risen from 7,000 to over 500,000, now divided into 57 Chapters and served by a staff of more than 200.

Sierra Club activists often have the dream for lands to be protected as parks. We rally grassroots support for these ideas by getting other community leaders involved, working with the local media for press coverage, and being persuasive with our elected officials to support and pass legislation to protect these important lands. Thus, the Sierra Club plays a prominent role in the establishment of national parks, and we continue to monitor the existing parks through the efforts of our grassroots membership.

Among the parks which the Club has worked hard to establish are Yosemite, 1890; Sequoia, 1890; Glacier, 1910; Rocky Mountain, 1915; Olympic, 1938; Kings Canyon, 1940; Point Reyes National Seashore, 1962; Redwoods, 1968; North Cascades, 1968; Voyageurs, 1971; Golden Gate National Recreation Area, 1972; Gateway National Recreation Area, 1972; Santa Monica National Recreation Area, 1978; Channel Islands, 1980; and, of course, our newest national park--Great Basin, 1987.

The Sierra Club was also instrumental in achieving the 1980 passage of the Alaska National Interest Lands Conservation Act, which added a record amount of lands in Alaska to our National Park System--Denali--the former

Mt. McKinley Park enlarged and renamed; Kenai Fjords, Lake Clark, Kobuk Valley; and the world's two largest national parks, Wrangell-St. Elias and Gates of the Arctic. Glacier Bay and Katmai were reclassified as national parks from national monuments; and national preserves were added--Bering Land Bridge, Noatak, Yukon-Charley, as well as Aniakchak and Cape Krusentern National Monuments.

EARTHWATCH:
THE VOLUNTEER RESEARCH CORPS

Watertown, MA...Why are black bear populations decling in a North Carolina sanctuary? How do butterflies in Papua New Guinea rain forests protect themselves from predators? Why are so many shark fossils found in Montana? Can a volcano create its own weather pattern? Were mammoths driven to extinction by humans 11,500 years ago, or were these ancient elephants the victims of a changing climate? These and many others are questions Earthwatch volunteers are helping university scholars to answer.

Dubbed a 'short-term scientific Peace Corps', Earthwatch has been matching natural resource professionals with citizens willing to pitch in and help since the nonprofit organization's founding in 1971.

Today Earthwatch sponsors expeditions in every field of scientific study-- from anthropology to zoology--by recruiting volunteers who provide both labor and funding to researchers around the world. There are archaeological excavations, surveys of plants, birds and animals, underwater and environ- mental impact studies, as well as research in public health, architecture, and folklore.

Among the projects Earthwatch is sponsoring in 1989 are a number of studies taking place in our National Parks. Dr. Rolf Peterson of Michigan Technological Institute uses volunteers in his long-term study of moose- wolf ecology in Isle Royale National Park, Michigan. Dr. Roy Horst of SUNY, Potsdam, has Earthwatch volunteers helping in his work on mongoose populations in Hawaii Volcanoes National Park. Dr. James Schmitt of Montana State is seeking geology buffs to determine dendro-geomorphology of debris flows on alluvial fans in Yellowstone National Park. Dr. George Engelmann of the University of Nebraska continues his excavations of small mammals from the Jurassic Morrison Formation of Dinosaur National Monument in Utah.

In recent years Earthwatch has been involved in studies as varied as the mapping of barrier beaches of the Cape Cod and Gulf Islands National Seashores, to studying the effects of fire on Tundra ecology in Alaska's Noatak River Biosphere Reserve, to mud sampling in the Florida Bay region of Everglades National Park--where volunteers collected 560 samples contain- ing 70,440 fish and crustaceans and 52,298 blades of grass! Little wonder that Dr. George Powell of the National Audubon Society applied for Earthwatch volunteers to help him on that project!

This year Earthwatch reports that it will mobilize some 450 teams, with over 3,000 volunteers, to staff projects in 46 countries and 20 states. The volunteers, ranging in age from 16 to 84, hail from all 50 states and about 20 countries. They are students and retirees, doctors and business people, artists and computer scientists--almost every imaginable occupation. Scholarship support for participation on expeditions is available for both teachers and students.

Geologist Dr. William Melson of the Smithsonian Institution has directed Earthwatch volunteers in his studies of volcanos in Costa Rica since 1971. He says, "What Earthwatchers lack in training and formal background, they make up in enthusiasm and willingness to learn. The variety of personalities, interests and backgrounds provides a rich experience."

Volunteers make a tax-deductible contribution to help fund the expedition they join. This share of the expedition costs, which range from $650 to over $2,000, covers all food, accommodations, field equipment and ground transportation for the expedition duration, but not the volunteer's airfare to the expedition's staging area. Volunteers generally join a project for a two-to three week stint. Researchers would generally have several successive teams of volunteers. Lodgings can range from tent camping, to the rustic comforts of old castles or village farmhouses, to the conveniences of major universities or research stations.

Clearly for many Parks Service Employees, Earthwatch would be a 'busman's holiday' letting them contribute their skills to fascinating projects in remote locations. Often volunteers use Earthwatch projects as a chance to learn new skills. Earthwatch materials emphasize that "No special skills are necessary, but all are welcome." Although some of the projects can use the help of professionals with laboratory or technological experience, and talents in surveying, photography, carpentry, cooking or diving are often needed, most expeditions welcome anyone with a curiosity, a willingness to work, flexibility and a sense of humor.

Earthwatch publishes a magazine six times a year which describes upcoming research projects, and is filled with articles and photos about findings and research in progress. Membership in the organization is $25 per year.

Researchers who want information on how to apply for volunteers to help in their work of inventorying or monitoring of natural resources, or in the preservation and protection of cultural resources, in National Parks should write for proposal forms to Earthwatch's academic affiliate, The Center for Field Research. Those interested in information on the over 100 projects which need volunteer participants should write to: Earthwatch Research Corps. The address for both Earthwatch and the Center is 680 Mount Auburn Street, Box 403 NP, Watertown, MA 02272, or call 617-926-8200.

IF YOU'VE EVER WISHED YOU COULD BE LIKE CHRISTOPHER COLUMBUS, JANE GOODALL, OR JOHN MUIR, HERE'S YOUR CHANCE.

Join an Earthwatch environmental research expedition. The days are long. The work is hard. But if you'd like to walk a mile in some pretty big shoes, write or call us: 680 Mt. Auburn St., Box 403Q, Watertown, MA 02272, (617) 926-8200.

EARTHWATCH
Helping You to Make a Difference

Boston   Los Angeles   London   Sydney

The next discovery could be yours...
on an EARTHWATCH expedition

Working with volunteers of all ages, help monitor huge leatherback turtles laying their eggs... Help African historians discover the village origins of their music... Help an archaeologist survey a newly discovered Maya ceremonial center.

Dozens of expeditions on six continents

Right now, over 100 Earthwatch expeditions are being mounted in every scientific discipline, bound for points throughout the world. As a team member, you'll be helping to fund the expedition you accompany.

A background in science isn't necessary. You'll learn as you go.

Join Earthwatch as a member

As an Earthwatch member, you'll receive a subscription to Earthwatch Magazine, the colorful chronicle of Earthwatch activities throughout the world. It contains descriptions and photos of all the expeditions.

Don't delay. Whatever your interest, it all begins with membership. Your tax-deductible contribution of $25 will make you a member.

EARTHWATCH
(617) 926-8200
Dept. 900 • Box 403 • Watertown, MA 02272

IF YOU KNEW HOW MANY DOLPHINS DIED TO MAKE THIS TUNA SANDWICH, YOU'D LOSE YOUR LUNCH.

Over 6 million dolphins were killed by tuna fleets in the eastern tropical Pacific over the last 30 years.

These dolphins weren't killed for food or for use in any product. They were killed purely to increase net profits.

It was just these dolphins' bad luck that schools of large, profitable yellowfin tuna often swim below dolphin herds. And in the late '50s, fishermen realized that if they could snare the dolphins, they could net tons and tons of the tuna below.

First, the dolphins are chased and herded with speedboats, helicopters, and underwater explosives. Then, an enormous net is set around the herd and drawn closed at the bottom.

Exhausted and entangled in the nets, many dolphins suffocate. Some are literally crushed to death.

The Marine Mammal Protection Act of 1972 has helped. But it hasn't

helped enough. Over 100,000 dolphins continue to die each year at the hands of the tuna industry.

Please donate your time or money to Greenpeace so we can continue our efforts to save the dolphins. If you must eat canned tuna, buy only Albacore or chunk white tuna which isn't caught "on dolphins."

Better yet, don't buy any tuna at all. It will only leave a bad taste in your mouth.

GREENPEACE
1436 U Street, Washington, DC 20009

EDITOR'S PREFACE TO THE GREENPEACE SECTION
By Robert Frankel

Resource management problems occur throughout most of the events in the course of human influence of our environment. These events can be classified under the following headings:

> exploration/discovery
> recovery/exploitation
> production/treatment
> transportation
> use
> waste disposal

Every man and woman on our planet with a rational mind must concede that the problems generated so far are most severe where they are the result of:

(1) man's manipulations of the earth's nonrenewable mineral resources

(2) pollution

(3) unrestricted hunting and fishing

Certainly these aren't all of the world's problems, only a few important ones. Our population is geometrically expanding, so naturally the demand for products and food grows.

Sloppily, inefficiently, and oftentimes greedily some of the world's commercial hunters, fisherman, miners and engineers have endeavored not only to supply the demands of society but also to create more demand for their products. The rush goes on to supply these ever-increasing demands of our planet's resources while ecological systems are upset and more and more animal and plant species dwindle.

The health of our natural world is faced with an epidemic not unlike the growing drug situation in our own culture. Obviously, acknowledging that these problems exist is our first step towards a solution. Research and action must follow.

Over the last hundred years or so the United States has taken positive steps in these directions by establishing national forests, wilderness areas, and national parks so that some of our world can be protected from the escalating exploitation of its resources. These areas have also provided areas for ecological research in a world where such non-protected areas are rapidly dwindling.

Unfortunately, that's not enough. Who will watch the watchers? **Who** has the financial resources and the facilities to observe and document man's abuses of our enfironment? Who can generate public awareness and outcry against those who are despoiling our planet? Who promotes techniques of recycling and the research and development of alternative energy sources? Who can promote these ideas and practices to international dimensions? Who is lobbying for the creation of not a national park, but an international world park in Antarctica?

The answer is Greenpeace, an organization which the volunteer staffers here at the National Parks Trade Journal wholeheartedly support and defend. We'd like to take this opportunity to tell you more about this important organization; and on the following pages you will find stories and pictures showing Greenpeace's involvement as well as interview with Twilly Cannon, captain of the Greenpeace vessel Vega.

The Greenpeace laboratory vessel, *Beluga*. This converted fireboat is touring the Great Lakes, and the St. Lawrence and Mississippi Rivers protesting the toxic poisoning of these unique ecosystems.

WHAT IS GREENPEACE

"Greenpeace is an international organization dedicated to preserving the earth and all the life it supports. With our unique brand of direct, nonviolent action, we fight to stop the threat of nuclear war, to protect the environment from nuclear and toxic pollution, and to halt the needless slaughter of whales, dolphins, seals and other endangered animals.

The Greenpeace philosophy of putting ourselves on the line to save animals from destruction and to bear witness to the pollution of our land, water and air has led to many significant achievements around the world, and to the renewed hope for the survival of all of the earth's creatures."

Excerpt from the Greenpeace Action Agenda

Starting in 1971 as a small group of people who sucessfully opposed nuclear testing on Amchitka Island in Alaska, Greenpeace has grown into a worldwide political movement with offices in the United States, Canada, Australia, New Zealand, the United Kingdom, Austria, Belgium, Denmark, France, Italy, Luxembourg, the Netherlands, Spain, Sweden, Switzerland, and West Germany. Recently Greenpeace expanded further, adding offices in Argentina, Costa Rica, and Ireland.

Here in the United States an elected board of directors sets the agenda for Greenpeace's work. Greenpeace directors carry out implementation of the agenda, coordinating staff members in regional offices. Greenpeace

In Antarctica, penguins and humans compete for the same small hospitable areas in this extremely fragile ecosystem now threatened with exploitation.

Gleizes/Greenpeace

The 190-foot M/V Greenpeace stands offshore the Greenpeace World Park Base at Cape Evans, Antarctica. The facility, housing the base crew, workshops, laboratory and communications equipment, is only a telephone call away from Greenpeace offices worldwide.

activists contribute a wide variety of skills and experience. The organization has enlisted help from hot-air balloonists, rock-climbers, scuba divers, navigators, engineers, scientists and legislative experts. Doctors, scientists, lawyers, and legislators have given their time and energy to the efforts of Greenpeace. Carpenters, mechanics, plumbers and electricians -- even employees of national parks have contributed their skills, time and money to the cause.

All members of Greenpeace are determined to continue their efforts until the world is a save and healthy place for all its inhabitants. In many cases Greenpeace has succesfully lobbied, demonstrated and petitioned against those who are harming our environment.

In other cases Greenpeace has met with frustration. Greenpeace-supported legislation and regulation has been invoked but largely unenforced. Target companies along with their governments have discovered loopholes or simply ignored governmental and international agreements.

For example, in the United States, toxic polluter Waste Management, Inc. has been caught violating local, state, and federal regulations while harming our environment. Sadly, their income from these wasteful and dangerous activities exceeded the fines imposed by our regulatory agencies. Our weak government has, in effect, sanctioned poor management and illegal dumping for a piece of the action.

Activities such as these must stop, and Greenpeace needs your help and support in this serious issue.

A STATEMENT FROM GREENPEACE

Greenpeace is an international organization dedicated to the protection of our natural environment through nonviolent direct action, education and legislative lobbying. Greenpeace has offices in twenty countries and more than 2.5 million supporters worldwide.

Through direct action, Greenpeace activists seek to stop violence against the earth without committing violence themselves. They fight to protect the environment from nuclear and toxic pollution, to halt the commercial slaughter of whales and seals and to stop the testing of nuclear weapons as a first step to ending the threat of nuclear war. Greenpeace also campaigns against the mining and reprocessing of nuclear fuel, the exploitation of the Antarctic continent and the destruction of marine resources through indiscriminate fishing methods.

Greenpeace exerts pressure upon national and international governing bodies and conventions through traditional lobbying and legislative techniques. Greenpeace commissions and conducts scientific research projects as part of its work worldwide, and submits evidence to various international fora.

Among the international conventions in which Greenpeace is active are the United Nations, London Dumping Convention, International Whaling Commission, Non-Proliferation Treaty Review Conference, International Union for the Conservation of Nature and Natural Resources, Convention on International Trade in Endangered Species, European Economic Commission, Antarctic Treaty Consulative Parties, and the Oslo and Paris Conventions on Dumping and Discharge of Toxic Materials.

Greenpeace receives its funding from relatively small but continuous individual donations from a very broad base of grass-roots supporters. Greenpeace supporters are kept informed about developments in environmental issues upon which they can have an impact. They are a primary source of the group's strength. Large corporate or government donations are not sought, however, as these are seen as potentially compromising to the organization's independence. Similarly, Greenpeace does not endorse individual politicians nor involve itself in the electoral or party politics of any of the nations in which it operates.

Since 1971, when Greenpeace first set sail to protest US nuclear weapons testing at Amchitka, Alaska, the organization has actively worked to show government and industry officials that the natural world is not theirs to destroy.

The MV Greenpeace on "Antarctica Day," February 1, the day of its arrival at the Bay of Whales, Antarctica. The journey of the MV Greenpeace was made to promote Greenpeace's campaign for the designation of Antarctica as a "world park." February 1986.

GREENPEACE and ANTARCTICA

In 1959, twelve nations signed the Antarctic Treaty, dedicated to the peaceful pursuit of scientific exploration and research of the last unspoiled wilderness continent on earth. Now, secret negotiations among twenty nations who have signed the treaty near completion. The object of these negotiations is apparently to quietly and efficiently divide among themselves the continent's potential mineral resources. Such a plan would destroy the ecological integrity of Antarctica.

Antarctica is arguably the rarest example of nature in a pure form. With some exceptions it remains largely unspoiled.

This vast expanse of ice and rock, together with the surrounding waters of the Southern Ocean, supports rare animal and plant species. The continent holds within its boundaries seventy percent of the earth's fresh water. Antarctica's terrestrial ecosystem has relatively few species forming a short food chain, thereby making it highly susceptible to human impacts.

The marine ecosystem is more complex, supporting populations of marine mammals and other aquatic life. Within the coastal waters and the Southern Ocean are only a few basic food sources for these creatures. If these simple food sources disappear from the effects of pollution or overzealous consumption by man, the entire ecosystem could collapse.

While the Antarctic Treaty has generally proved to be a model of scientific cooperation, there have been serious infractions. A French airstrip develop-

Greenpeace crews unload the re-supply helicopter from M/V Greenpeace in preparation for 1986-87 overwintering by four Greenpeace volunteers at World Park Base, Antarctica.

Courtesy 1986 Greenpeace/Loor

ment, begun in 1983, brazenly destroyed parts of penguin habitats and rookeries while leveling islands to fill the passages in between. Earlier an American-installed nuclear facility was removed, along with tons of contaminated soil, from the base at McMurdo.

Overfishing has contributed to the decline and near extinction of several fish species in Antarctic waters. According to government surveys, some species might not recover. While Finfish stocks decline, fishermen have focused on Krill, an important link in the Ocean's food chain. Already some surveys have noted the absence of previously observed "super swarms" of Krill.

Only two percent of Antarctica's shoreline becomes ice free during the summer. Wildlife colonies concentrate in this region, and humans are having a threateningly dangerous impact. Unique habitats could be obliterated as basis and their support facilities continue to expand in the "ice-free zone."

Tourism and colonization have led to human generated waste disposal problems. Biodegradable wastes are preserved by the subfreezing Antarctic climate. As for the Antarctic Treaty Consultative Parties' Code of Conduct for Waste Disposal, Greenpeace has documented violations by various research stations of different countries.

On the other hand, I was glad to take note that the personnel of the Greenpeace World Park Base packed out their wastes -- just as a responsible visitor to any wilderness area should.

Colonization and tourism problems are important issues concerning the Antarctic environment. Drilling, mining and production of Antarctica's mineral resources, if permitted, could devastate any or all nearby wildlife should an accident happen. We all know such accidents have occurred in the past. There are no minerals beneath Antarctica that cannot be more easily exploited outside of the continent. Seeking some few years' supply of oil in Antarctica is a misguided attempt to forestall the inevitable search for alternatives to fossil fuels.

A WORLD PARK

Greenpeace has a superior vision for Antarctica's future. The continent should be preserved as a World Park, a zone of peace, and an international research laboratory for future generations. The concept of an Antarctic World Park is embodied in Greenpeace's "Antarctic Declaration," a document establishing principles for managing Antarctica and ensuring its protection. Many organizations and hundreds of thousands of people, among them scientists and politicians, have already signed the Declaration.

GREENPEACE IN ANTARCTICA

Since 1986 Greenpeace has undertaken one of its most difficult challenges in its 17 year history, establishing and maintaining the first international, non-governmental base in Antarctica. Devoted exclusively to research and preservation, the members of World Park Base monitor the effects of human impact on the continent's vulnerable ecosystem. They have documented environmental abuses by neighboring bases, underscoring the need for Greenpeace's watchdogging effort.

Through its continued presence Greenpeace hopes to insure that improvements to the waste-disposal situation are not merely cosmetic. We know Greenpeace belongs there to spread a better environmental awareness to the whole of Antarctica, and we hope that Antarctica becomes the first World Park.

GREENPEACE ROCKS THE SOVIET UNION

Greenpeace has made history with the first major release of western rock music in the Soviet Union.

The LP entitled, 'Greenpeace - Breakthrough' is a double album on the Soviet Stat label, Melodiya Records. The greatest names in rock music have donated their biggest hits to the project. The Greenpeace album includes songs by U2, Pretenders, Eurythmics, Dire Straits, John Cougar Mellencamp, Peter Gabriel, Bryan Ferry, Simple Minds, Bruce Hornsby & the Range, INXS, Basia, Belinda Carlisle, R.E.M., Sting, Martin Stephenson and the Daintees, Talking Heads, Waterboys, Bryan Adams, Aswad, World Party, Thompson Twins, John Farnham, Sade, Terence Trent D'arby, and the Grateful Dead.

Melodiya Records has pressed and distributed 5 million copies. Sales in the Eastern Bloc are expected to exceed 10 million copies.

This is the first time such a recording has been released by Soviet authorities. It will also be their largest pressing of a rock album. Although they have released records by groups such as the Beatles, Jethro Tull and the Moody Blues in the past, the Greenpeace album will be the first opportunity Russians will have to purchase new western rock. Outside of Moscow and Leningrad many of the legendary western artists are completely unknown.

Released earlier this year, the album master and artwork was delivered to Moscow last September.

The proceeds of the Greenpeace album in the Soviet Union are being divided between Greenpeace and the International Foundation for the Survival and Development of Humanity - an international organization established last year to bring experts together from the East and West to work on common problems like pollution and the depletion of the ozone layer.

The album was put together 'pro bono' by Ian Flooks and his London-based booking agency "Wasted Talent."

Artwork for the album is being completed by British award-winning designer Neville Brody. Esclusive photographs for the project were shot by Anton Corbijn.

David McTaggart, Chairman of Greenpeace, comments: "This album is a great big greeting card to young people in the Soviet Union from Greenpeace and the artists. It's going to introduce them not only to the best of western rock but also to Greenpeace and the idea of people working together across national boundaries to build a safe, clean world."

GREENPEACE'S WASTE TRADE UPDATE

Greenpeace is seeking a global ban on the trade of all wastes which will release toxics to the environment. At the same time, Greenpeace seeks bans of waste import and export in individual countries and regions.

The Greenpeace Waste Trade Update is published regularly and is available in Spanish, French, and English.

The sources of information for these articles are Greenpeace offices, international news services, environmental and political activists, and government officials throughout the world.

If you have information to contribute to the next issue, please contact Ann Leonard, author of Waste Trade Update. We will credit the source of information, unless otherwise requested.

If you require information about specific trade schemes, policy developments, and trends regarding the international waste trade, contact Jim Vallette, Greenpeace International Waste Trade Campaign researcher.

And if you would like to be added to the mailing list for this newsletter, or would like a copy of Greenpeace's 70 page inventory of proposed and completed trades, please contact Fred Munson, Greenpeace Toxics Campaign assistant.

GETTING INVOLVED WITH GREENPEACE

Getting involved with the efforts of Greenpeace is easy. It can be as simple as writing your elected representatives in either local, state or federal government. Or writing to officials of other governments, even representatives in the United Nations.

Letters to leaders of industry and commerce can help -- they may be able to ignore one or two, but not thousands or even millions. Nothing is more important to us all than the future of our world.

Greenpeace actively recruits volunteers with any kind of skill. Turning a wrench, maintaining equipment, or simply providing a few hours of time and/or labor is just as important to the cause as plugging a discharge pipe or climbing a smokestack.

One really doesn't have to be expert at anything to lend support. All that is needed is time and commitment to Greenpeace's goals. It can be as simple as purchasing checks with the Greenpeace logo. (see page .)

Everybody has some free time to spare, and we hope you will join us. Those few of us without enough time to get actively involved may wish to send donations. Greenpeace is a non-profit organization, yet all of us profit by making our world a safer, healthier place.

The Greenpeace Quarterly is published four times a year. To receive the Quarterly and support Greenpeace in the U.S.A. (a non-profit, tax exempt organization), we request an annual donation of $15.00 for individuals and $30.00 for families sent to:

Greenpeace U.S.A.,
1436 U St., N.W.,
Washington, D.C. 20009
(202) 462-1177

INTERVIEW WITH TWILLY CANNON, CAPTAIN OF THE *VEGA*

Last summer Dave Anzalone and Bobby Hicks of the Trade Journal staff accompanied the Greenpeace sailing-vessel *Vega* on a Fleet Week demonstration in San Francisco Bay. Back in port Bobby and Dave took the opportunity to take photographs of the vessel and her crew and interview her captain, Twilly Cannon.

D.A.: When did you start aboard the *Vega*?

T.C.: I began this tour last July, and we'll probably be here on the west coast for another year.

D.A.: What qualifications do you have for this position?

T.C.: I had a lot of sailing experience before Greenpeace. I've had a captain's license since I was nineteen. I've done transoceanic sailing and sail deliveries. The job is not strictly a boating job. You have to wear a lot of different hats: being sensitive to the needs of the press, making political decisions, plus interpersonal stuff that one normally wouldn't field. The boat is the focus of the tour, but it doesn't comprise the tour. We have the crew, land-based people and other campaigners working with the boat. The *Vega* is often the center for twenty or twenty-five people; like it or not, they turn to the skipper to arbitrate some decisions which are completely unrelated to the boat.

D.A.: Why do you sail with Greenpeace?

T.C.: I think Greenpeace makes a positive contribution to the environment. Often the results are not as tangible as at other times but I've had enough experinces where I've done direct actions and work for Greenpeace where I have seen tangible results. For example, we did a direct action in Canada last year; as we were in the midst of it the government announced that they were going to halt the Japanese driftnet fishing off the Canadian coast. That was clearly a response to our action.

I participated in a direct action near Seattle, where a pentachlorophenol - producing plant had been contaminating Elliot Bay with dioxins. They had been put on court probation, which they were ignoring. Since our direct action against them they've had a much better record of compliance.

D.A.: So you do see success in your efforts.

T.C.: Yes. Another, less tangible way of measuring our success is to look at the reaction of the other actors in the power structure. Today you saw the concerted effort of the Coast Guard to interfere with our activities. We were of no threat to them, but if our activities weren't going to have some effect they wouldn't be bothering with us.

Greenpeace Zodiac "PIA"

D.A.: What's the most exotic situation you've encountered while with Greenpeace?

T.C.: One of the situations I most enjoyed was when we tried to publicize a semi-secret Canadian nuclear-warfare laboratory in inland waters near Vancouver, B.C. As part of that action we landed a group of elderly women called the "Raging Grannies". They symbolically occupied the base and tried to show it for what was, we felt, an illegal operation. As a result, Canada's department of National Defense admitted they had no legal right to operate there and prohibit the use of those waters by fishermen and recreational boaters. I was working with an unusual group of people: the press, the Raging Grannies, and Greenpeace.

D.A.: What was the most exciting or dangerous Greenpeace action you've been involved with?

T.C.: On the first action of the Beluga tour we demonstrated against an aging aluminum company that was just, well, atrocious in their pollution. We sailed on the Greenpeace vessel *Beluga*, and this particular company was one of the companies primarily responsible for the decline of the beluga whale population. It was suspected that they would have heavy security at the plant. We infiltrated in the middle of the night with climbers and a video

261

team, scaled the smokestacks and deployed the banners. We were up there several hours before the company was aware of our presence.

D.A.: How high were the smokestacks?

T.C.: Several hundred feet. It wasn't that difficult of a climb. For a rock-climber it was fairly simple. The whole infiltration process was exciting. The company overreacted and we were able to capitalize on a number of their mistakes. We got away with a good kickoff to the tour.

Recently we did an action at a hotel that prides itself on its security. We were able to crack it, getting several key rooms; and, as the international treaty members were convening, we deployed a fifty-foot wide by three stories tall banner on the side of the hotel. The delegates had to pass under the banner on their way in to vote. I really enjoy things like that.

D.A.: Do you have anything to say for our Parks' readers?

T.C.: I've met a lot of National Parks employees because I've spent a lot of time in the parks, especially those out West, where I've gone rockclimbing. I really enjoy the parks and I encourage park employees to have an effect on their parks. I don't see the Park Service acting as an opposing weight to counterbalance the wrong kind of development. On a personal level I am disgusted by the willingness to make parks more like wilderness theme parks rather than places to enjoy an ecosystem in its natural state. My message to park employees is: use your inside influence to work for the benefit of the parks and the natural environment.

D.A.: What advice do you have for prospective Greenpeace volunteers?

T.C.: Greenpeace works with a lot of volunteer power. Often one can't "plug in" instantly. There are times when we have needs, and there are times when we can't use people. If you want to volunteer you have to be persistent. You also have to come across with what skills and abilities you have that makes you valuable to Greenpeace, both intellectually and physically. It's a demanding job, similar to public service work in that no one gets paid a lot, the hours are very difficult, and often one is away from home. I'm not trying to discourage folks, but when you see us out there in the zodiacs or an action on a bridge or a building, you're seeing only the tip of the iceberg of organization and work. There are many less glamorous hours, and we spend a lot of time on Vega just gruntin' away, trying to get to that next stop. It can be a grind after a few months. National Park employees are mostly environmentally aware people, and it's natural that they may join an environmental organization like Greenpeace in the future.

D.A.: Any thoughts for the future?

T.C.: My career is not about being a captain of a vessel, it's about being an environmentalist. I'm on Vega because I have the skills to make the tour

263

go, to be successful, to bring the issues to the folks and let them choose what they want to do about these problems in their communities. I'm perfectly willing to shift into other roles for Greenpeace where I can be most effective.

D.A.: Captain, thanks for the voyage and the interview; it was really a pleasure.

T.C.: Thanks for coming out with us. I'm really glad you guys were able to come out here.

Vega captain Twilly Cannon, beteran of numerous Greenpeace "actions" from Canada to the South Seas prepares for encounter with the Sixth Fleet in San Francisco Bay.

TROPICAL RAINFOREST UPDATE
By Randy Hayes

"Never doubt that a small group of thoughtful, committed citizens can change the world; indeed, it's the only thing that ever has."

Margaret Mead

The ancient, remote rainforests seem unlikely to affect our daily lives. Yet today and every day, their disappearance will make our tax burden larger, the cost of living higher, the fascinating cultures of the world fewer, and perhaps the chances of survival on earth slimmer.

Rainforests cover less than two percent of the globe, yet they are home to between 50 and 60 percent of all types of living things on our planet, as many as 5 million species of plants, animals and insects. The world's tropical rainforests are located within a 3,000 mile-wide band stradling the equator. Less than half of the original acreage survives. The main concentrations are in Amazonia, Southeast Asia, and Central Africa. The main causes of deforestation are cattle ranching, logging, road-building, agriculture and industrial developments such as hydro-electric dams and mines. The forests have evolved to a delicate ecological balance that can easily be permanently destroyed, without hope of recovery.

The rainforest is the richest, oldest, most productive and most complex ecosystem on earth. The National Academy of Sciences reports that two and a half acres could contain an estimated 42,000 insect species alone. The forests also have an abundance of useful plants, particularly medicinal plants. Fewer than one percent of tropical species have been examined for their possible use to humanity.

Rainforests are the traditional home of hundreds of tribal societies. They rely on the forest for food and shelter. Moreover, rainforests capture, store and recycle rain, thus preventing floods, drought and soil erosion.

We are connected to the rainforests in more ways than we think. Not only do rainforest ecosystems support hundreds of thousands of tribal forest people, but they provide food and medicine and regulate rainfall which supplies clean water for millions of people outside of the forest. Yet our connection is much more profound. Consider that the Earth is the only planet we know of that supports life.

These biologically rich forests are the natural laboratories of evolution. Their trees are the oldest living beings on earth--surviving for hundreds of years. They are the old growth or ancient forests. Global deforestation threatens the planet's ability to support life. Stable weather patterns on which we rely

on for growing food and for water are being dangerously disrupted by the global warming or "Greenhouse Effect". Human diversity is being eradicated by the loss of forest tribes of indigenous peoples. An ecosystem diverse in species is more stable than one with just a few species.

Our planet is a web of ecological systems that depend upon each part of the whole to support all life. We never quite know what we are doing when we remove one part. Old growth forests are a critical part. They are like the lungs of the planet, regulating the breathing between the atmosphere and the body of the earth. Even dead wood plays a part in the overall health of a forest ecosystem. Insects, and fungi break down the wood and enrich the soil. The myriad of life of old growth forests are the blueprints of natural evolution. This natural diversity cannot be replicated or reestablished. A mere pine tree plantation or simple reforestation project is biologically impoverished. It is certainly not a functional substitute for a diverse ancient old-growth forest.

The atmosphere, soil and water, called biosphere, is no thicker than a coat of paint on a football. It is a complex ecological system linking plants, animals, soil, air, water, and every form of life on the planet. It all works together in a steady state system of dynamic balance. When you alter any one part **you affect the other parts.**

We humans are only one minute part of the biosphere. However, we behave differently. We set ourselves apart and call all the other coinhabitants such as tropical rainforests "natural resources". Our survival depends on preserving the biosphere. It is the stuff of existence, the framework of life on earth. We ultimately have to abide by its ways or rules. This is called 'natural law'. The ecosystem can carry on without us but we can't live without it. Seeing nature or tropical rainforests as no more than a collection of resources for human consumption is indeed dangerous.

The projections are that by the year 2050 (less than one person's lifespan), virtually all of the world's tropical rainforests will be gone forever. We are the last generation on earth to have a chance to save these ancient old growth forests.

As citizens of the industrial world, we hold some of the keys to the rainforests' survival because the industrial societies of Europe, Japan, and the United States are largely responsible for the problem. Our tax dollars and investment capital finance many destructive projects in the tropics. Corporations in which we own stocks and from which we buy products are responsible for the forest clearing. And our patterns of consumption and wastefulness also contribute to the problem.

The Rainforest Action Network (RAN) is an organization working both nationally and internationally to protect the world's tropical rainforests. Their methods range from banner hangings and letter-writing campaigns, to boycotting products that destroy the rainforest and organizing demonstrations against corporations that contribute to rainforest destruction. One of RAN's chief goals is to inform the public on how they can take action to preserve rainforest habitats. They offer two publications, the monthly *Action Alert* and the quarterly *World Rainforest Report*, and produce numerous fact sheets and brochures targeting specific rainforest issues.

A yearly subscription is $25.00, $15.00 for students and low income people. Subscribers receive 12 issues of the *Action Alert* with information about current activities taking place which are causing deforestation. It also provides readers with ideas for direct action.

RAN sponsors Rainforest Action Groups (RAGs) across the country and provides a RAG Manual which outlines all the necessary information to set up a local rainforest group. For more information contact:

Rainforest Action Network
300 Broadway #28
San Francisco, CA 94133
(415) 398-4404

The Problem

Global deforestation threatens the planet's ability to support life.

• Wildlife and plant species are being annihilated. Evolution itself is being retarded.

• The intense biological diversity of natural or old growth forests can not be replicated by reforestation projects.

• Stable weather patterns on which we rely on for growing food and for water are being dangerously disrupted by the global warming or Greenhouse Effect.

• Cultural diversity is being eradicated by the loss of tribal peoples.

Rainforest Action

A major effort must be launched to:

• Protect them forever.

• To restore surrounding damaged areas to some semblance of their natural state.

• To ensure ecological balance and sustainable productivity for all people.

• **To ensure a future for our world.**

Chris Mitchell

ROCK GROUP *GRATEFUL DEAD* JOINS FIGHT TO SAVE WORLD'S REMAINING TROPICAL RAINFORESTS

UNITED NATIONS/NEW YORK (September 13) -- The rock group Grateful Dead announced they are joining the fight to save the world's remaining tropical rainforests. The band -- which recently sold out eight scheduled concerts at Madison Square Garden in three hours -- played a special benefit concert on September 24th, 1988 at the Garden for activist groups Cultural Survival, Rainforest Action Network, and Greenpeace.

"They're wiping out the rainforest at the rate of 50 million acres a year -- that's the equivalent of England, Wales, and Scotland every year -- or one square mile every six minutes. In sixty years they'll all be gone. As a person, a musician, and a citizen of earth, I object," said Jerry Garcia, lead guitarist for the Grateful Dead. Bob Weir, rhythm guitarist with the band, added: "Consider that rainforests are essential to our survival. We're already paying the price of rainforest loss with the record-breaking hot temperatures we had last summer from the Greenhouse Effect. But scientists say the worst is still ahead -- changing weather patterns, disrupted food production and mass famine -- unless we start doing something now."

"Look, half of the world's organisms live in the rainforest," said Mickey Hart, percussionist for the band. "The world can't afford to lose this variety. Diversity is precious. Evolution couldn't happen without it. The loss of rainforests also means the loss of indigenous cultures -- music, rhythm, dance and human knowledge, specifically, a profound understanding of man's biochemical relationship with nature," he continued.

The band -- which has a long history of social commitment dating back to its inception twenty-three years ago -- selected three organizations known for their direct action approaches to saving rainforests -- Cultural Survival, Rainforest Action Network and Greenpeace -- as the principal beneficiaries of the benefit concert at Madison Square Garden, which raised close to a million dollars.

Randy Hayes, director of Rainforest Action Network, explained why it's important for people in developed countries to care about rainforests: "I think it's critical to bring the message home because here's where the problem starts -- with consumer demand for products made from raw materials taken from rainforests, and with our own tax dollars in the form of U.S. foreign aidloans used to finance rainforest-killing development in Third World countries. The destruction of rainforests begins right here in the U.S., in Japan and in Western Europe. The fight to save rainforests must begin here too."

The band members emphasized that the September benefit was just the start of their involvement and that their commitment to rainforests is long term. Peter Bahouth, Chairman of Greenpeace USA, stated: "All of us participating in this benefit want to be careful not to gloss over the complexity of this issue. We're all fully aware that lots of political, social and economic factors affect the fate of rainforests. There's no one magic bullet that's the solution. It's going to take a lot of people -- here in the U.S., in Japan, in Western Europe -- working to change things. We need to act as consumers and as citizens to change government and corporate policies -- specially international banking and foreign aid policies -- that are the root cause of rainforest destruction," he continued.

Rainforest Action Network's Randy Hayes added that all three groups are highly sensitive to working with activists in rainforest countries: "I think that it's important to stress that we're not just telling people who live in rainforests what to do, imposing our environmental values on them. All three groups -- Rainforest Action Network, Greenpeace and Cultural Survival -- are listening to the indigenous people who live in rainforests and who are fighting to save them. They're doing their part in their countries -- risking their lives -- to stop the killing of rainforests. We're saying it's time for us to do our part like not eating fast-food hamburgers or roast beef sandwiches made with rainforest beef, or not buying teak furniture, or telling our congressmen to stop the World Bank from using our tax dollars to finance big power dams in the Amazon, whick indigenous tribes are fighting to stop."

Dr. Jason Clay, director of Cultural Survival, added: "I think the last point is critical. This isn't about environmental elites in developed countries telling people in rainforest countries what they should do. We're not environmental colonialists. We're supporting the efforts -- oftentimes heroic --of indigenous people in developing countries fighting to save their environments, their cultures, their way of life. They're asking for our help because they know the problem starts here with us. We're responding to them. They're putting their lives on the line. Right now, Amazon Indians in Brazil are giving their lives -- more than on killed every day -- fighting to save their rainforests. The least we can do is give up our fast-food burgers or roast beef sandwiches, or write a few letters to our representatives in Washington, D.C."

Greenpeace USA's Bahouth also stressed the continuity between the problem as it exists in developing countries and efforts to address the problem in developed countries: "We're working to stop the flow of agro-toxics -- pesticides and herbicides considered too deadly for use in the U.S. but cynically sold to developing countries for use in export cash crop production on land that's usually cleared from rainforests. In the case of these deadly, outlawed agro-toxics, there's no question the problem starts here and has to be stopped here. U.S. companies produce the agro-toxics. And U.S. tax dollars as foreign aid often is used by developing countries to pay for their pesticide imports. It's a vicious circle. Agro-toxics -- produced here but banned here -- find their way back to our dinner tables as poisonous, cancer-causing residue on imported food. Greenpeace is working to break that circle."

The three rainforest organizations are using the funds they received from the benefit concert to support porjects designed to help indigenous tribes and rainforest activists in developing countries and to increase public awareness and concern about rainforests in the U.S.

> "If I wasn't a rock star I'd be sailing with Greenpeace." Quote from Grateful Dead rythm guitarist Bob Weir during recent interviews with N.P.T.J.

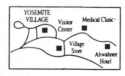

GRATEFUL DEAD
1988

Left to right/ Bob Weir, Jerry Garcia, Mickey Hart, Phil Lesh, Brent Mydland, Bill Kreutzmann.

TROPICAL FORESTS MAY GROW PLANTS TO CURE HUMAN ILLS

By Joy Aschenbach
National Geographic Society

Naturally caffeine-free coffee beans. Juice that makes you skinny. A contraceptive that's effective for two years after just one dose. Long-sought cures for cancer and AIDS.

Such wonders may come out of the jungle, not the laboratory. Tropical forest plants or their derivatives already are found everywhere from the hospital operating table to the family breakfast table. Yet only a small percentage of the tens of thousands of such plants have been adequately analyzed for potential uses.

Tropical forests, sources of such familiar products as cacao, rubber, and exotic woods, are also untapped reservoirs of genetic information. One way to help save these forests from destruction is to make their rich diversity profitable.

"It's not just conservation in the traditional sense. Some plants can pay for themselves," says Mark J. Plotkin, plant-conservation director for the World Wildlife Fund. "Where is the panacea from synthetics?"

Plotkin, an ethnobotanist who has carried a machete and climbed trees to gather plant samples from the Amazonian rain forest of Suriname, has hopes to treat human skin fungus with sap from a certain nutmeg tree, and to cure human earaches with the juice of a rare fungus that grows on rotting logs.

Among some 50 species of wild coffees on the island of Madagascar, he believes, at least one may produce beans with little or no caffeine. Such a miracle bean could be crossed with those of flavorful commercial beans.

"There are about 3,000 different tropical fruits, a wealth of delicious flavors and good nutrition to be tapped, and we only use banana, pineapple, mango, and papaya in a major way," says Noel D. Vietmeyer, who studies the economic potential of plants for the National Research Council of the National Academy of Sciences.

"We're looking for the fruit that's got what it takes to become an international star, to be the next papaya," he tells National Geographic. He is seeking funds to review all 3,000 and choose the 50 with the most potential. One certain to be on the list, he says, is mamey, Cuba's brown-skinned, grenade-shaped national fruit. Its bright red flesh has the texture of avocado and a sweet taste with a hint of chestnut.

Renewed interest in tropical forest plants prompted the National Cancer Institute in 1986 to commission a five-year search of the tropical forests of

274

An Indian medicine man in the Amazonian rain forest of Suriname shares his knowledge of jungle plants with Mark J. Plotkin, plant-conservation director for the World Wildlife Fund. A single healer in an Amazonian tribe may use more than 100 plant species for medicinal purposes alone. Scientists are collecting thousands of samples from the world's tropical forests in hope of finding a wealth of new medicines, including cures for cancer and AIDS.

Southeast Asia, Africa, and Latin America for natural anti-cancer agents. The project was later expanded to include the dread AIDS, acquired immune deficience syndrome. About 10,000 plant samples have been collected so far.

The Latin America search is emphasizing the plant knowledge of traditional Indian healers or medicine men, says Michael Balick of the New York Botanical Garden, who oversees the cancer project's plant-gathering from that region.

"We are the last generation of field scientists who can learn what they know," he explains. "The information the old healers posses is being lost. It's not being passed on to their sons or daughters."

A single healer in an Amazonian tribe may use more than 100 different plant species for medicinal purposes alone, says Mark Plotkin. Once when he was stung by wasps, an old healer ground up the bark of a shrub and rubbed it on the sting. Within five minutes, Plotkin says, the bump was gone.

About 75 percent of the world's people rely on traditional medicine for primary health care. Tropical forest plants are used to combat everything from heart ailments and childbirth difficulties to pimples and dandruff.

A quarter of all modern medicine's prescription drugs, worth more than $15 billion annually in the United States, include plant extracts, many of tropical-forest origin. An ingredient from Madagascar's rosy periwinkle contributes to a 95 percent chance of remission for victims of lymphocytic leukemia, usually children.

Such medicines do not get from forests to drugstores overnight. It takes about 10 painstaking years. In the past decade, relatively little development of new wonder drugs has originated in tropical forests.

Biologist Walter H. Lewis of Washington University in St. Louis, who spent part of the past six years in the Amazonian rain forest of Peru, believes that one of the plants Jivaro Indians use may be effective against hepatitis B virus and another, for birth control. Laboratory testing is under way.

Among the world's estimated 260,000 species of higher plant forms, there is reason to hope for the cures humans seek. Only about 1 percent of these plants have been thoroughly analyzed. Based on what's been found so far, "in the 99 percent, there has to be something," Michael Balick says. "It's just a question of our being persistent."

> *"The man who goes alone can start today; but he who travels with another must wait till that other is ready."*
> *Henry David Thoreau*

Awards Program to Improve the Quality of Life Started by Philanthropist and University of Louisville

By Paul Desruisseaux
Louisville, KY.

For 10 years H. Charles Grawemeyer, a millionaire and philanthropist, has spent his working days in a tiny, basement office just off Muhammad Ali Boulevard in downtown Louisville, developing plans for a program that he hopes will make the world a better place. He has been pursuing his goal with ideas, with money, and with the University of Louisville, of which he is both a graduate and a benefactor.

Mr. Grawemeyer is the inspiration—and the money—behind an ambitious program of international awards to recognize extraordinary ideas, particularly those that could help improve the quality of life for people all over the world.

"I strongly believe that a great idea can change the world," he says. "What we are trying to stress with these awards is how individuals can dramatically help humanity by developing new ideas that have practical applications."

Enormous Interest Among Scholars

Within the next two years, the full program of five annual awards, each bearing a cash prize of $150,000, will be in place. The structure and guidelines for awards in psychology and religion are now being developed. Next spring the first awards for ideas in education and in "improving world order" will be announced. Last week the third annual award in music composition was presented.

Although only in their infancy, the University of Louisville Grawemeyer Awards, as they are officially known, have generated enormous interest among scholars in many countries. They also have occasioned considerable pride on the part of the University of Louisville.

When first proposed by Mr. Grawemeyer, however, the awards program was not immediately viewed as a great idea. The $10-million or more he was planning to dedicate to the project was seen as having much greater value to the university if it could be used to finance new academic programs, or sponsor scholarships, or endow professorships.

He recalls explaining his idea to the university's president, Donald C. Swain:

277

"He seemed pretty much against it."

Says Mr. Swain: "My initial reaction was, of course, to be very grateful for his generosity. Then I pointed out that the university had lots of needs, and I identified some of them. But Charlie is very single-minded, and once he gets an idea he sticks with it until it's fully developed--and only *then* makes his decision."

"The more we talked, however, the more I saw how truly imaginative this idea was," says Mr. Swain, "and how it would allow a lot of exciting things to happen at the university."

Mr Grawemeyer decided to start the program with just one award. "And I told Don Swain I'd forget the whole thing if, after a few years, people clearly felt it was a dumb idea that wasn't working."

Once the program was under way, there were few questions about its importance and usefulness to the university.

Says Mr. Swain: "The idea of bringing world-renowned people to the university, of picking out and identifying the very best ideas in these different fields and bringing them to greater public attention—these are things that a university ought to be involved in doing. And the fact that this is being done here helps bring greater recognition to the University of Louisville."

Several administrators and faculty members at the university have worked with Mr. Grawemeyer on the development of the program and, in particular, the procedures for selecting winners. But the program was and remains, as Mr. Swain puts it, "a Charlie Grawemeyer idea," one that now has an endowment worth close to $13-million backing it up.

The idea goes back a dozen years, when Mr. Grawemeyer, who is now 74, was planning to retire and sell the company—Plastic Parts, Inc., of Shelbyville, KY.—that had helped him accumulate his personal wealth.

A 1934 Louisville graduate and a longtime contributor to the institution, Mr. Grawemeyer earlier had transferred to the university a small foundation he had used as a vehicle for his philanthropy. However, he retained control over how the fund would be used to benefit the university during his lifetime, and—in a special arrangement—he was allowed to continue personally managing the assets, which at the time amounted to only about $25,000.

He distributed income from the fund to support programs, scholarships, and library acquisitions. "But it became clear to me that this fund would grow to be much greater than I'd originally anticipated," he says, "and I began to think about how it could best be used."

Focus On New Areas

An admirer of the Nobel Prizes, Mr. Grawemeyer wondered if a similar program might be developed, one that would focus on areas untouched by the Nobels. "I picked five that seemed important to me," he says.

He selected music composition, he explains, because music has always been a part of his life and his family's—he and his wife had been musicians, and their three daughters all had either taught music or performed professionally.

He wanted the awards to be worth about as much as Nobel Prizes, which at the time were set at $150,000—a sum that since has been increased by about $100,000.

"I knew it was going to take about $750,000 to do this, and doing it every year would require an endowment of about $10-million," explains Mr. Grawemeyer. "I then had about $1-million in the fund at the university, so I set myself the goal of trying to build that into $10-million."

Ten years later, the fund is worth almost $13-million. "That's a lot more than I'm now worth," says Mr. Grawemeyer. Over the past decade he contributed about $4-million to the fund, but the rest of its growth was the product of his shrewd management of the investments.

"It was all done through trading in common stocks, although it has involved quite a bit more risk than the university's foundation could reasonably be expected to take," he explains. "But I knew that's what it would take to reach the goal. The current strategy involves less risk—all of the money is in mutual funds, but aggressive-growth funds."

It was not until five years ago, when Mr. Grawemeyer was sure the value of his fund would indeed pass the $10-million mark, that he shared his vision of an awards program with officials of the university.

Members of the Louisville faculty help screen nominations for the awards, and a panel of judges makes a final recommendation to the university's trustees. Mr. Grawemeyer sits as a judge, but he makes it clear that his vote is counted only once.

To illustrate the point, he tells how he has voted for only one of the first three winners of the award for music composition. This year it went to Harrison Birtwistle, a British composer recognized for an opera. The previous winners were Gyorgy Ligeti, a Hungarian living in West Germany, and Witold Lutoslawski, a Pole.

Mr. Grawemeyer had not wanted the awards to be in his name; he envisioned them as the University of Louisville Awards. "We really had to twist his arm," says Mr. Swain, who ultimately convinced Mr. Grawemeyer that such a label could create problems for the publicly supported university if taxpayers were to infer that the state funds were financing the awards.

Mr. Grawemeyer had feared—justifiably, it turns out—that publicity from the awards would bring him lots of solicitations for donations. "I get besieged with requests whenever there is publicity about this," he says. "I just write back and explain how all of my charitable dollars are out at the University of Louisville."

An Inspiration To Donors

Although he was born in Louisville and has lived here all his life, Mr Grawemeyer was not very well known before the awards program was established.

Over the years he's done all kinds of things for the university and the community, but you never heard much about him until these awards," says Elaine Musselman, the president of a Louisville-based insurance company and a university trustee.

Colette M. Murray, the university's vice-president for development and alumni relations, says Mr. Grawemeyer's actions have inspired other donors to the university, which has raised close to $50-million in a capital campaign now in its final phase. "I think people see that what he has done makes their gifts to the university even more valuable," she says. "One of the reasons the awards dinner has been so successful is that most of the people who attend are other donors who come to honor Charlie."

Mr Swain, the university president, says he has never regarded Mr. Grawemeyer as a typical major donor. "One day I walked into my office and found on my desk a scruffy brown envelope with a handwritten note from Charlie attached. It said, essentially, that he thought I'd be interested in this, and inside was a million dollars in stock that he was giving to the university."

W. Landis Jones, chairman of the political science department at Louisville, has been working with Mr. Grawemeyer on the award for "improving world order," which will recognize an idea that promotes better relations among nations. Before enlisting Mr. Jones's help, Mr. Grawemeyer audited one of the professor's courses. "When he came to see me about the award," says Mr. Jones, "I thought he'd come to talk about courses he might enjoy."

Mr. Jones says the response from political scientists to the new award has been overwhelming.

Mr. Grawemeyer hopes the award competition will nurture the development of ideas that politicians and government officials could adopt as part of their policies.

The award in education, he says, might lead to the discovery of ideas that, for example, could help close the knowledge gap between developed and third-world countries, a gap he says is growing larger all the time.

The award in psychology, he says, might "encourage people who can find out how the brain works, and how it can become more productive and come up with better ideas."

Over all, says Mr. Grawemeyer, he hopes the awards will bring prominence to the important ideas.

"I also hope," he adds, "that we can find somebody who has an idea that shows the nations of the world how to live together without going to war to accomplish their goals."

N.P.S. Journeyman Walt Castle at the workbench.

SURVIVAL OF WOLVES
Northern California Hybrid Wolf Pack
By Lori Fox

The dominant society in the United States and Europe has failed to understand the wolf as much as it has failed to understand the indigenous peoples of North America, taking land, sources of food, and lives by right of God, might, and Manifest Destiny. This ties in with religious doctrine: Christianity that preaches the attitude of man's dominance over the earth and all of its children vs. native religions which teach that all lifeforms are related and dependent upon the earth for their survival.

In *Of Wolves and Men*, Barry Lopez says that mankind (referring to the Anglo Saxon breed) uses the wolf as a mirror to reflect all that is considered base and evil within humanity, and thus the wolf has become the all-time favorite scapegoat. Pick up any children's book about animals--nine times out of ten, wolves will be left out altogether, or if included, are portrayed as evil, dangerous, blood-thirsty beasts, while animals such as tigers, bears and crocodiles, which are much more dangerous than the wolf in the wild, are depicted as noble, cute, and even cuddly.

Russell Rutter and Douglas Pimllott, in *The World of the Wolf*, conclude that the varying attitudes towards wolves are based upon the differences in human population densities; the lower population density of humans in wolf habitats throughout North America meant fewer incidences of rabies, whereas condensed human populations throughout Europe led to countless wolf attacks upon humans, with frequent rabies epidemics among wolves. Thus, Dr. Doug Clark, as quoted in Rutter and Pimlott's book, summarizes that the fierce wolves of European history were all rabid. Non-rabid wolves do not attack humans, and there has yet to be a single documented attack on a human by a wild, non-rabid wolf throughout all of North America.

Wolves once roamed throughout most of the Northern Hemisphere. Today, they exist in small, isolated populations in northern North America and a few areas of Europe and Russia. The dominant society has managed in a few short centuries of poisons, traps, guns, and airplanes, to undo the handiwork that nature took millions of years to perfect. Man and wolf first began to cohabit from between 12,000-20,000 years ago. From this relationship developed the over 800 varieties of domestic dogs we now recognize. All the characteristics that we admire and cherish in these mutant offspring of wolves originated in the wolf, and yet our society does not recognize the wolf's claim to them. Rather, we endeavor to destroy him in the name of predator control and domestic animal husbandry. Translated, this means less competition for the human sports hunter and lax ranching practices.

Fortunately, the future yet dawns bright on the horizon for the wolf. Many, many clubs, organizations, and societies, as well as wolf-focused publications, have sprung up across North America and in parts of Europe that are dedicated to ensuring the wolf's survival in the last remnants of his once great territory. Many people own and/or breed wolves and wolf dog crosses (called wolf hybrids) as companions, fiercely defending their right to do so at the same time expressing that these animals are definitely not for everyone. It's as if by "owning" or being "owned by" this small piece of the wilderness, they are helping to preserve the animal they so admire.

One of the brightest stars in the skies of tomorrow regarding the survival of the wolf is the Wildlife Education and Research Foundation's Rabies Research Program, which is focusing it's efforts on proving the effectiveness of the rabies vaccine on wolves and wolf hybrids. The results of this controlled research project, which are expected to confirm the effectiveness of the vaccine, will benefit both privately owned wolves and wolf hybrids as well as wolves in zoos and in the wild. Hopefully, this program will pave the way for even more future beneficial actions directed towards the plight of the wolf.

Questions and tax deductible contributions to WERF may be directed to: *Lori L. Fox*, President, *Northern California Hybrid Wolf Pack*, P.O. Box 2204, Wawona Station, Yosemite National Park, CA 95389, 209-683-3567.

Robert Frankel

284

DELTA IV SUPER SKINS™

Mount Timpanogos, Provo, Utah — Home of Delta IV, Incorporated

A SYSTEM OF 7 adhesive and non-adhesive skins designed to serve virtually every climbing skin need.

COMPETITIVE PRICES with discounts:

Pro discounts for instructors and ski patrol members.

Discounts for outdoor professionals employed by ski area base facilities, the U.S. Park Service, and USFS.

CLASSIC I MODEL — Mechanically-attached nylon skins that use no adhesives and require no permanent attachment to ski.

MINISKIN I MODEL — A nylon skin only two feet long for use on slopes of moderate incline. Fast on, fast off. Customer-applied adhesive requiring no permanent attachment to ski.

MINISKIN II MODEL — Same as Miniskin I model but uses a factory-applied adhesive.

ADHESIVE I MODEL — Save a bundle on top quality nylon skins by applying your own adhesive. The Tail Loc™ eliminates duct tape forever.

ADHESIVE II MODEL — Same as Adhesive I model, but without the Tail Loc™. This is the least expensive top quality skin available anywhere.

MOUNTAINEER MODEL — An imported mohair adhesive skin of the finest quality.

BACKCOUNTRY MODEL — A top quality imported nylon adhesive skin.

For more information please send for our brochure and prices. You will also receive product test results from a leading ski magazine, customer testimonials, and discount information.

Delta IV, Incorporated
P.O. Box 871
Provo, Utah 84603

Phone toll free 1–800–627–7039

OCEANIC DOLPHINS

By Deborah Johnson

There are approximately thirty-four known species of salt water dolphins, of which one species swims in fresh or salt water. There are also five known species of freshwater dolphins. All dolphins belong to the *delphinidae* family, having numerous conical teeth with variations in number and arrangement. All dolphins have highly developed echolocation capabilities, highly evolved social structures, and are gregarious. The species best known to man, through television, films, oceanarias and research facilities, are the bottlenose dolphins and the killer whales.

The bottlenose dolphins are the most common species kept in oceanarias and research facilities. In captivity, they are curious, alert, cooperative and friendly to humans and other dolphins. They are wary and difficult to capture, but, once captured, adapt readily to their confinement. In the wild, they are often seen riding the surf in shallow water.

Physically they have the typical *delphinidae* body form, long but somewhat stocky. Their melons are well defined where the beak meets the forehead. The lower jaw extends beyond the upper, curving slightly upward at its tip. They are dark grey on the dorsal area to a lighter grey on the flanks, and white or pink on the ventral area. They have a prominently falcated dorsal fin located on mid-back, medium sized flippers well spread and somewhat rounded at the tips, with the leading edges curved toward the body. These dolphins reach up to thirteen feet long and as much as 1,450 pounds at maturity. There are eighteen to twenty-six sharp, small, conical teeth in each jaw. Dolphins feed on small fish, eel, catfish, mullet and squid. Herds usually consist of several hundred dolphins, broken into pods of about a dozen. They are found worldwide in temperate and tropical waters.

Technically a dolphin, killer whales are by far the largest-sized member of the dolphin family. They also adapt well to captivity. While in their natural habitat or in captivity, they have had ample opportunity to attack humans, and there is no record of any humans being killed from such an attack. Killer whales, so long considered a rapacious murderer of the deep, are actually capable of gentle, responsive and sensitive behavior. In the wild their family units remain intact over long periods. As they "vocalize" constantly with one another, it is suggested that they are always in constant communication.

Killer whales have long, thick, extremely streamlined bodies. Their heads are bluntly tapered with definite indentations forming the rounded upper lip. Their blowholes are located slightly to the left on the forehead. Their coloring patterns are striking, and vary slightly from herd to herd. This variation is apparent when comparing killer whales from different regions.

Jet black is the predominant color, with clearly-delineated snow white undersides. This white area narrows along the ventral ridge to just past the anus, and rises to separate patches of white, curving towards the tail on both sides. There are also white patches on each side of the head above the eyes, extending almost to the flippers.

In male killer whales, the dorsal fin may grow to six feet in height; whereas in females this fin reaches to no more than three feet. Also, males have wider flippers. Adult males may grow over thirty-one feet long and weigh upwards of nine tons, while for females the figures are upwards of twenty-seven feet and four and a half tons.

Killer whales have ten to twelve conical teeth, curved slightly back and inward, on each side of each jaw. Their diet consists of fish, cephalopods, birds, sea turtles, and they have been observed and filmed while attacking and feeding on porpoises, seals, and the larger whales. Herds of killer whales range in number from as few as two or three to twenty-five to thirty members. Herds of several *thousand* have been reported in Icelandic waters. Killer whales have a wide distribution and inhabit all of the world's oceans from polar seas to tropical waters, although cooler regions seem to be preferred.

Friendly and cooperative in confinement, both bottlenose and killer whale dolphins are popular and common to oceanarias and research facilities. Their physical characteristics and coloring vary greatly from each other, yet their feeding habits include similar diets, with the exception that killer whales feed on larger marine mammals as well. Both species can be found worldwide with the bottlenose preferring warmer, tropical waters, and the killer whales preferring colder, polar waters.

The bottlenose dolphins and the killer whales are the marine animals best loved by mankind. Through exposure to books, films and television showing the gregarious and loving nature of these species, man has begun to realize that they are some of the most precious gifts the oceans have to offer.

Editor's note: Never in my life have I had a more exhilarating experience than when I snorkeled alongside a herd of bottlenose dolphins in the waters of Channel Islands National Monument off Southern California. See more on underwater parks elsewhere in this edition.

THE DREAM OF THE BLUE WOLF

Terra went to sleep one fine evening and dreamed a dream. In her dream she saw the buildings of a big city. It was civilization at it's peak. Then, the city skyline faded. Things went blank. All that remained was the sensation of something forming.

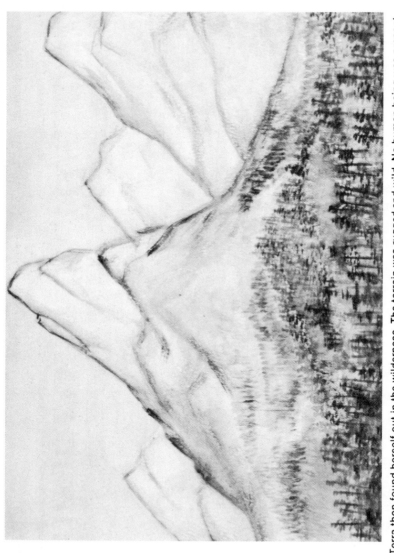

Terra then found herself out in the wilderness. The terrain was rugged and wild. No human being was present.

As Terra looked upon the land, she noticed a trememdous energy penetrating her body. Every cell within her felt it. This same energy vibrated in the mountains, the rivers, and in the sky. Terra felt the full impact of the grandure of nature. It was an awesome experience for her. She felt a deep respect, an appreciation for the power of nature.

288

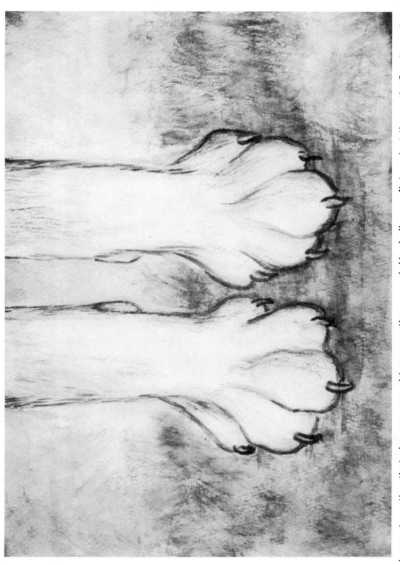

Terra began to notice that she was crouching upon the ground. Her belly was flat against the earth. Courious about this, she looked down at herself and saw that her hands were paws. Blue paws!

Terra turned her head over her shoulder to look at herself. She was a blue wolf. Her fur shimmered in the light.

Terra found that being a blue wolf was a delightful experience. She looked around and discovered she had a companion who was a blue wolf just like her.

Terra and her partner began to travel together. They trotted over rocks and around a hill. There they were met by a cold icy wind. They turned away from the chill and traveled in a different direction. The land became warmer in this new direction.

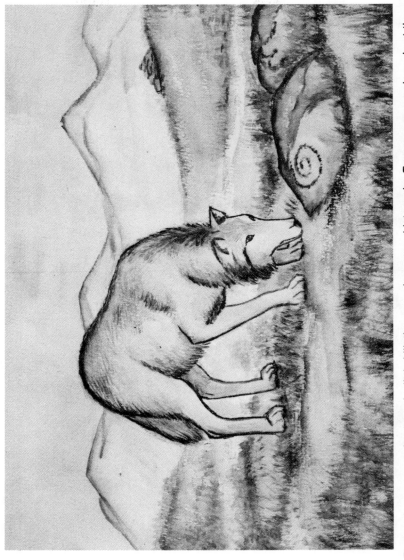

The, as they were coming 'round a little hill, they saw signs carved into rocks. Terra was very curious about these signs and began to follow them. Together the two wolves climbed up some enormous boulders that were worn smooth. There they found a little stream. They followed the stream and it led them to a meadow in the mountains.

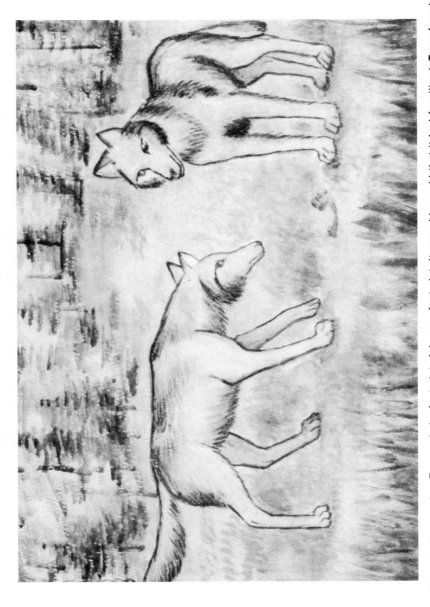

There in the meadow Terra spied a footprint. A human footprint. It was old, so old that it had fossilized. Terra found this intriguing. She moved to the center of the meadow and asked, who were these people? Answers came.

These people were the ancient wise ones. They knew how to live at one with nature. They knew the wisdom of the universe. They were the old wise ones.

Terra sat in deep contemplation of what she had just learned. Then, Terra awoke from her dream. She felt a wonderful joy. She became greatly inspired by her dream. She wanted to know more about it. She decided to learn what the ancient wise ones knew.

Dreamed, written and illustrated by Terry Birch

293

SELECTIONS FROM THE WRITINGS OF PARAMAHANSA YOGANANDA

The beauty of the world bespeaks the creative motherly instinct of God, and when we look upon all the good in Nature, we experience a feeling of tenderness within us.

1986 Engagement Calendar/May 5

Affirm divine calmness and peace, and send out only thoughts of love and goodwill if you want to live in peace and harmony. Live a godly life yourself and everyone who crosses your path will be helped just by being with you.

1986 Engagement Calendar/July 28

Live each present moment completely and the future will take care of itself. Fully enjoy the wonder and beauty of each instant. Practice the presence of peace. The more you do that, the more you will feel the presence of that power in your life.

1986 Engagement Calendar/August 18

Feel the love of God; then in every person you will see the face of the Father, the light of Love which is in all. You will find a magic, living relationshipuniting the trees, the sky, the stars, all people, and all living things; and you will feel a oneness with them. This is the code of divine love.

1986 Engagement Calendar/November 3

295

Mankind is engaged in an eternal quest for that "something else" he hopes will bring him happiness, complete and unending. For those individual souls who have sought and found God, the search is over. He is that Something Else.

1986 Engagement Calendar/October 13

If you radiate love and good-will to others, you will open the channel for God's love to come to you. Through meditation and service to mankind you will develop divine love, the magnet that draws to you all good.

1987 Engagement Calendar/November 2

God the Beautiful is manifest in the synchronized scenery of nature. His breath is heaving in the wind; His divinity is smiling at us in the flowers. The qualities of love and peace and joy that grow in the garden of human hearts are reflecting His goodness, His beauty.

1987 Engagement Calendar/March 16

Underlying all life is the silent voice of God, ever calling to us through flowers, through scriptures, and through our conscience -- through all things that are beautiful and that make life worth living.

1987 Engagement Calendar/April 13

Practice consideration and goodness until you are like a beautiful flower that everyone loves to see. Be the beauty that is in a flower, and the attractiveness that is in a pure mind. When you are attractive in that way, you will always have true friends.

1987 Engagement Calendar/May 18

Realize that the same lifeblood is circulating in the veins of all races...We are Americans or Hindus, or other nationalities, for just a few years, but we are God's children forever. The soul cannot be confined within manmade boundaries. Its nationality is Spirit; its country is Omnipresence.

1987 Engagement Calendar/September 21

Change your thoughts if you wish to change your circumstances. Since you alone are responsible for your thoughts, only you can change them. You will want to change them when you realize that each thought creates according to its own nature.

1987 Engagement Calendar/September 28

You should look at life unmasked, in the mirror of your experiences...Look at the perpetual current of emotions and thoughts that arise within you. Go into the heart of your aspirations, dreams, hopes, and despairs. Dive deep into the mute cravings of your inner self. Life is manifesting itself through all these channels and demanding that you seek understanding with your highest intelligence, wisdom, love, and vision.

1987 Engagement Calendar/November 30

Even if a person covers himself with a veil you can see that someone is there. So is nature like a great veil bulging with God's presence. He is hidden there, but you take just a casual look, not penetrating to see the shy Indweller.

MEQ pg 393

An Almighty Power has linked us all together. Whenever you help others you are helping yourself.

Paragram on AMBITION

Life should be chiefly service. Without that ideal, the intelligence that God has given you is not reaching out toward its goal. When in service you forget the little self, you will feel the big Self of Spirit.

Paragram on SERVICE

If you do not choose to be happy no one can make you happy. Do not blame God for that! And if you choose to be happy, no one can make you unhappy....It is we who make of life what it is.

SPIRITUAL DIARY/April 25

Rather than always be striving for personal happiness, try to make others happy. In being of spiritual, mental, and material service to others, you will find your own needs fulfilled. As you forget self in service to others, you will find that, without seeking it, your own cup of happiness will be full.

SPIRITUAL DIARY/April 27

Photo by Dave Anzalone

PACIFIC CREST TRAIL
Washington - Oregon - California

The Pacific Crest National Scenic Trail extends 2,600 miles from Canada to Mexico. It passes through 24 national forests, (including several wilderness areas), five national parks, five state parks, four Bureau of Land Management Resource Areas, and many areas of private land.

The trail was established as part of the National System of Recreational and Scenic Trails by the National Trails System Act of 1968. Although the trail extends along mountain ranges, there are stretches where there is no well defined "Pacific Crest".

The trail passes through some of the most scenic areas in Washington, Oregon and California. Elevations range from near sea level at the Columbia River between Washington and Oregon to 13,200 feet near Mount Whitney in the Sierra Nevada. Elevations average 6,000 feet in California, 5,000 feet in Oregon, and 4,000 feet in Washington.

Whatever your starting point and however long you plan to spend, the Pacific Crest Trail offers challenge and beauty to match your pace and interests.

The PCT crosses 19 major canyons, passes by 1,000 lakes, and climbs 57 mountain passes. It also crosses the Mojave Desert with its unique flora and fauna.

Temperatures range from very hot in the desert of southern California to well below freezing in the mountains. Midsummer snowstorms may occur in the high mountain passes. Sudden drops in temperature from the 90's to below freezing are not uncommon. The trail is usually passable from July 1 to October 15 and snowfree from August 1 to September 30.

The concept for the trail was first proposed in 1932 and the route was explored in the late 1930's.

A permit is not required for travel on the PCT in Washington and Oregon. In California, a permit is required for backcountry travel through most wilderness areas, all national parks, and the Angeles, San Bernardino, and Cleveland National Forests. Contact the appropriate office for permit information.

The trail is designed for travel on foot or with horses or pack stock. Vehicles of any kind are prohibited.

The PCT crosses mostly public land but there is a fair amount of private land along the way. Without the cooperation of private landowners the trail could not have been completed. When hiking the trail, please keep in mind that private land is not available for camping, grazing stock, or building campfires.

HELP
WANTED

YCC CHANGING THE LIVES OF TEENS

By Tina S. Sonnier

When I was 15, summer meant movies, music and mostly hanging out. Yet for 30 teenagers based at Badger Pass, enrollees in the United States Youth Conservation Corps (YCC), this summer has meant lots of hard work.

The YCC was organized under a 1971 congressional act designed to foster summer work educational programs in national parks. Back then, almost every national park had a program. Today, Yosemite offers the only remaining full seven day residential program.

Enrollees work a non-typical eight hour day. Non-typical because they don't merely go to work each day, then return home to do whatever they want. They live, work, and play as part of the program for eight weeks.

Their job duties range from clearing forest, fencing, making leach fields for High Sierra camps, re-establishing trails, installing bear boxes, revegetation, meadow restoration, painting and picking up litter.

They are a completely self-sufficient group. They cook their own food, set up their own spike camps and enforce rules of community living. For many of the participants, it is their first extended time away from home.

How does a group of 15 to 18 year old young adults do all this? Under special guidance and instruction of crew leaders, a project leader, and Bill Thomas, Yosemite's YCC coordinator for the past eleven years.

Courtesy Tina Sonnier

299

"The YCC was designed to give kids a chance to experience their national parks," Thomas said. "For me, it's a continuous source of pride in our American youth. The work these kids can accomplish is incredible," he said.

"Safety is number one, and this has been an accident-free year. In 1978 there were 35 accidents, but much of the program's success results from its continuity. Today, we are accident free," Thomas said.

Crews worked in Vogelsang, Ostrander Lake, Tuolumne Meadows, Mather District, Badger Pass and Yosemite Valley. Their compensation is the national minimum wage based on: a 40-hour week, newly learned skills and the chance to participate in many Yosemite activities.

There are nearly 2,000 bear boxes in the park, all of which YCC installed over the past four years. "Bears are really smart animals, the boxes are to protect the bears from becoming habituated to human food," Robert Johns, assistant crew leader, said.

For recreation, the group climbed to the top of Half Dome, hiked to Bernice Lake, danced at Wawona, fished and did plenty of backpacking.

This year's group is composed of enrollees mostly from the Yosemite area, yet some enrollees came from as far as Texas and Arizona. "We are definitely seeing a rise in applicants from all over the country because we have the last full residential program," Johns said.

Sequoia National Park has a five day program with six participants.

"Yellowstone ended their program this year on short notice. The equipment was purchased and enrollees were packing to spend the summer there, but there was just no money for the program," he said.

Courtesy Tina Sonnier

300

"Two trailers filled with equipment are just sitting in Yellowstone," Jeff Hickman, crew leader, said. "YCC actually saves the government money and brings in new blood for the park, but they can't afford to implement it," he said.

"YCC benefits the parks greatly. The work these students accomplish equals one-half the cost of manual labor," Johns said. "This is the only section of the park service that gets to do work in all areas of the park also."

Luckily, Yosemite's program has been able to survive for the past two years because of a special fee legislation which now sends a percentage of money collected at entrance gates back to the national parks where it was collected. Thomas hopes to see the Yosemite program return to its original size of 40 enrollees.

Private enterprise helps greatly. "Thanks to the Curry Co. and Mr. Hardy's generosity, we have full use of Badger Pass facilities and free shower use in the Valley. We would not be able to survive without this help," Thomas said.

Nearly 800 enrollees have passed through the Yosemite program since 1971 contributing more than 200,000 labor hours. Many went on to their careers in the national park service or forestry areas.

Enrollees (15 females and 15 males) were divided into three crews. Waking at 6 a.m. and sleeping in wilderness became an every day occurence at spike camps. The crews averaged more than 80 miles by foot across Yosemite.

"Girls learn how to set fence posts, and the guys learned how to cook. Everyone leaves with new knowledge in many different areas," Hickman said.

This month, enrollees will return to their homes to begin school again and adjust to normal routines. "I just hope I can remember how to use the VCR," one enrollee said.

Courtesy Tina Sonnier

HAVE THE
WHOLE WORLD
IN YOUR HANDS

The Worldwatch Institute invites you to read the most widely used public policy document in the world today--State of the World 1989.

Since its inception six years ago, our "annual physical exam of the planet" has shown that its vital signs are rapidly approaching a danger point.

State of the World 1989 sketches a portrait of a world at risk. The natural systems on which humanity depends are crumbling under the pressures of ever-rising population and a growing global economy that fails to take them into account.

As a result, our croplands are washing away, our forests disappearing, and the protective ozone layer eroding. The very temperature of the earth seems to be on the rise--posing a threat of unprecedented dimensions.

Using an approach that ties together all the earth's natural systems and their interdependence with humanity, State of the World is the only work that gives a complete portrait of the perils that we face--and a prescription for change.

For only $9.95, you can join the more than 200,000 concerned citizens who receive our annual State of the World report--it's like having the whole world in your hands, one convenient volume, 250 pages in length. The book is fully referenced and indexed and contains more than 50 useful tables and figures.

And for only $25, you can receive a Worldwatch Subscription, including a copy of State of the World 1989 and a whole year's worth of Worldwatch Papers, the authoritative and comprehensive series of small books on individual topics such as ozone depletion, biodiversity, toxic wastes, recycling, energy efficiency, etc.

Knowledge is power. Get the information you need so you can act. Mail in the coupon on the next page today.

302

SOME OF THE FACTS YOU WILL LEARN FROM STATE OF THE WORLD 1989:

- [ ] The five warmest years of this century have fallen in the '80s
- [ ] Environmental refugees are the single largest class of displaced persons
- [ ] By 2050, Bangladesh and the Maldives may no longer be habitable
- [ ] The world's armed forces are equivalent to the population of Argentina
- [ ] In Peru, the country's international debt is detectable in the height of its children

FILL IN THE COUPON BELOW AND MAIL TODAY!

_____
(Name)

_____
(Address)

_____
(City/State/Zip)

- [ ] **State of the World 1989**
  - ___ Paperback, $9.95
  - ___ Hardcover, $18.95

- [ ] 1989 Worldwatch Subscription
  Includes paperback edition of <u>State of the World 1989</u> and all Worldwatch Papers released during 1989--total $25.00

Enclosed is my check or purchase order for U.S. $ _____

NOTE: Prepaid orders are postage paid. Minimum $3 postage and handling charge on unpaid orders.

Make check payable and mail coupon to:
Worldwatch Institute
1776 Massachusetts Ave. NW
Washington, DC 20036

PLANNING FOR THE OUTDOORS, SLEEPING WARM AND SOFT CANTEENS

3rd Edition Equipment Update

By Rob Frankel

Last time, Lewis Goldman covered the basics of layering for warmth plus newer lightweight materials to reduce your load when packing it in. For this edition we sampled a lightweight sleeping bag and a convenient system for using water in the backcountry. These products are useful and are found in my backpack.

Aside from material goods, your head is the most valuable piece of backcountry equipment. No one can overemphasize the necessities of planning and using common sense when outdoors, or anywhere. Adventuresome folks like Ellie Hawkins or Tim Messick et. al. could not have achieved their goals without careful planning.

Truly exceptional guides and outdoorspeople can make plans entirely in their heads. For the rest of us however, lists, schedules, maps etc. become a somewhat tedious reality. A trip plan can take a few minutes or a few hours to compose, mentally and/or on paper. Smaller trips involving less commitment require less planning.

Regardless of size, a plan is meant to be a personal guide, not a rulebook. Plans should be modifiable. The importance of planning is not only do you think about your future, but also that obstacles in your path can be evaluated before you reach them. Surprises are nice, but nasty ones are seldom fun.

It's a good idea when walking to keep one's head up and not concentrate on the toes (except in rattler country). Planning is simply another way to concentrate on what's ahead. Stay alert and aware. Rest is an essential. Try to sleep comfortably and avoid contaminated water. Here are the products:

Sleeping Warm

Nowadays we have a wide selection of midweight sleeping bags available through mail-order catalogs and retailers. For this edition we decided to test Caribou Mountaineering's Solstice multi-season bag. I chose the 5' 11'' regular length (I'm an inch shorter). Rated at 5 degrees and insulated with Dupont Quallofil insulation this bag is relatively light at only four pounds. The stuff-sack fits well when placed vertically in my backpack and overhangs each side only slightly when strapped horizontally outside the pack.

Lightweight, comfortable and compact, this bag is reasonably priced three-season bag. The Solstice, coupled with a hot-water device such as the Upstream soft thermos/canteen can make the winter camper warm at night without having to invest in a second bag or shell. As with all sleeping bags, keep it dry and clean (follow washing instructions carefully for best satisfaction). For more information contact Caribou Mountaineering, P.O. Box 3696, Chico, CA 95927.

Staying Warm and Hydrated In The Outdoors

Just prior to going to press, our NPTJ staff learned of several new products for the outdoors that we felt our readers might like to know about. These items are from Upstream Products of Los Gatos, California, and they are designed to keep you warm and hydrated. Since these are two areas of prime concern to rangers, skiers and national parks personnel, we decided to review the items for this issue.

Staying Warm

Upstream Products has two new products (which they call Coldbusters™) that keep you warm and we have used them both. They are called the Waist-belt Thermos and the Pac-A-Therm® Insulated cushion with soft thermos insert. The Waistbelt Thermos is a soft insulated "fanny pack" worn around the waist that can be filled with up to 2½ quarts of liquid. It may be used as a bodywarmer by pouring in boiling hot water and wearing under an overcoat. Heat from the Waistbelt Thermos drifts upwards and tends to be trapped under the coat, warming the upper body. The Insulated Cushion with Soft Thermos Insert (or heated cushion for short) consists of an inner 5-quart insulated Soft Thermos and an outer insulated bag which has specially designed openings for warming the hands and feet. Heat is provided by pouring boiling hot water into the inner Soft Thermos. When the heated cushion is sat upon, heat drifts upwards, warming the user. Hot drinks such as instant coffee, tea or cocoa, may be made with hot water from these two Coldbusters,™ and this really helps to beat the cold. Either of these two Coldbusters™ can be filled with boiled water and will keep a sleeping bag or bed warm all night.

Staying Hydrated - Safely Hydrated

When you're thirsty, it can be very tempting to take a chance on drinking untreated water from natural streams and lakes. This temptation arises mainly because the water is cool and easy to get to. Upstream's new products make cool *safe* water easy to get to. This is mainly due to three reasons: The bags *fill easily with safe water,* they, *keep the water cool,* and they're *easy to drink from.* Two hands are needed to operate most water filtration pumps. A third hand is often not available to hold a bottle to pump into. Upstream solves this problem by providing adaptors that connect the clean water output of the pumps directly to their bags. The bags are just set down while being filled. They're far easier than water bottles to fill with safe water. Upstream has adaptors available to fit all commercially available portable water filter/pumps for $2.95 or less. Upstream has a drinking hose with mouthpiece that attaches to any of the containers and doesn't leak. This attachment makes it easy to drink with one hand without removing your backpack. The bags also will fill easily with the use of an unbreakable funnel which attaches to the bag outlet.

The bags can be partially filled and frozen during warm weather. The resulting insulated lump of ice provides cold drinking water for a long time.

The pocket on the outside of each water bag is a very handy place to keep a water filter and adaptor in between uses. Note: The easier you make it to use filtered, safe water the more you reduce the temptation to drink directly from questionable lakes and streams.

Insulation - State of the art insulation, sandwiched between cloth layers, totally surrounds the contents - for an effective thermal barrier, second only to a vacuum thermos bottle. Good insulation means that you don't have to find a stream and get out your water filter every time you want a safe cool drink.

Lightweight - Upstream's 5-quart thermos weighs half of what most one-quart thermoses weigh.

Replaceable Liner system - The liner that comes with the bag should last for many years, but it's comforting to know that it can be replaced for $2.95 if it ever comes punctured or badly tainted. This feature has certainly been missing from numerous bota bags I've had to throw away after a short period of use.

The bags are very collapsible, and take up a minimum of space when empty or partially full, making them easy to pack in and out.

The outer covering of the bags is rugged construction - tough 400 denier packcloth. There are no zippers to break. These bags were clearly made to last many years.

The heavy inner liner resists abrasion and impact. Dependable o-ring seals are used wherever needed.

The bag's inner liquid-retaining liner appeared to be very durable. With my loaded backpack on, I jumped on the container, and it didn't leak a drop. It will withstand boiling or freezing temperatures.

The instruction sheet that comes with the bag points out that a brand new liner usually has a "new" plastic taste, similar to a brand new bicycle water bottle. I followed the directions for removing this taste and it disappeared. I added 2 oz. of vinegar to a quart of water and poured the solution into the bag. Then I expelled the air, tightened the cap, and let the solution soak for half an hour or more. Lastly, I poured out the solution and rinsed the bag thoroughly. The whole process took about an hour, and most of that time was spent in just letting the bag soak.

The cord which connects the cap to the bag will not tangle, unlike bota bag cords.

Upstream has three sizes of insulated bags available - the 2½ quart Waistbelt Thermos, the 2-quart Soft Thermos, and the 5-quart Soft Thermos, which is made to fit the Insulated Cushion. There are a few 2-quart and 5-quart non-insulated bags available too, though most people will probably prefer the insulated containers.

Showering attachments, extra hose sections, mouthpieces, and other accessories are available by contacting the manufacturer at this address: Upstream Products, 24991 Skyland Road, Los Gatos, CA 95030.

Would you like to see your product reviewed here? Send a sample to: Equipment Editor, care of N.P.T.J. Sorry, we cannot guarantee return of merchandise.

Photo by Harvey White

Our equipment editor taking the plunge...

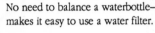

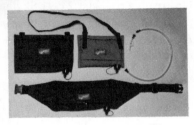

Mini-Planetarium Makes Stargazing Magic!

NightStar. A virtual library of star charts all rolled into one—with none of the distortion inherent in conventional sky maps. The secret? A star globe made of soft, flexible plastic, deflated and sealed into the shape of a bowl. At a roll of the fingertips, **NightStar's** flexible walls slide over a "horizon ring" (situated within the rim of the bowl) to duplicate the night sky exactly—*for any location on Earth!*

NightStar *Classic*

*The original **NightStar.***
Now with glow-in-the-dark stars!

8 inch **NightStar** dome (3 colors on blue).
Rigid steel internal horizon ring.
48 page activities handbook.
Snap-on time dial.
Latitude finding tool.
Planet finder overlay strips.
Red lens pocket light.
Full color storage box.

MODEL 2000RG

NightStar *Traveler*

The foldable planetarium that fits in your pocket!

8 inch **NightStar** dome (white on blue).
Flexible rubber internal ring.
Instruction booklet.
Clear plastic travel tube.

MODEL 3000LT

NightStar *Explorer*

School model—for classroom or home use.

8 inch **NightStar** dome (printed in white on blue).
Rigid steel internal ring.
48 page activities handbook.
Snap-on time dial.
Latitude finding tool.
Planet finder overlay strips.
Plain white storage box.

MODEL 2200RE

Pocket Light

Squeeze this versatile little light and a soft red glow brings **NightStar** alive! Or remove the red lens cap for a bright beam. For use with all **NightStar** models—or as a handy map or night light. *Very popular with children!*
4000FB: 4"x6" blister pack.
4000F: Less blister pack.

Learning & Teaching Astronomy with NightStar

Activities booklets using **NightStar** as a starting point for exploring 30 basic astronomical topics with children and adults new to astronomy.
Learning, Item 2305: 8-1/2"x11", 40 pages, 37 illustrations, 30 activities.
Teaching, Item 2306: Same as **Learning** *plus* guidelines for parents and teachers. 64 pages.

Point of Purchase Display

Item 3000D: Colorful space-saving display unit holds up to 6 *Travelers.*

Information or CA orders (408)462-1049 • Out of state orders (800)782-7122 • Fax (408)462-2496
Manufactured by The NightStar Company, 1334 Brommer St., Santa Cruz, California 95062, U.S.A.

Press On!
By General Chuck Yeager and Charles Leerhsen
Bantam Books $17.95 Nonfiction 256 pp.

"PRESS ON!: FURTHER ADVENTURES IN THE GOOD LIFE", A NEW VOLUMN OF MEMOIRS FROM CHUCK YEAGER

General Chuck Yeager, the World War II fighter ace who shot down a Messerschmitt jet with a prop-driven P-51 Mustang, and then went on to become the first person to fly faster than the speed of sound, is also the author of one of the most widely read non-fiction books of the decade. The critically acclaimed *Yeager: An Autobiography*, written with Leo Janos and published as a Bantam Hardcover in July 1985, sold over one million copies in hardcover alone and was a #1 bestseller for more than three months.

Now Chuck Yeager, the author, returns to relate more of his experiences as test pilot, outdoorsman, husband, father, and the focus of "this hero business" in *Press On! Further Adventures In The Good Life*.

"As a barefoot kid in bib overalls, I used to wander the West Virginia woods for countless hours, always wanting to see what was around the next bend, beyond a big boulder, over the next rise," Yeager writes in his new books opening paragraph. "I was just an incredibly curious kid with a vague notion that one of these days I'd discover some grand, new wonder, maybe a place that would be some kind of Shangri-la, where the trees and rocks and water formed a scene more beautiful than anyplace else on earth." That promised land, the Sierra Nevada Mountains, and the annual two-week trek across its most rigorous terrain he takes with his best friend and fellow World War II fighter pilot Bud Anderson, is one of the quintessential adventures in *Press On*! With several carefully chosen companions, Chuck and Bud climb to an altitude of nearly 14,000 feet, hiking some eighteen miles in a day with full packs to live off the land, fishing for golden trout which are later cooked over a campfire and eaton off old tin plates.

Their journey will never be construed as a yuppie-style day in the woods. Yeager personally checks the backpacks of all newcomers. "Man, you should hear the howls of protest when I pull out their favorite sweater or their backup pair of designer blue jeans. It's hard to convince some guys that they can get by with just one pair of jeans for two weeks, and one shirt, but there's just no room for extra weight." While the object of their trek is to have fun...and Yeager relates how they've had some outrageous times over the years...discipline and precision are the essence of what their trips are about these days, he says, with "the idea being to eliminate all things not strictly necessary to our well-being, and to keep risks to a minimum."

The Sierras adventures and similar trips to such exotic places as the wilds

310

of New Zealand are but the latest examples of a basic tenet in the Yeager philosophy that kept him in good stead in his combat and research flying: "I'm the type of person who is inclined to take a risk and go for it." The author wonders "what good does it do to stop in your tracks and start fretting? About all you can do when the going gets tough, is just keep going forward and press on as determinedly as you can."

General Yeager takes us back to his home town of Hamlin, West Virginia, one of the poorest regions in the country, to visit his mother and sister... and to examine his roots. As his wife Glennis notes, "rather than being impressed by all the attention he gets, he's amused, I think, that the world would want to celebrate and shower lucrative offers upon someone for a set of characteristics...resourcefulness, strength, peace of mind, and sometimes brutal honesty...that were so common among the poor anonymous folk of Hamlin." The General recalls those women and men like his father and grandfather whose influence on his life values was profound.

Through her firstperson recollections of their courtship, early life together, and post-military experiences, Glennis Yeager is a co-star of *Press On*! Another is Colonel Bud Anderson, his best friend of forty-six years. "Andy," the most successful fighter pilot in their World War II fighter squadron, is the man whom Chuck admits trying to model his own flying style after. Their mutual military backgrounds and extracurricular interests notwithstanding, Yeager believes that Andy is laid back, easygoing and sensible compared to him, and respects him for being so. In his first-person "voice", the Colonel offers his own perspective on his buddy's philosophy ("Chuck's not terribly interested in looking backward...") and his ability to handle danger ("He never took a chance where he didn't strongly believe he would come out all right. If he appeared reckless, it was a calculated controlled, knowledgeable recklessness").

The star of the story, General Yeager is especially forthright with his opinion of the various aspects of the lionization he's received of late. Of Tom Wolfe, who immortalized him in *The Right Stuff*, Yeager says, "A nice guy... but I've never understood a lot of what he was driving at. Once a few years ago, he sent me a bunch of his books to read but I've never got past the titles, they were so weird...I prefer Louis L'Amour any day." While Yeager enjoys his recognition, he neither takes it too seriously or lets it interfere with his doing what he enjoys doing or avoiding what he won't do. His heroes are men almost no one ever heard of: Grandpa Yeager, his Uncle Richard and his Dad. Without much in the way of worldly possessions, they were rich in self-confidence and peace of mind. Moreover, says the author, "they truly knew how to live. That's what it's all about."

311

WE SWAM THE GRAND CANYON:
The True Story of a Cheap Vacation that Got a Little Out of Hand
By Bill Beer

WE SWAM THE GRAND CANYON: The True Story of a Cheap Vacation That Got a Little Out of Hand - *Bill Beer*. Mountaineers, $15.95 ISBN 0-89886-151-9.

April 10, 1955: the water temperature was 51°F, and a fierce wind buffeted two men as they entered the Colorado River at Lees Ferry. The author and John Daggett had set out to swim the river through the Grand Canyon. At a time when fewer than 200 people had run the river in boats, this was daredeviltry—and illegal. Their equipment was primitive: Army-surplus rubber boxes to carry gear, thin rubber shirts, woollen long johns and swim fins; they also took a movie camera to record the adventure. Twenty-six days and 280 miles later, bruised and battered, they left the river at Pierce Ferry. Beer relives the miseries and exhilaration of that singular journey, a gripping story of endurance. In an afterword, he discusses other, legal trips through the Grand Canyon (he has swum the occasional rapid from a boat) and assesses the present state of the environment; he has high praise for the Park Service. This will appeal to readers who enjoy adventure.

SNOW-SHOEING

THIRD EDITION
By Gene Prater

Nothing appeals more to the cabin-feverish than the opportunity to enjoy the icy beauty of a winter landscape at a speed less than breakneck. For the winter hiker who seeks wilderness solitude, not ski-slope crowds, the only way to travel is on showshoes. The newly revised and updated third edition of *Snowshoeing*, by Gene Prater (The Mountaineers, Seattle) will put you on showshoes and into the freedom of the outdoors.

In this edition, the ancient activity of snowshoeing is brought up to date with Prater's explanations on everything from equipment to snowcamping; the beginner will literally take it step by step, from when he puts on his first pair of "beavertails" to his first snowshoe race. Detailed chapters on the snowshoe itself (covering the basic Yukon, Beavertail, Bearpaw and Western types), the bindings, appropriate clothing and equipment help the beginner to best outfit themselves for the type of snow they may encounter, the terrain they will be travelling and the weather conditions they should expect.

For the expert, Prater offers an entire chapter devoted to racing, and sections throughout the book are crowded with technical tips on how to make already familiar techniques easier; this is information which is helpful to those who work in the snow, as well as those who play. In this updated version, every element of the sport is considered from two angles--eastern snowshoeing versus western snowshoeing. The sometimes vast differences in terrain, weather, even types of snow between the two regions are discussed and dealt with. The book progresses from physical pre-conditioning to walking on snowshoes to traction devices and balancing aids, and includes chapters on snow conditions, routefinding, snow camping and snowshoe racing. Chapters on winter safety and injury and illness insure that once outdoors, the snowshoer enjoys a safe and satisfying experience. With its black-and-white photos, illustrations and practical, easy-to-follow advice, *Snowshoeing* facilitates the transition between winter couch potato and outdoor explorer.

About the Author: Gene Prater is a well-known authority on the subject of snowshoeing. A resident of Ellensburg, Washington, he has led snowshoeing seminars in New England for the Appalachian Mountain Club, and in the Rockies and the Pacific Northwest. A snowshoer since he was 12 years old, Prater has written extensively about showshoeing.

Books are available through most book and outdoor stores, or can be ordered directly from The Mountaineers: by phone with a VISA or Mastercard at 1-800-553-HIKE, or by mail with a check or credit card. All orders must be prepaid; no charge for shipping (4th class) and handling.

Mary Beth Hennessy (left) and Wendy Reynolds (right) issue wilderness permits and provide information to backcountry users in the wilderness permit station in Yosemite Valley.

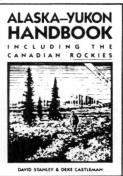
315

ACROSS THE OLYMPIC MOUNTAINS: THE PRESS EXPEDITION, 1889-90

In 1889, while Washington celebrated its statehood, another history-making event was underway--the first exploration into Washington's last frontier: the Olympic Mountains' interior. Sponsored by the *Seattle Press*, six men, four dogs and two mules embarked on a six-month journey during one of the most severe winters on record. Their struggle against a hostile, unknown environment is recounted by Robert L. Wood in *Across the Olympic Mountains: The Press Expedition, 1889-90* (The Mountaineers Books, Seattle).

Although Seattle in 1889 boasted 40,000 residents, the formidable mountain range to the west was still a "great unknown land like the interior of Africa." Then-Governor Elisha Ferry called for an expedition of discovery during an interview with a reporter from the *Seattle Press* (forerunner to the *Seattle Times*). The *Press* took up the call and in weeks rounded up six mountaineers to "unveil the mystery which wraps the land encircled by the snow capped Olympic range."

Called the Press Expedition, the group opted to brave the winter hazards by departing in December in Order to thwart the springtime plans of other parties. After building a boat that sunk twice in icy waters, losing a mule over a precipice and abandoning the other one, and constructing toboggans that collapsed before traversing half a mile, the men packed up 1,500 pounds of essentials on their backs and made the rest of the journey on foot. In less than a month, one member left the party and went back to civilization. The remaining five often subsisted on meals of spruce bark or soup made of flour and water. Although the distance they covered amounted to only 85 miles, the steep mountains and deep valleys hindered progress; they averaged less than one-half mile per day on a journey taking six months. Gaunt and exhausted, the Press Expedition reached the southern side of the Peninsula in May 1890, made their way down to Aberdeen, and telegraphed their success to the world.

Author Robert Wood interweaves journal entries, photos and newspaper accounts of the expedition with his own detailed knowledge of the Olympics. A long-time favorite of outdoor and mountain leterature collectors, the classic has been brought back into print in response to increasing numbers of requests and in time to coincide with Washington's Centennial celebration.

About the author: Robert Wood, nicknamed "Old Grizz," has climbed, hiked and cross-country skied the Olympic Mountain region extensively. A Seattle resident and past editor of Seattle Mountaineers bulletins, Wood is an expert on the exploration history of the Olympic Mountains. He has written **Men, Mules & Mountains: Lieutenant O'Neil's Olympic Expeditions, Olympic**

Mountains Trail Guide, and has co-authored *Monte Cristo* (all published by The Mountaineers).

Books are available through most book and outdoor stores, or can be ordered directly from The Mountaineers: by phone with a VISA or Mastercard at 1-800-553-HIKE, or by mail with a check or credit card. All orders must be prepaid; no charge for shipping (4th class) and handling.

In the days before television

Do Something To Save The Planet

Use this card

For some people, saving the planet is a life-long commitment. But it takes more than idealism to make a difference. It also takes money.

That's why Working Assets is proud to offer you the world's first environmentally responsible credit card. One that lets you work to save our endangered planet... just by doing what you already do.

Become a cardholder and we'll automatically contribute $2 to time-tested organizations like Greenpeace, the Environmental Defense Fund and Rainforest Action Network.

Then, every time you use your card, we'll contribute another five cents. *All at no cost to you.*

Which means that every day you and thousands of other concerned cardholders will be helping to save the planet.

Call 800-52-APPLY

Working Assets Tools for Practical Idealists™

WHY USE WORKING ASSETS SERVICES?

Because they turn everyday activities into acts of generosity. Each time you use a Working Assets tool to shop, fly or call long-distance, money flows to non-profit groups... *at no cost to you!* Here's how:

What You Do	Donation
Use Working Assets VISA or MasterCard	5¢ per purchase
Use Working Assets Long Distance Service	1% of your net long-distance charges
Use Working Assets Travel Service	2% of your travel purchases

Then, once a year, you vote on how to allocate the funds. Since 1986, Working Assets members have generated over $350,000 in donations.

WHY WE DO THIS

Every day of the year, Americans use credit cards, make long-distance calls and travel. We thought, if just a small fraction of these charges could be diverted to social and environmental uses (at no cost to the user), the impact would be tremendous. And that is precisely what Working Assets does.

WHERE THE MONEY GOES

Working Assets supports organizations working for peace, human rights and the environment. Recipients include Greenpeace, Environmental Defense Fund, Trust for Public Land, Amnesty International, Oxfam America and more.

Call 800-52-APPLY

Working Assets Tools for Practical Idealists™

320

PACIFIC CREST OUTWARD BOUND SCHOOL:
One Way to Experience the Wilderness

Many people have heard of Outward Bound but can't quite pinpoint what it actually is or does, perhaps because it encompasses many things. Outward Bound is one way of experiencing the wilderness in our country.

Outward Bound is the oldest and largest wilderness-based adventure education organization in the world. It is a non-profit school that teaches people more about themselves through challenging activities in a wilderness setting. The experiences allow the students to gain greater self confidence and self esteem, learn the importance of teamwork, test their leadership skills, and push past some pre-conceived personal limits.

As one student said "We are better than we know, perhaps if we are made to see that, for the rest of our lives we will be unable to settle for less."

The Pacific Crest Outward Bound School, founded in 1966, has taught over 24,000 students in the mountains, rivers, and deserts of Washington, Oregon and California. Course lengths range from 4-22 days and anyone 14 and older can participate.

The majority of the courses are open enrollment, but the School does offer courses designed for specific age groups or restricted to a certain type of student. Some examples are: high school leadership (15-17), adults over 50, youth-at-risk, women over 30, families and corporate executives.

People of all ages, backgrounds and skill level enroll in Pacific Crest Outward Bound courses. Many of them are new to outdoor activities and most are in average physical condition.

Coarse Components

All Pacific Crest courses include a number of distinct phases:

- Training phase - students learn the basics of the course activities; first-aid, campcraft, hydrology or glacier travel. Rockclimbing and rappelling are usually included.

- Expedition Phase - students, building on knowledge gained during the training phase, take on more responsibility for their activities and group actions.

- Solo Phase - a time for reflection and introspection. Students spend time alone in a designated area. Daily safety checks are made by staff.

- Final expedition - students undertake a longer expedition, without direct supervision from the staff.

- Fitness run - a physical activity designed to allow a student to test himself at his/her own pace.

Pacific Crest Outward Bound School is coming up on its twenty-fifth year of service to the public, and recently received a letter from a woman that participated on one of the first courses offered by the school.

"Dear Pacific Crest Outward Bound School,

As an alumni I can say that my course remains, more than 20 years later, the most meaningful personal experience I've had. Although Outward Bound seems to be a physical experience, it is more cerebral and spiritual than anything else. As a revelation-giver, it is superb. In every way I learned I was much more capable than I thought. And in the painful moments of facing and admitting my actual limitations I learned to accept them and get around anyway.

How is it I hiked and climbed, slept and shared many weeks with strangers, mastered mountains and glaciers, diminished my human importance in wind and weather of ageless woods, fields and God-made monoliths at the age of 21 and found myself totally reinforced so many years later? How could this experience affect me so wholly and thoroughly? How does it relate? Because I learned all about me and I use it every day to get up life's mountains and to sleep in life's peaceful fields. Thank you."

Wendy Shawn

JOIN OUR ROCK GROUP.

Rappelling off a 60-foot cliff is a tremendous confidence builder. Outward Bound is involved in outdoor programs that teach wilderness skills that can help you survive urban life. You are led by professional, safety-aware instructors who help you build inner strength to tackle new experiences and be successful. You'll captain a river raft through white water, hike the backwoods trails and make camp a hundred miles from any stress and strain. For our free 24-page catalog, write PACIFIC CREST OUTWARD BOUND SCHOOL, 0110 S.W. Bancroft Street, Portland, OR 97201.

TOLL-FREE NUMBER
1-800-547-3312 or
1-503-243-1993

Art Director Brian Webb by Lower Yosemite Falls

HE COMES FROM A BROKEN HOME.

© Kevin Schafer

Every day 140,000 acres of tropical forest are axed, burned, or clear cut. The result: this margay — and thousands of other species that call these forests home — are teetering on the brink of extinction.

Tropical forests help regulate the Earth's climate. And they shelter ⅔ of all Earth's species — unique life forms that give us priceless medical, industrial, and agricultural benefits.

The Nature Conservancy works creatively with partners throughout Latin America to safeguard tropical habitats. But we need your help, so join us. Write The Nature Conservancy, Latin America Program, Box CD0031, 1815 N. Lynn Street, Arlington, VA 22209. Or call 1-800-628-6860.

It's a question of proper housekeeping in the only home we've got.

Conservation Through Private Action

HELPING OUT IN THE OUTDOORS
By American Hiking Society

NATIONWIDE

AMERICAN HIKING SOCIETY VOLUNTEER VACATIONS PROGRAM

The American Hiking Society sends crews each summer, winter, and spring to work in national parks and forests, wilderness areas, and state parks. Armed with pick and shovels, the crews build new trails, maintain existing trails, and help with a variety of projects designed to make these areas safe, attractive, and accessible. The work is hard and the rewards are great. AHS Volunteer Vacation crews are made up of people 16 and older who are in good physical condition and desire to combine an exciting and fun vacation with hard work to preserve the nation's wilderness resources. Any travel and food expenses incurred are tax deductible, as is the $30 registration fee. Food, training, tools, and supervision are provided by the cosponsoring government agency. Watch for AHS Volunteer Vacation projects throughout this directory. For information and a 1989 schedule, send a long self addressed, stamped envelope to:

Contact: Kay Beebe, Director
AHS Volunteer Vacations
P.O. Box 86
North Scituate, MA 02060

APPALACHIAN MOUNTAIN CLUB

The AMC, the nation's oldest (1876) recreation/conservation organization, sponsors a smorgasbord of weekend, weekly, and 10-12 day public service projects. For weekends join an AMC Chapter project in the Northeast (D.C. to Maine).

Adopt-A-Trail, or participate in Trail Days. Alternatively, participate in one of 3 unique weekly Volunteer Crew Base Camps in NH, MA, or NY. Or during July and August pitch in on 10-12 day backcountry service projects in Alaska, Maine, Montana, and Wyoming. Leaders, training, tools, some equipment, and room and board are provided in many cases. The projects are open to individuals, families, and groups. Our brochure gives details on all opportunities. Help us give something back to the backcountry.

Contact: Volunteer Coordinator
AMC Trails Program Box 298H
Gorham, NH 03581 Phone 603/466-2721

THE STUDENT CONSERVATION ASSOCIATION

The Student Conservation Association offers positions nationwide (including Alaska & Hawaii) year round. Job descriptions vary and are based upon personal interests (career, geographic, academic, etc.). RESOURCE ASSISTANTS to assist professionals in Resource Management projects. Specific positions available in archaeology, geology, wildlife management, forestry, backcountry patrol, visitor assistance, and many others. Qualifications vary according to position; some may require specific academic training, others require outdoor skills and knowledge. Benefits include round trip travel, free housing, a weekly stipend to cover food expenses, and a uniform allowance.

Contact: Dean S. Klein
Student Conservation Assoc.
P.O. Box 550
Charlestown, NH 03603 Phone: 603/626-5741

SIERRA CLUB SERVICE OUTINGS

Combine the enjoyment of a backcountry outing with the satisfaction that comes from doing something positive for the environment. People on service outings perform outdoor work of all kinds. It's not all work—half your time in the field is free to enjoy the outdoors. The Sierra Club coordinates service trips throughout the U.S., with an occasional foreign outing. You must be a member to participate.

Contact: Outing Department
Sierra Club
730 Polk St.
San Francisco, CA 94109 Phone: 415/776-2211

U.S. GEOLOGICAL SURVEY VOLUNTEER PROGRAM

An earth-science oriented research institute with major centers near Washington, Denver, and San Francisco, as well as smaller centers mainly in the west. Research and volunteer work may be indoors (labs, libraries, computers, drafting) or outdoors (sampling, recording, mapping). Field work requires

331

active volunteers, and some geologic knowledge is always an asset. Pay is not available, but in some cases expenses for field work may be available. Geologists study ore deposits, faults and earthquake problems, environmental problems, landslides, fossils, and earth history. Volunteers may be students (16) years or older), foreign, or underemployed, or retired. We regret we are unable to help with travel expenses.

Contact either: Mary Orzech, U.S. Geological Survey
MS-912, National Center
12202 Sunrise Valley Dr.
Reston, VA 22092 Phone 703/648-6631

Or Contact: Harold Drewes
U.S. Geological Survey MS-905
Federal Center
Denver, CO 80225 Phone 303/236-5647

US FISH AND WILDLIFE SERVICE

Year-round opportunities are available throughout the U.S. on national wildlife refuges, national fish hatcheries, wildlife and fishery research facilities, and other Fish and Wildlife Service offices. Volunteer work is varied, challenging, and rewarding. It may include WILDLIFE SURVEYS, VISITOR INFORMATION SERVICE, TRAIL MAINTENANCE, PHOTOGRAPHY, CLERICAL AND MAINTENANCE WORK, BIOLOGICAL RESEARCH, and more. For complete details, contact the office nearest you:

(AZ, NM, OK, TX)

Contact: Volunteer Coordinator
U.S. Fish and Wildlife Service
P.O. Box 1306
Albuquerque, NM 87103

(CA, ID, HI, NV, OR, WA)

Contact: Volunteer Coordinator
U.S. Fish and Wildlife Service
500 N.E. Multnomah St.
Portland, OR 97232

(AL, AR, FL, GA, KY, LA, MS, NC, SC, TN, PR)

Contact: Volunteer Coordinator
U.S. Fish and Wildlife
Richard B. Russell, Federal Bldg.
75 Spring St. S.W.
Atlanta, GA 30303

(ALASKA)

Contact: Volunteer Coordinator
U.S. Fish and Wildlife Service
1011 E. Tudor Rd.
Anchorage, AK 99503

(CO, KS, MT, NE, ND, SD, UT, WY)

Contact: Volunteer Coordinator
U.S. Fish and Wildlife
Service Denver Federal Ctr.
Box 25486
Denver, CO 80225

(CT, DE, MA, MD, ME, NH, NJ, NY, PA, RI, VT, VA, WV)

Contact: Volunteer Coordinator
U.S. Fish and Wildlife Service
One Gateway Center No Sign 700
Newton Corner, MA 02158

(IA, IL, IN, MI, MN, MO, OH, WI)

Contact: Volunteer Coordinator
U.S. Fish and Wildlife Service
Federal Bldg., Fort Snelling
Twin Cities, MN 55111

BUREAU OF LAND MANAGEMENT

Volunteer work opportunities on the public lands administered by the BLM ARE ALMOST AS DIVERSE AS THE LANDS AND RESOURCES WE MANAGE IN THE WESTERN STATES. Some examples include: WILDLIFE: conduct wildlife surveys to determine numbers and habitats of various animals; install watering devices to enhance habitats. RECREATION: Assist rangers on wild and scenic rivers; construct picnic tables or build fire pits; develop recreational trails and campgrounds. FORESTRY: Thin seedling patches and plant sapling stands. Volunteers are also needed in such programs as computer science, lands and minerals, historic and cultural resources, cadastral survey, and in various office, research, and support jobs. Benefits vary with the position, and may include housing and reimbursement for out-of-pocket expenses. All volunteers receive training and are covered for work injury and tort claim liability. For information refer to the district or resource listed for specific areas in this directory or contact the volunteer coordinator in the state office listed below.

ALASKA

Contact: BLM State Office
701 C St. (Box 13)
Anchorage, AK 99513 Phone: 907/271-5555

ARIZONA

Contact: BLM State Office
3703 N. 7th St. (P.O. Box 16563)
Phoenix, AZ 85011 Phone: 602/241-5504

CALIFORNIA

Contact: BLM State Office
2800 Cottage Way (P.O. Box 1449)
Sacramento, CA 95825 Phone: 916/978-4746

COLORADO

Contact: BLM State Office
2850 Youngfield Street
Denver, CO 80215 Phone: 303/236-1700

EASTERN STATES

Contact: BLM State Office
350 S. Pickett Street
Alexandria, VA 22304 Phone: 703/274-0180

IDAHO

Contact: BLM State Office
3380 Americana Terrace

Boise, ID 83706 Phone: 208/334-1771

MONTANA

Contact: BLM State Office
222 N. 32nd Street (P.O. Box 36800)
Billings, MT 59107 Phone: 406/657-6461

NEVADA

Contact: BLM State Office
300 Booth St. (P.O. Box 12000)
Reno, NV 89520 Phone: 702/784-5451

NEW MEXICO

Contact: Joseph M. Montoya
BLM State Office
P.O. Box 1449
Santa Fe, NM 87501 Phone: 505/988-6316

OREGON

Contact: BLM State Office
825 N.E. Multnomah St. (P.O. Box 2965)
Portland, OR 97208 Phone: 503/231-6277

UTAH

Contact: BLM State Office
324 S. State Street
Salt Lake City, UT 84111
Phone: 801/524-3146

WYOMING

Contact: BLM State Office
2515 Warren Ave. (P.O. Box 1828)
Cheyenne, WY 82003 Phone: 307/772-2111

WESTERN STATES

U.S. FOREST SERVICE INTERMOUNTAIN REGION AND RESEARCH STATION

We have many volunteer opportunities within the states of Idaho, Montana, Nevada, Utah, Wyoming, and a small portion of eastern California. Details on these volunteer work opportunities, along with information concerning free housing, subsistence, and the person to contact for more information are all located in our Volunteer Opportunities Directory.

The directory covers 44 different types of work. Some examples are: ARCHAEOLOGY, CAMPGROUND HOST, FIRE LOOKOUT, GROUP VOLUNTEER OPPORTUNITIES, HYDROLOGY, MINERALS, OFFICE WORK, TIMBER MANAGEMENT, VISITOR CENTER, WILDERNESS RANGER, WILDLIFE, WRITER, etc. Mention HELPING OUT IN THE OUTDOORS when you write or call and we will include a free map of the Intermountain Region with your copy of the directory.

Contact: Regional Volunteer Coordinator
USDA FOREST SERVICE
324 25th St.
Ogden, UT 84401 Phone: 801/625-5175

EASTERN STATES

APPLACHIAN TRAIL CONFERENCE

The 2100-mile long Appalachian Trail is one of the longest marked footpaths in the world, winding along the high ridges and peaks of the Appalachian Mountains from Maine to Georgia. Dedicated volunteers initiated, constructed, and have maintained the trail for over 60 years. The Appalachian Trail Conference (ATC) is a nonprofit organization responsible for the protection and management of the trail. The ATC represents over 20,000 members and 60 volunteer clubs. Members spend many thousands of hours each year working on the trail to keep it in good condition for the hiking public, and to protect the resources from damage. Projects in 1989 will include work in national forests and parks, and park trail lands along the length of the AT. We will design and build new trail, do dock work, move logs, build shelters, and correct erosion problems during our work period from June 2 to October 31. Anyone 18 or older in good physical condition is welcome.

Contact: ATC Crew Information
P.O. Box 807
Harpers Ferry, WV 25425 Phone: 304/535-6331

PACIFIC NORTHWEST

PACIFIC NORTHWEST NATIONAL PARKS & FORESTS ASSOCIATION

Serving a vast area of the Northwest, the association assists the Park Service, Forest Service, and BLM in their educational and interpretive missions. We provide books and other materials to 82 small bookstores located throughout the public land areas we serve. Together, we help the growing numbers of visitors to know, enjoy, and respect America's outdoors.

VOLUNTEERS and SALESPEOPLE are needed year-round to help sell and maintain inventory in our larger outlets. In the Seattle headquarters, we use volunteers for all types of office work including EDITING, DESIGN LAYOUT, and LIBRARY assistance. Requirements: 18 years or older, high school education, physically able to handle the job. Benefits include training, supervision, and equipment.

Contact: Mrs. Mary Ellen Rutter, Executive Director
Pacific NW National Parks & Forests Assoc.
83 S. King St. Suite 212
Seattle, WA 98104 Phone: 206/442-7958

The State of Yosemite

by Garrett De Bell

Twenty years ago Robert Cahn, a good friend of mine and of the National Parks, wrote a prize winning series for the Christian Science Monitor. This series *"Will Success Spoil the National Parks?"* helped draw attention to environmental and social problems theatening our parks.

During the next controversial decade Yosemite National Park became the focus of an unprecedented planning effort to address these concerns and fears of possible overdevelopment. This was followed by years of action by the National Park Service; Congress; The Yosemite Park and Curry Company, the Park's concessioner; and environmental organizations. As an environmental consultant to the Curry Company for the last fifteen years, I have been privileged to work on a wide range of projects to help protect Yosemite. By my assessment Yosemite today is in the best shape in a very long time, and more importantly the trend toward improvement continues steadily. Unfortunately the media chooses to focus on the problems that remain, often exaggerates these, and ignores the improvements that have been made. This makes it very hard for those concerned about Yosemite to get accurate information.

Here is a summary of some of the major improvements:

Endangered species have returned. The Peregrine Falcon has returned and has nested successfully in both Yosemite Valley and Hetch Hetchy. The Bighorn Sheep has been reintroduced and is reestablishing itself.

Many buildings have been removed. Several structures have been removed. These include: Big Trees Lodge, a small hotel in the Mariposa Grove of Giant Sequoias; all of the employee houses between the old Village site and Curry Village. In a cooperative effort, the National Park Service, Curry Company, Yosemite Association, and the U.S. Army dismantled and removed an abandoned sewer plant, allowing approximately 3 acres of Yosemite Valley to revert to nature.

Some support operations have been relocated outside Yosemite. A hotel reservation center, purchasing department, freightlining operation and some of the hotel and store warehousing operations were relocated from Yosemite Valley to Fresno. An industrial laundry serving the hotels and restaurants was removed from Yosemite Valley.

Wildlife protection has improved. The most dramatic change in Yosemite's wildlife has been due to the NPS Bear Management Program through which bears have been denied access to garbage and human food. This helped them to return to their natural foraging habits.

The greater Yosemite environment is protected. Through Congressional action, supported by the Park Service, environmental groups, and the Curry Company, most

338

of Yosemite is now protected as Wilderness; the two rivers in the park, the Tuolumne and the Merced, are both protected in the Wild and Scenic Rivers System, and Mono Lake and the eastern boundary of Yosemite are protected as a National Forest Scenic Area.

Global environmental impacts addressed. Curry Company has pursued an affirmative environmental program to lessen environmental impacts. Perhaps most important have been the efforts to reduce the impacts of chlorofluorocarbons on the atmosphere, because of their harmful effect on the ozone layer and their contribution to the greenhouse effect. Chlorofluorocarbon aerosols were removed from Yosemite's stores. Last year polystyrene foam products were phased out of Curry Company stores and restaurants. Most recently a system has been installed to recycle freon from automotive air conditioning systems as an alternative to dumping the freon into our atmosphere.

Recycling of solid wastes. Yosemite's recycling program handles all common materials such as aluminum, cardboard, glass, and paper. In addition, some exotic materials are recycled such as automotive antifreeze and the freon mentioned above. All recycling saves resources, saves energy, reduces the use of fossil fuels and thus [reduces] the greenhouse effect.

Restoring the backcountry. Through cooperative efforts that involved the Park Service, Curry Company, The Sierra Club, and Yosemite Association, much of the previous impact has been eliminated. Twenty-five sites impacted by major debris such as plane wrecks and by abandoned equipment have been cleaned up.

Automobile congestion reduced. Automobile congestion is one of the most popular complaints about Yosemite. While it is still possible to get pictures of crowded parking lots and streets, much has been done. A free shuttle system lets people get around the developed area of Yosemite Valley without the need for cars. Shuttles also service the Mariposa Grove of Big Trees and Badger Pass. A campground reservation system allows people to reserve a site and avoid the drive to Yosemite in the futile search for a non-reserved campsite. Bike paths now allow safe biking in Yosemite Valley without having to use roads. A Traffic Management plan turns day visitors away on the very few days when the roads and parking in the east end of Yosemite Valley are full.

More to do? Of course more needs to be done to protect Yosemite. Air quality needs to be improved, automobile congestion further reduced, remaining impacted areas restored, and global issues solved.

The Yosemite Park and Curry Company Environmental Program has been recognized by the "National Take Pride in America Award". The award was presented to Yosemite Park and Curry Company at a White House ceremony presided over by President Bush in July of 1989. Yosemite Park and Curry Company President Ed Hardy, and Environmental Consultant, Garrett De Bell, journeyed to The White House to accept the award. The award recognized the comprehensive environmental program as a leader in the nation. Only ten other companies were given the award and there were no other winners from the State of California.

Spend
The Summer At
Sea World.

Spend your summer in paradise at the world's largest oceanarium. Sea World of California, located in San Diego, will be hiring hundreds of students for summer jobs. Explore the opportunities available in Merchandise, Operations, Food Services or Entertainment.

To receive an application, please write to: Ruth Munoz, Sea World of California, 1720 South Shores Road, San Diego, CA 92109. Or call (619)226-3848.

Sorry, but we are unable to provide housing.

EOE M/F/H/V

Sea World.

© 1990 Sea World, Inc.

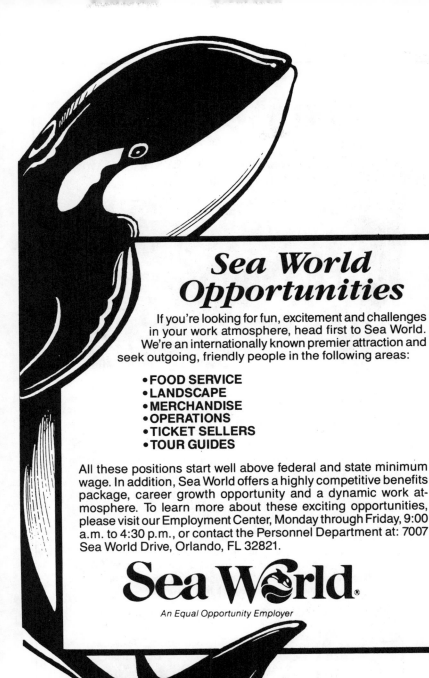

Live and Work in California's Sierra Mountains

Royal Gorge
Cross Country Ski Resort

BOREAL

SODA SPRINGS

Ski Area Jobs Available on Donner Summit

Lift Operators	*Food Service*
Ski Rental Shop	*Ticket Sellers*
Hospitality	*Ski School*
Ski Patrol	*Maintenance*

Location

Donner Summit is located in California's beautiful Sierra Nevada mountains.

Lake Tahoe: 25 miles
Reno: 45 miles
Sacramento: 85 miles
San Francisco: 175 miles

Employee Benefits

▶ Free skiing at 5 resorts; alpine, snowboarding and cross-country.

▶ Employee discounts on skiing at more than 20 other resorts.

▶ Employee discounts on meals, rental equipment and lessons.

▶ Free skiing for dependents.

COMPETITIVE WAGES

CALL OR WRITE FOR AN EMPLOYMENT APPLICATION

Donner Ski Ranch
P.O. Box 66
Norden, CA. 95724
(916) 426-3635

Royal Gorge
P.O. Box 1100
Soda Srings, CA 95728
(916) 426-3871

Boreal/Soda Springs
P.O. Box 39
Truckee, CA 95734
(916) 426-3666

345

346

Prescott College: The Southwest Is Our Classroom

High in the forested mountains of central Arizona, Prescott College has created an innovative approach to higher education. This independent four-year college offers small classes, extensive field work, a close community atmosphere, an intimate campus, and, most significantly, the opportunity for students to design their own educational path.

"By the time most people find their way to Prescott College, they have done a lot of searching..." It is a unique college which embraces a pioneering educational philosophy including the idea that learning is a lifelong, continuing process. At Prescott College, students gain self direction, insight, and creativity.

Education at Prescott College is as much an adventure of the spirit as it is a physical and mental engagement with the world. Educational journeys take students to remote parts of the Grand Canyon, the Sea of Cortez and to many other parts of the world. Exploration takes place, also, within individuals, and in the broader world of thoughts, knowledge and learning. The attempt to blend direct experience with academic education is best seen as an effort to reintegrate life and learning. When students can learn as honestly and purposefully as they walk and eat and sleep, Prescott College will have accomplished its mission.

Prescott College's home, Prescott, Arizona, is nestled in the Bradshaw Mountains. It has been described by *Arizona Highways* as "Everybody's Hometown" and is known for its friendly atmosphere and small town charm. The community has a vital, growing spirit which strives to balance the needs of a high quality, environmentally conscious lifestyle with an expanding economy.

Founded in 1966, Prescott College's seeds lie in the resolutions of the Ford Foundation's Symposium to design an innovative and effective college. The first premise of the symposium was that disciplines within the liberal arts and sciences should be integrated. Colleges should be interdisciplinary as well as multidisciplinary. Students should become synthesizers of many realms of knowledge rather than specialists in specific areas. It was time for the liberal arts to look at life through the eyes of the sciences and the sciences to look at life through the eyes of liberal arts.

Second, the school should continue to be a pioneer in initiating innovative academic programs. Prescott College would not hesitate to launch unusual strategies in order to best further it's students educational interests.

Almost a quarter of a century later, Prescott College has retained the same premises under which it began, but has evolved. Three basic elements have emerged as essential focuses. The education is largely experiential, recognizing that students often learn as much by doing as by listening and reading; there is a lower than normal student faculty ratio, ten to one; and students design their own individual courses of study,

347

aiding them in the process of "learning to learn."

Instruction at Prescott College includes faculty participation with students through real experience in internships, reasearch in the wilderness, and field studies, as well as in classrooms. Prescott College is small; it has an enrollment of about 200 students annually. Attempts are made to offer all courses necessary and students are encouraged to take as independent studies any courses which are not offered directly. Independent studies are mentored by a faculty member or a dean approved community mentor.

At Prescott College, each course is unique, with the regional boundaries selected to match each student's special interests and field of study. Within hours of Prescott are the varied landscapes of Arizona, the Mountains of Colorado, the Pueblos of New Mexico, the Sea of Cortez, the Pacific Ocean, Mexico and the Grand Canyon.

Prescott College offers the Bachelor of Arts Degree in the following areas: Southwest Studies, Environmental Studies, Human Development, Humanities, and Outdoor Action. Bachelor of Arts Degrees are also available in other areas individually designed by students and faculty.

Education at Prescott College is as much an adventure of the spirit as it is a physical and mental engagement with the world. Students gain self direction, insight and creativity through experiences within themselves as well as within the larger macrocosm of the world.

For more information, please contact: Derk Janssen, Director of Admissions, 220 Grove Avenue, Prescott, AZ 86301.

Want To Learn More?

by Don Albrecht

Have you ever desired a deeper understanding of the philosophical meanings of wilderness? Have you ever wished to be able to identify plants or animals, or to know their niche in the ecosystem? Have you ever wanted more training in how to handle yourself — and others — in almost any outdoor situation?

If so, then there is a place where you can go to learn about these things, and many more facts, skills, philosophies, interpretations, and angles than you thought imaginable. It's a small college situated about a mile from the shores of Lake Superior at the top edge of Wisconsin. Nearby are the Apostle Islands (protected since 1970 by the U.S. National Park Service; Apostle Islands National Lakeshore), several national forests, dozens of state and county lands, streams and abundant natural resources. It is a private, liberal arts and environmental college named after the part of the world where it was established in 1892 — Northland, a liberal arts/environmental college, in Ashland, Wisconsin.

For the past 18 years, Northland has paid particular attention to its environmental focus. It was in 1971 that Northland began its Environmental Studies and Outdoor Education programs. Both majors emphasize Northland's location.

Not far from the campus in Ashland, Wisconsin, is the Apostle Islands National Lakeshore where 21 of the 22 islands are protected by the National Park Service. These islands include a wide range of wildlife and vegetation and are where activities such as camping, hiking, sea kayaking, skiing, and learning abound. Five of the islands have lighthouses. And in addition to being accessible for recreation, the islands offer a place where students can gain invaluable on-site experience. Northland College and the Apostle Islands National Lakeshore cooperate on internship programs open to qualified students.

Don Albrecht

352

Also nearby are two large national forests; the Chequamegon (800,000 acres) and the Nicolet National Forest (655,000 acres). These and other federal and state lands are administered by agencies that have similar cooperative programs, allowing Northland students to gain experience and training. Often, there have been cases where a student would attend a course, such as Ecosystem Interpretation in Earth Science in the morning, and then be working — for pay or for credit — in a forestry lab in the afternoon.

Northland's Environmental Studies curriculum is designed to do two things: to offer the development of skills in a particular field of study and to develop an appreciation for the breadth of everything that gives form to our environment. Two divisions are open for in-depth study: Biophysical and Sociopolitical. The former is designed to make graduates problem-solvers, especially within the realm of the natural sciences, but also with broader understandings of cultural perceptions about environmental relationships. The Sociopolitical emphasis concentrates more on the social sciences as they relate to problem-solving.

The college's Outdoor Education program uses direct experience to expand and enhance environmental principles. Students begin by taking a core of courses aimed at instilling such basic concepts as biology, geology, wilderness emergency care, ecology, teaching techniques and group dynamics, among others. The core for all students also includes some basic liberal arts course work, such as communication, natural and cultural history, English and fine arts.

Then, students of Outdoor Education can elect to further specialize in several specific areas. These include: Natural History, Special Populations (graduates work in social work, therapeutic recreation for disabled, delinquent youth, or emotionally disturbed people, for example), Recreation and Leisure Services, Native American Studies, Teacher Education, Writing, or any of Northland's other 19 major fields of study. This opens up a whole range of job possibilities given the individual's interests, skills, and talents.

Graduates of Northland's Environmental Studies or Outdoor Education programs have gone on to become environmental monitoring consultants, naturalists, wilderness instructors, park rangers, biological technicians, fisheries biologists, foresters, youth rehabilitation counselors, historic site managers, or any of dozens of other examples.

Both programs offer many opportunities for organized field study experiences, both domestic and foreign. Examples of past expeditions include journeys on the Athabasca and Churchill Rivers in Canada, the Boundary Waters Canoe Area of Minnesota, Michigan's Porcupine Mountains or the Sylvania Tract. Northland's four-week spring session allows extended trips to such places as the Western Rocky Mountains, the Southwestern United States, and the Black Hills of South Dakota. New locations around the globe are being considered as future sites. Under consideration are such locations as the rivers of Mexico, the forests of Costa Rica,

353

and the active volcanoes of Hawaii.

International studies have allowed Northland students to test wilderness skills in Canada, study biology, rain forest ecology, ornithology, and Mayan culture in Mexico, and mammalogy in East Africa. Foreign study tours with a cultural emphasis have traveled to Greece, England, Japan, and the Soviet Union.

There are many other academic and social spinoffs from these programs and Northland's location in the North Country of the upper Great Lakes region. One is the Sigurd Olson Environmental Institute, an outreach arm of the College established to enhance public understanding of environmental issues facing the region. For more details, write the college's Admission Office for a brochure detailing the Environmental Studies and Outdoor Education programs, and other information about financial aid, and the other academic programs. The address is: Northland College, 108 Wakefield Hall, Ashland, Wisconsin 54806.

Brett Parkhurst

356

Nature Can Be A Healing Environment For Campers

Chopping firewood, cooking meals over an open fire, and taking a canoe trip — these are just some of the activities that campers do at Eckerd Wilderness camps. Sounds like fun, right? But there's more to it than originally meets the eye. These camps are part of the Eckerd Wilderness Education System, a year-round, residential therapy program set in a nuturing environment for emotionally troubled youth. They are designed to provide an alternative to institutionalization for kids with behavioral problems, such as persistent running away from home, difficulty in forming close relationships with others, habitual truancy, or poor self-esteem.

The Eckerd Wildnerness Educational System is one of the programs provided by Eckerd Family Youth Alternatives, Inc. (EFYA). Since 1968 when Jack and Ruth Eckerd founded the first camp in Brooksville, FL over 6,500 young men and women have been served. The Eckerds built the camps because they realized there are plenty of places to lock up a kid, but not enough places to send troubled youth who need to live away from their homes while receiving additional guidance. Part of the Eckerd philosophy stems from the belief in the healing power of nature. By taking troubled kids off the streets and putting them into the woods they are in a better environment to be healed.

Each camp is designed to serve 50 - 60 youth at risk between the ages of 10 and 17. The youth live in small groups of ten campers and two counselor/teachers. The counselors, known as chiefs, are responsible for the progress and welfare of each camper in the group. They live with the group in a wilderness campsite 24 hours a day, 7 days a week, providing a positive adult role model.

Campers live without electricity, phones, radios or in-between-meal snacks. But they also live without bars, locks or walls. Each campsite has a variety of sleeping, cooking, library and tool tents.

Group members work together to develop "action-oriented" plans that involve constructing their own shelter, cutting wood for camp fires and cooking, creating their own recreation and meal plans, and taking extended trips. The learning process is built around an "experienced-based" educational curriculum.

Problem-solving sessions are commonplace and are the backbone of therapy. When a kid has a conflict it takes priority over everything else. Before the group proceeds to the next activity they stop to discuss and solve the problem.

The intent of the program among the campers is to develop positive changes in attitude, self-image and understanding of others, as well as to increase the individual's sense of responsibility.

EFYA has taken the successes of the camping program and expanded in new directions, while still maintaining their stated mission: to provide quality alternative

programs to children, youth and young adults. They currently operate programs in 7 states - Florida, New Hampshire, Maryland, North Carolina, Rhode Island, Tennessee and Vermont. The three other programs are Eckerd Youth Development Center (EYDC), which serves Florida's adjudicated male delinquents; the Eckerd Youth Challenge Program (EYCP), serving adjudicated males in a non-secure residential setting; and the Florida Conservation Corps (FCC), a work/study program for underemployed/unemployed youth between the ages of 18 - 20. The FCC works toward improving individual capabilities while preserving the natural environment.

For more information on employment opportunities as a camp counselor or any of the other EFYA programs contact:

Eckerd Family Youth Alternatives
Personnel Office
P.O. Box 7450
Clearwater, FL 33518
Phone: (800) 554-4357 or (813) 461-2990

ENVIRONMENTAL JOBS!

Executive through entry level, seasonal and internships!

JOB-SCAN has it all!

ARE YOU LOOKING FOR A NATURAL RESOURCE JOB...

☆ Each month **JOB-SCAN** offers over 36 pages of environmental and natural resource opportunities from federal agencies and conservation organizations from coast to coast. Fisheries Biologist, Park Ranger, Wildlife Rehabilitator, Preserve Worker to name a few. Articles written with both the **CAREER CHANGER** and the **STUDENT** in mind offer career insights, job hunting advice, and environmental "think pieces" as well!

ARE YOU LOOKING FOR EMPLOYEES...

☆ As an **EMPLOYER**, listing in **JOB-SCAN** will bring you a national audience targeted for your kinds of job opportunities **AND** it is absolutely **FREE** to list with us. FAX capabilities are available for last minute entries.

COULD YOU USE INEXPENSIVE, NATIONAL ADVERTISING...

☆ With your camera ready **GRAPHIC AD**, your college, company or organization will be seen by individuals interested in all facets of the environment. Make full,1/2 or1/4 page **JOB-SCAN ADVERTISING** work for you!

If you answered **YES** to any of these questions,
let **JOB-SCAN** be your guide!

SUBSCRIPTION RATES (Sorry, no billing)
6 mo/$22, 1 yr/$39 Single/$4 (Outside US add $4)

Call or write:
JOB-SCAN, Linda Rounds, Editor
c/o SCA, PO Box 550ᴛɢ
Charlestown, NH 03603
(603)826-4301
FAX (603)826-7755

360

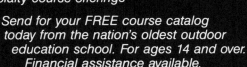

**GREGORY
MOUNTAIN SPORTS**

DOWN LAUNDRY
&
REPAIR SERVICE

WE PROFESSIONALLY WASH
(NOT DRY CLEAN !)
ANY DOWN OR SYNTHETIC
SLEEPING BAG, COAT,
COMFORTER, OR...?

REASONABLE RATES
&
SUPER RESULTS !!

FOR MORE INFORMATION
WRITE OR CALL

110 So. El Camino Real
Encinitas, Ca. 92024   **619-436-1630**

Wiggy's Bags
Simply The Best

IF YOU SPEND LESS, NATURALLY YOU GET LESS.
BUT, IF YOU SPEND MORE, YOU STILL GET LESS, WHY:

WIGGY'S BAGS are the lightest weight sleeping bag for each temperature range regardless of insulation used.

WIGGY'S BAGS are the most compactible for each size. Each of our mummy models is available in 5 separate sizes. We fit individuals comfortably from 5'4" to 6'6".

WIGGY'S BAGS are the most durable. Our guarantee is for a life time of use. If a seam opens, a zipper breaks or the insulation deteriorates, (such as losing its loft or separation, clumping in one place or another) we will repair or replace the bag at no charge to you for a life time. Wiggy's Guarantee is "Simply the Best!"

WIGGY'S BAGS are washing machine washable at home, (when you purchase a WIGGY'S BAG your only obligation is to launder it when it gets dirty; once a week, once a month or once a year. Laundering will always enhance the loft of a Wiggy's Bag).

WIGGY'S BAGS are Simply the Best with respect to function, fit, durability and cost.

Wiggy's Inc. FOR FREE CATALOGUE, WRITE OR CALL
P.O. Box 2124 • Grand Junction, CO 81502 • (303) 241-6465

NATIONAL PARKS TRADE JOURNAL NETWORK

NATIONAL PARKS

Acadia
Badlands
Big Bend
Blue Ridge Parkway
Bryce Canyon
Canyonlands
Capitol Reef
Carlsbad Caverns
Crater Lake
Death Valley
Denali
Everglades
Glacier Bay
Glacier
Glen Canyon
Grand Canyon
Grand Teton
Great Smokey Mountain
Hawaii Volcanoes
Hot Springs
Isle Royale
Katmai
Lake Mead
Lassen Volcanoes
Mammoth Cave
Mesa Verde
Mt. Rainier
North Cascades
Olympic
Oregon Caves
Ozark National Scenic
  Riverways
Petrified Forest
Rocky Mountain
Sequoia/Kings Canyon
Shenandoah
Theodore Roosevelt
Virgin Islands
Voyageurs
Wind Cave
Yellowstone
Yosemite
Zion

VOLUNTEER/ ENVIRONMENTAL ORGANIZATIONS

American Hiking Society
American Rivers
Appalachian Trail Conference
California Conservation Corps
Cal. Dept. of Parks & Rec.
Earthwatch
Greenpeace
Nature Conservancy
Nat'l. Parks & Conservation Assn.
Peace Corps
Rainforest Action Network
Red Cross
Sierra Club

Working Assets
Worldwatch
Youth Conservation Corps

SKI RESORTS

Aspen Highlands
Aspen Skiing Company
Bear Mountain
The Big Mountain
Boreal
Boyne USA
Breckinridge
Copper Mountain
Deer Valley
Dodge Ridge
Donner Ski Ranch
Estes Park Holiday Inn
Grand Targhee
Heavenly Valley
Hidden Valley
Holiday Valley
Keystone
Killington
Kirkwood
Mammoth Mountain/
  June Lake
Mount Bachelor
Mount Hood
Mount LaCrosse
Mount Mansfield
Mount Rose
Mount Snow
Park City
Purgatory
Shawnee Mountain
Sierra Ski Ranch
Sierra Summit
Snow Summit
Snowshoe
Soda Springs
Squaw Valley
Steamboat
Stevens Pass
Sugal Bowl
Sugarbush
Sunday River
Vail/Beaver Creek
Whiteface Mtn./Lake Placid

THEME PARKS

Sea World of California
Sea World of Florida
Sea World of Texas

DISTRIBUTORS

Alpenbooks
Ansel Adams Gallery
Baker & Taylor
Bigfoot Mountaineering
Blackwell North America

Bookpeople
B. Dalton Booksellers
Garret Park Press
Gordon's
Input Culture Co.
Little Professor Book Ctrs.
National Park Service
New Careers Center
Paperbacks for Educators
Pine Tree Market
Recreational Equip., Inc.
The Ranch Bookshop
U.S. Forest Service
VistaBooks
Wellington's Books
Wilderness Press
Yankee Book Peddler
Yosemite Association

EDUCATIONAL INSTITUTIONS

Astronomical Society of the
  Pacific
Audubon Expeditions
Ball State University
Berkshire School
California State Colleges
California State Universities
Connecticut College
Denver Institute of
  Technology
East Stroudsburg University
Eckerd Family Youth
  Alternative
Emporia State University
Hastings College
Houghton College
Marlboro College
Middlebury College
National Outdoor Leadership
  School
North Carolina State
  University
Northland College
Ohio State University
Pacific Crest Outward Bound
Paul Smith's College
Prescott College
Sierra Nevada College
Texas Tech. University
The Thacher School
Tufts University
University of California
University of Missouri
University of Texas-El Paso

PUBLISHED REVIEWS

American Libraries
Arizona Republic
Bookpeople Autumn 1989

CSAA Motorland
Chevy Outdoors
Dallas Morning News
Fresno Bee
Knapsack Magazine
Los Angeles Times
Mariposa Gazette & Miner
Milwaukee Journal
National Parks Magazine
Natural Science Teachers
  Association
New Age Community
  Enterprises
New Art Examiner
New York Times
Outdoor Retailer
Outdoor Writers Association
  of America
Shape Magazine
Sierra Magazine
South Bend Tribune
Whole Earth Review
Yosemite Sentinel

UPCOMING REVIEWS

Adirondack Magazine
Arkansas Game Magazine
Backpacker Magazine
Bakersfield Californian
Black Collegian Magazine
Bloomsbury Review
Buzzworm Magazine
Camping/RV Magazine
Collegiate Career Woman
Colorado Outdoors
Connections Magazine
East Side Journal
Globe Magazine
Good Times
Minnesota Volunteer
National Business Equipment
Outside Magazine
San Francisco Chronicle
Sporting Goods Mfrs. Assn.
The Sun
Theme Parks/Tour Attractions
Whole Earth Access

SPONSORS

Adventure Ease
Amtrak
Beattie Systems
Birkenstock
Camp Chilnualna
Casio Corporation
Corporate Ski Incentives
Daylab
Evolution USA
Green Tortoise
Gregory Mountain Sports

Hi-Tec
ICS Books
Marriott Corporation
Modern Homesteader
Moon Publications
Mountaineers Books
Mystic Color Lab
Nautical Pacific Recreation
Northern Outfitters
Outdoor Wilderness Fabrics
Ponderosa Printing
Quacker Packer
The Redwoods
Royal Robbins
Sierra Trading Post
Sierra Productions
Stackpole Books
S.E.I.U. Local 752
Upstream Products
U.S. Army Reserves
Vertical Adventures
Wawona Neighborhood News
Wiggy's

INTERVIEWS

WILLIAM SHATNER:
Famous actor and director.
On location in Yosemite to
film Star Trek V.

WILLIAM MOTT: Recent
director of the National Park
Service.

CHUCK YEAGER: Record-
breaking aviator, Air Force
General. Spends ten days
each year backpacking in
National Parks.

ROYAL ROBBINS: Famous
mountaineer and white-water
kayaker. Pioneered classic 1st
ascents and descents. Writer
and outdoor businessman.

★ ★ ★ ★ ★ ★ ★ ★ ★

"Hope you join us for the '90s — The Outdoor Environmental Decade!"

Index of Ski Areas / Winter Resorts

Index of National Parks

Index of Product & Service Advertisers

Index of Product & Service Advertisers
(continued)

Index of Outdoor Schools

Index of Theme Parks

NOTES

NOTES

NOTES

NOTES

NOTES